Adoption Combat Zone

DECEPTIONS AND COLLATERAL DAMAGE

OUR TRUE STORY
OF INTERNATIONAL ADOPTION

Kathe Ray

Purple Cloth Books
NOVI, MICHIGAN

Copyright © 2018 by Kathe Ray.

All rights reserved. No part of this publication may be reproduced, distributed or transmitted in any form or by any means, including photocopying, recording, or other electronic or mechanical methods, without the prior written permission of the publisher, except in the case of brief quotations embodied in critical reviews and certain other noncommercial uses permitted by copyright law. For permission requests, write to the publisher, addressed "Attention: Permissions Coordinator," at the address below.

Kathe Ray/Purple Cloth Books
P.O. Box 260
Novi, Michigan 48376-0260
www.adoptioncombatzone.com
248-704-6677

Book Layout ©2017 BookDesignTemplates.com

Ordering Information:
Quantity sales. Special discounts are available on quantity purchases by corporations, associations, and others. For details, contact the "Special Sales Department" at the website address above.

Adoption Combat Zone/Kathe Ray. —1st ed.
ISBN: 978-1-7320426-0-5

Contents

Forward 8

Introduction 12

Family X – Families in Crisis 19

    If only I had known... 19

    What are they thinking? 35

Who We Were 41

Our First Adoption 45

    First recommendation if you are considering adoption .. 46

    Hosting Agencies 49

    Legalized Human Trafficking 53

Orphan Alcoholics 65

    Institutionalization 66

Piling More On 75

    Biological Children/Teens 75

    Yahweh 79

    Fear 82

Our Second Adoption 85

    Unexpected Decisions! 87

    EMOTION 89

    The Sales Pitch 91

- Pay attention to the signs ... 94
- FRAUD ... 98

Love and Abuse ... 101
- Orphan savings accounts ... 102
- Orphans Biological Family ... 103
- Abuse by an adoptee against an adoptive parent ... 106
- TRIANGULATION ... 108
- Please Don't Correct Me Correcting My Kids ... 110

Finally Arrived Home ... 115
- The Lies Came Out ... 116
- VK – VKontakte ... 118
- Running Away ... 120
- Control ... 121
- NORMAL PARENTING DOES NOT WORK! ... 122

24 Hours One Day in Our Life ... 125
- ROOMS ... 131
- A "Friend" ... 135

Escalation ... 139
- Counseling ... 140
- Grateful ... 141
- More Running Away ... 142

Electronics 146

GUILT 148

PROBATIONARY PERIOD! 149

A Snowstorm and Rejection 151
YES! We Padlocked the Refrigerator 159
Introduction of "Horrid Man" 167
Human Trafficking Too Close for Comfort 181
    Adoptive Family PTSD/Trauma 186

Triangulation 191
Return of "Horrid Man" 197
More Missing Money 201
Another Gestapo (I mean CPS) Witch Hunt 207
Triangulation Part II 219
Domestic Violence 225
Vacation! What Vacation? 231
    NEGLECT CHARGES by CPS 234

Tattoo Man 247
    DOCUMENT. DOCUMENT. DOCUMENT. 248

Catching the Thieves 251
CPS Confrontations Continued 265
Tom Moved Out 269
    Domestic Abuse 276

Back in Ukraine! 277

Gone Again, and Again, and Again...	283
Gone for Good!	287
Surprise! You Don't Instantly Feel Great Again!	297
Hollywood Lies about Adoption	299
Annual Reports	305
Viktor Reappeared	309
Working to Recover	315
Some Final Thoughts	319
Empathy	320
The Last, Last Word!	329
Resources	349
I Am Grateful	361

*This book is dedicated to my husband Tom and my teenagers;
Garrett & Katherine. Together we decided to go on this
adoption journey and although it was crazy hard I'm grateful
we did it together. We will all be better because of the hard stuff
we endured! Yahweh will give our family
beauty through the ashes.
I love you to infinity!*

*And to the thousands of families who are living or have lived
"In the Trenches" of devastating adoptions. You are brave and
dedicated and selfless. You are heroes!*

And to Yahweh, because without You I am nothing!

Reviews for Adoption Combat Zone

Kathe Ray delivers a gripping account of her family's struggle with international adoption in Adoption Combat Zone. Devastatingly honest, it peels back the layers of deception and exposes hosting, adoption, and governmental agencies for what many are - corrupt vehicles trafficking emotionally and mentally damaged children across international lines through manipulation of unsuspecting adoptive parents. The greed behind the reckless driving of these forces is sickening, and the carnage of broken families to be finished off by CPS and other such organizations is shocking. Little else stands between the complete shredding of their family fabric except for their complete devotion to each other and their unwavering, though sorely tested, faith in Yahweh. Through a nearly four-year battle, Kathe and Tom are left shell-shocked by adopted teens who cannot reconcile the transition from their native land to America. The injections of quotes by numerous families who have suffered similarly leaves the reader aching for a resolution on their behalf - the REAL victims.

- Rebecca Bailey, Author of "To Touch the Hem."

"Kathe has done an amazing job of telling her gut-wrenching story of international adoption. Adoption Combat Zone is not anti-adoption but rather an educational tool for those considering international adoption. Many of us have sacrificed our children on the altar of adoption and live with the pain and guilt it brings each day. Kathe pours out her heart and in doing so, gives us a glimpse into the depth of her hurting soul, as she advocates for adoption reform. This book will bring you to tears, yet give you hope that the truth is being revealed and that a reformation will take place regarding adoption. I know this was tough for Kathe to write but she was created "for such a time as this" and I pray that beauty will come from her ashes as she shouts this from the rooftops to ensure others are spared from the potential pain and horror of the Adoption Combat Zone."

-Becca Hill, adoptive mom

Forward

WE OFFERED THE KEY TO A LIFE THAT COULD BE

I grew up in Toledo, Ohio. I went to the same grade school for eight years, and the same high school for four years. We lived in the same house. I describe my childhood as a "Beaver Cleaver" upbringing with a stay home mom and a dad who worked Monday through Friday. We had sit down meals every night. I was in the middle of eleven children, and even though my parents didn't have much money, it was a simple 60's/70's life and I look back with fond memories.

Kathe was not so fortunate. Her childhood was filled with continual chaos and uncertainty. Because she was the oldest of five, Kathe was expected to be more like a second mother. Much responsibility, but no power. By the time she was nine, she was expected to see to it that meals were prepared, rooms were cleaned, and other siblings were dressed and off to school. She was constantly under the threat of beatings and being yelled at was a daily occurrence. She became a person she didn't want to be; bossy and demanding; like a drill sergeant. If things didn't get done, there would be severe punishment, and she was always first in line. She was continually told she "was the oldest" and therefore she "was responsible." The punishment for failure was either a belt or large paddle with holes drilled into it. Twenty lashes or whacks was not uncommon.

As they grew, her siblings resented her forceful demeanor. She became the target of their anger and bitterness. She was caught in the middle between her parents and siblings. There was no winning. This was her childhood. Every single day.

Then there were the many moves. Her parents uprooted and moved the family so many times Kathe can't even remember them all. As she matured, she questioned why they had to move AGAIN, many times with only a few days' notice. There was never a straight answer. There were no established roots. Unlike me, who had a life of normalcy, Kathe had a life of being beaten, coerced, and being unloved. She never made friends since she never knew how long they would live at that address. Adult relatives who knew the circumstances refused to step in and protect her. THEY DID NOTHING! This led to her wanting to rescue anything and anyone who crossed her path. She could not stand by and do nothing.

When I met Kathe, I viewed her life up until then as normal and similar to mine. I think as a rule, that's what most of us do; we see others through our own paradigm. She married me (for which I am exceedingly grateful) and we built a family. I never gave much thought to how those childhood experiences would affect her adulthood, and how it shaped her to be someone who so willingly would sacrifice herself for someone else. She has a keen sense of right and wrong and she immediately sets out to right all wrongs with which she comes into contact. Justice and loyalty are very important to her. She is a very loving and caring mother to our children and was determined to be the opposite of what she experienced.

Kathe felt we had the power to change a youth's life and give them the key to a better life. We both did. So together, we started this adoption journey.

Tom Ray

Speak up for those who cannot speak for themselves;
ensure justice for those being crushed.
Yes, speak up for the poor and helpless,
and see that they get justice.

Proverbs 31:8-9

For adoptive families around the globe.

Introduction

August 2012 forever changed our family. That was when the world of adoption became personal. I have gone back and forth on writing this story so many times. On one hand, I never want to think about what we went through ever again. I want the memories buried so deep they never resurface. I have started and stopped writing many times. The last break was several months. I've wondered if I'm doing all of this and it's not even going to make a difference. It's so hard reliving our story by writing and re-writing; for each time refreshes the events.

I cry. I wish we had never adopted. I wish I had never heard of hosting. I wish it were all a bad dream. I want a do-over.

Then a nudge comes along. It might be another family reaching out for help or advice. Or seeing a request on social media from someone fundraising to adopt. Or waking up from a dream knowing Yahweh (God) was speaking to me. I know the story must be told. Yet I dread the thought of reliving through the telling. I have spent so much time working to be positive again. Happy. Joyful. Healed. I think about a title of a book I recently read. "In a Pit with a Lion on a Snowy Day" by Mark Batterson. I can relate. Only my pit was with several very hungry lions, a blizzard to end all blizzards and I was stark naked. Yeah. But there was some good that came of it. So, this story is being told for several reasons.

- As a wakeup call on the adoption factory - I mean culture - I mean industry - NO…I mean **business** and to shine a bright light on the entire process which has ripped apart thousands of wonderful, caring, godly, and good-hearted families! Physically, emotionally, mentally, and financially. An industry which thinks nothing of lying to procure money from a family who is trying to do the right thing and then disappears once everything falls apart, only to move on to the next loving, caring family who wants to do the right thing. All in the name of "saving" orphans and helping a child or teenager have a shot at a future. Using hearts and emotions to make boatloads of money. Nothing perpetrates fraud in international adoption like money and having so much money attached to this process makes it inherently open to fraud. Where money is involved, especially to this degree, corruption will be found, and fraud is rampant in the business of adoption.

1Timothy 6:10. For the love of money is a root of all sorts of evil, and some by longing for it have wandered away from the faith and pierced themselves with many griefs.

This is a business that is founded on great lies and masked by some truths and half-truths. It is built on the backs of orphaned children and "aging out" teenagers, most who will be forced to leave the orphanage once they turn 14, 15, 16 or 17. Adoption is a business and there is an absurd amount of money flowing through it, mostly from decent American and Western European families whose heart strings are pulled by the agencies and individuals who stand to profit the most. Those families who want to make a difference in the life of a child and who later learn that most orphans in the world really aren't true orphans at all, but "social" orphans. They often have mothers, fathers, uncles, aunts, siblings and grandparents. Maybe these relatives aren't as stellar as our American high and mighty standards might want them to be; nonetheless they are family. Many just don't have the money to support their children. The lies, the hidden facts and lies of omission, the money and the corruption are very real.

- For families thinking about adopting. To show them there is another side, an ugly side, of adoption. Families about to go blindly in, thinking they are rescuing, saving, or helping an orphan. Thinking they are giving an adoptee the hope of a future. Families who don't know adopting could have the potential impact of an atomic bomb on their family. That "doing what Yahweh wants us to do" and "taking care of the widows and orphans" might just turn their peaceful home into a war zone of divorce, burned down homes, raped and molested biological children, physically and emotionally abused adoptive parents, fathers and/or mothers in jail or with records that will prohibit them from ever again finding gainful employment, careers ruined, jobs lost, or biological children removed from the family, and on and on and on.

Entire families torn apart.

To all, I say there are other ways to make a difference. Ways to help orphans that won't destroy families in ways most can't imagine. This work serves as an Ezekiel warning to families considering adopting. Know what's possible. Be aware. Do your due diligence. Make an informed decision based on facts, not on emotions. Research common disorders found in adopted children/teens such as Reactive Attachment Disorder (RAD), Fetal Alcohol Spectrum Disorders (FASD), and Adoption Post Traumatic Stress Disorder (PTSD); to name a few. And know that <u>every single one of us</u> who is living in adoption hell right now **NEVER** thought it would happen to us. Or we thought we could handle the hell. Or we thought we knew how bad the hell could be.

We were wrong. Dead wrong.

- For governmental agencies like CPS (child protective services). Yes, they are supposed to protect children; after all that is what their name implies. But when said child or teen has an evil vendetta against a family or family member, taking all that child/teen says at face value wreaks destruction on the family unit. There is no "innocent until proven guilty" in this arena and there needs to be. This is one institution in America where officials are both judge and jury and adults are assumed guilty from the get-go. Many officials have a vested interest in guilty findings and they are virtually uneducated about adoption related trauma and disorders.

When the truth comes out that the child/teen was lying about mistreatment by their adoptive family, there needs to be consequences on the adoptee; something to discourage revisits "to the well" of false accusations. When CPS begins an investigation, safeguards need to be put into place to protect the whole family. When the child/teen is suspected of having a disorder such as RAD or other attachment/trauma issues, there needs to be immediate protection of the entire family, <u>including</u> the parents, which <u>doesn't</u> include removal of the biological children from the home. More education on RAD and other trauma and attachment disorders would be invaluable for social workers and other investigating officials in these agencies so they can appropriately identify what they are encountering.

> ***Just learning a family has adopted should throw a red flag into the investigation and an entirely different process should be implemented <u>immediately</u>!***

- Just like CPS, the entire law enforcement and court system needs education in adopted trauma children/teens and how their dysfunctions are destroying good families. Officials are used to rubber stamping situations like these but have no understanding how children/teens with disorders like RAD, FASD and other trauma and attachment issues are manipulating outcomes by faking emotions and injury. Too many excellent parents are losing the good fight for their families because the present court system is all in favor of only doing what's "best" for the one who is hell-bent on destruction. The courts and police are playing right into the hands of these master manipulators; some as young as four-years-old.
- Lastly, to give hope to those weary warriors fighting the daily, hourly and minute-by-minute battles. Know that someone has come through to the other side. Although our family is forever changed, and we still fight some trauma demons, things are getting better, and easier, one day at a time, with Yahweh's help. If we can overcome, so can you!

As I begin this writing journey I give thanks to my Creator, Yahweh (God), for without Him I would not be able to function. I give thanks to Him for the continued healing of my family, for wisdom, for knowledge, for understanding, for discernment, for guidance, for protection, and for being with me on a minute-by-minute basis on most days. I ask Him to speak through me as I write and ask Him to give me guidance on what to say to you to help you understand the enormity of this adoption problem, and to give peace and hope to those of you who are fighting these battles in your homes.

I wrote this book for the thousands of families who are *"In the Trenches"* and to those who've reached out to me; desperate for solutions for your families. I pray for your families. I pray for a change to this insane and broken system. I pray for support for you and your loved ones. I pray to make a difference. I pray for this light to shine brightly upon the adoption industry so real changes can take place; changes that help and protect both orphans **AND** families. I pray for the orphans of this world; that they receive the much-needed assistance, love and support without destroying families in the process.

Finally, I know there are happy stories of adoption. Lots of them. Maybe you have one. Maybe you know someone with one. Maybe you were adopted, and it was all good. My goal with this book is to prompt changes to the system so that there are more safeguards in place for adoptive families, should they happen to find themselves in a situation like ours and like the many other families living in hell right now. So that there are more stories like yours and less like ours. I thank Yahweh you have a great story. I wish they were all like yours. More than you will ever know, I wish ours had been. If it had been, you wouldn't be holding this book right now. This is why I'm sharing our story.

The Plight of the Orphan

This was a postcard I was given by our hosting organization. A message used repeatedly and blatantly all over social media, especially before the summer and winter hosting periods.

> *Today is August 31st and in Eastern Europe that means that it's "graduation day" when the 16 -18 year olds "graduate" from orphanages. Every year on August 31st an entire group of orphans is sent out of the orphanages across the land. Most of these teenagers are without adequate life skills, without much more than the bag on their back and well wishes to find a place at one of the trade schools. No family, no mentors, no chance for adoption and no hope. Within a few short years over 80% will find themselves trapped in lives of poverty, crime, prostitution, addiction, incarceration or dead, many from suicide.*

Wow does that ever tug at the heart strings. Well, at least it did mine five years ago. Now I know the truth. I ask myself how much of this lifestyle by aged out orphans is by choice and how much by circumstance. In the aftermath of our adoptions our adopted teens were given ideal circumstances and yet they still chose the above lifestyle anyway. It did not serve our family or the orphans to adopt them and bring them into our family. For them it simply changed location. For us, well…read on…

CHAPTER 1

Family X – Families in Crisis

Throughout these memories I will interject stories from other families. These are actual stories from **more than 350 families.** I will call them **ALL "Family X"** to protect their privacy. Many of them are living in fear their adopted son or daughter will find them, harass them, or even kill them, or these parents are being pressured by different governmental agencies, so it's imperative they remain anonymous. Some have been persecuted by their hosting/adoption organization and some by their own relatives and church members. (I'm ashamed at how much of Christian America has turned its back on these families who have sacrificed so much for orphans.)

If only I had known...

On social media I belong to some groups who are parenting through horrific adoptions. I asked them to share one "I didn't know prior to adoption...", or "If only I had known..." or "I never knew before adopting..." or "When I adopted..." comment for this book. Some are here in the beginning; the rest of their accounts are sprinkled throughout. Each one from a single person/family. Honestly, even writing our story and with the hundreds of messages and emails I've gotten in response to my blog, I had no idea how widespread this problem with adoptions really is and how many families are suffering through adoption related trauma. This mere handful of stories represents thousands who have adopted and those who are now enduring trauma and upheaval. Some believe they are alone in this journey and they have no one to talk to about their daily struggles.

As you read our stories, remember, these were all parents who put themselves, their families, and their finances on the line to simply ***"make a difference in the life of a child."***

If only I had known...

- I never knew I would invest as much brain power thinking about how to get him out of my home as I spent trying to bring him into my home.
- I didn't know that while adoptions only represent 4-5% of the total population, they represent more than 50% of kids in residential treatment.
- I never imagined that I would find my beloved dog bloody and stabbed to death on my front porch one morning. I never imagined being told **"You are next"** when she saw me standing there sobbing. I never imagined that people wouldn't believe me when I told them about it.
- I walk into adopted daughter's (17) room this morning and see she's peed all over everything. She took things out of a box in her closet and peed on them. Then she ripped up her jeans.
- I feel like I owe the whole country an apology for bringing this complete derelict here. I'm sorry America.
- Leftovers. She was picking at the big bowl. I asked her to get a small bowl and dish up some if she wanted it. She responded, "But I want this." I said, "Get your own bowl and get out of the big bowl so you don't contaminate it for the rest of us." So, she spit in it.
- **I never thought I would have to sleep on the couch for 15 months with one eye open to make sure no one in my house was murdered.**
- When I adopted I didn't know I would be locking up scissors, knives, glass in picture frames, and anything sharp to ensure the safety of my family.

- **That my husband and I would divorce after 27 years of marriage.**
- I didn't know the damage adopting would do to my younger children.
- I didn't know I would hear other people planning a risky adoption (profound/unknown special needs, out of birth order, 2 or more at once, older child to new parents, older with younger children at home, etc.) and cringe inside.
- I didn't know I would forever wonder if we could have healed her. I didn't know children could be so broken so young that they didn't want healing.
- I literally had no idea children could be psychopaths and that no, sometimes you cannot "love" them better.
- As well-informed and ready as I thought I was I really had no clue someone like him existed.
- When we adopted I never thought having a safe wasn't safe enough.
- **I had no idea that a five-year-old could possibly be a psychopath.** How does that happen and why are these children allowed to be farmed out for adoption?
- I didn't know a minor child of 12 years old could be found guilty of committing domestic violence.
- **I didn't know the world would judge us so harshly.**
- When I adopted I never realized the trigger November (National Adoption Month) would be when Facebook® came out with the frame "touched by adoption"- our entire family has been literally touched by adoption.
- I didn't know a child could feel threatened by genuine love.
- Before we adopted I didn't know showing love to a person would actually – to them – give them enormous power over you, and in their mind tell them they now control you.
- **I didn't know that I wouldn't like the mom I became to my other children.**
- I never knew I would develop PTSD from adopting.
- That I would spend my days telling him not to lick the car. Yeah.
- When I adopted, I thought I was giving three teen boys a home and a family they had always wanted. I had no idea I was bringing three con

artists into my home who used us to get to American soil where they would lie, steal, and tell even more lies.
- **When I adopted my host child, I didn't realize everything he portrayed was a lie during the several weeks hosting period.**
- When I adopted, I expected a forever family, but instead received a forever broken family.
- **When I adopted my older teens, I didn't realize the trauma it would cause to me and my other children.**
- When we adopted we didn't realize that every adult we had contact with in that country was lying to us about him. I don't know how to stop hating those people.
- I never knew I would become a hyper vigilant detective my own home.
- **I didn't know my child would stop at nothing to watch porn. He is 7.**
- I never knew that a young teenage girl could be so addicted to online porn that she would do anything to gain access to it.
- I never thought I could resent a child so much!
- When I adopted I expected to like my kid. I expected to enjoy being his mom. I expected rainbows and unicorns because that's what everyone else on my friend's list had. I never expected to feel like an absolute schmuck and a failure because my kid was having so many problems and all those others had perfect adoptions.
- I didn't realize I would ever be part of this group. (Adoption trauma group on social media.) In fact, I never knew such a group existed. And the fact that there needs to be groups like this one is so incredibly sad.
- I had no idea I would be hiding food in every room other than hers. I never dreamed I would have to divide what we ate by number of people and set limits.
- I never realized I would develop PTSD and anxiety from the behavioral issues my adopted kids have.
- When we adopted I had no idea I would spend my weekends trying to get him committed.

- I never thought I would have to write names on oranges, so he wouldn't eat all of them and leave none for anyone else. (He still ate the others anyway and I found orange peels with their names under his mattress.)
- **I didn't realize a 5-year-old could destroy a family** and cause all of us to have PTSD. I couldn't wait to adopt our son. I was so excited! Now I HATE the word ADOPTION. Our family will never be the same.
- When I adopted, I never knew we'd end up in the frightening situation of living with a teenager diagnosed with Antisocial Personality Disorder - a sociopath.
- I NEVER imagined people would say I was a bad mother (after raising seven other AMAZING children).
- **When I adopted I never thought my other children wouldn't be safe from a sexual predator in their own home.**
- I had no idea how much adoption would test my marriage and family.
- I always, always wanted to adopt. I was the biggest advocate. And now I can't even stomach the thought. We will never be the same.
- That I would have to lock up money, hide food, create and remember passwords on ALL electronics, and warn neighbors, relatives, and friends to not let my son have any internet access because of his porn addiction.
- That my handsome son would have a test result of a 48 IQ but be a master manipulator who wedges discontent into every relationship he has in common with me and other adults. They all think he's delightful and that I'm a mean and terrible mom.
- I never imagined my adopted daughter would tell me we "stole" her from her family when she'd lived in an orphanage as long as she could remember. Huh?
- **I never thought adoption would be such a lonely, solitary road.**
- How humiliating it would be to go around to my neighbor's homes to tell them not to allow RAD boy access to their internet because he wanted to go on porn sites.

- I never thought I would HATE my adopted son's name. Or get anxiety when I hear random people named the same name.
- "When I adopted." I didn't know a phrase or feeling could make my stomach instantly churn. Wow! That escalated quickly!
- When I adopted I never thought I would ever put a chain and lock on my refrigerator and put locks on the pantry.
- When I adopted I didn't know how normal kids could seem in the orphanage, because they are trained and taught they must be to be adopted. Who then turned into horrible children as soon as you spend all your money and get them to America.
- When I adopted I never dreamed I would be told that everything was my fault and I stole her from her real friends and family even though she had been in the orphanage for many years and asked us to adopt her.
- **I never thought I would be told that someone's violence TOWARDS ME was all MY FAULT because a child cannot be blamed for their actions.**
- When I adopted I thought I was saving two cute boys from a life of crime in another country when actually I brought two extremely dangerous psychopaths here to terrorize our family and victimize others.
- I never imagined adults would coerce a child into saying they wanted to be adopted, then lie to us about his mental instability and rage.
- That it would be so exhausting and brutal, not only living with a psychopath in our home, but attempting to find a solution that works for all of us in this broken system.
- That people would give my adopted daughter chance after chance but give us none.
- Before adoption I didn't know a daughter could have a crush on her father and try to take my place as his wife.
- **I never thought one small child could ruin and destroy a family.**
- Before adoption I didn't know a child could be so physically violent as to scare and hurt adults. I didn't know others wouldn't believe me.

- I never thought I would be living with a broken man. My husband is absolutely the kindest human on the planet and he wanted to adopt so badly. To have our adopted daughter, 14, turn him in for sexual abuse broke him into a million pieces. All because she was mad we wouldn't let her stay up all night watching T.V.
- Before adoption I never felt like Bridget Fonda in Single White Female©.
- I often wonder if the pre-adoption therapist who told us we would "have it easier than most because we cherry picked the lot" knew exactly what was in store for us.
- **As an adoptee myself** I never thought I'd be anything but PRO adoption. Now I secretly want to shake someone who tells me they want to adopt and tell them to wake up and run the other way as fast as they can **before their life turns into a nightmare.**
- I never imagined what it would be like to have absolutely no power in my own home. That it would be run by a 9-year-old I wouldn't have been able to fathom.
- I didn't know how isolated and broken I would become. I actually thought it would connect me more with the greater community of families - instead, I'm more alone than ever.
- I never expected to be so desperate that I would mull over ideas of causing both me and the adopted child to die as a solution to make it better for the rest of my children and my husband.
- That I would be all alone except for my abuser and that no one would believe me about the abuse because they only see her as an "angel". I wonder some days if they will believe me when they find me dead or will they still make excuses for her?
- **When my own death became the best-case scenario that I prayed for every day. *sigh*.**
- Adoption will never make up for miscarriage / abortion loss.
- I never knew adoption would mean I would gain a son and his behaviors would make me lose my mind. I never knew that poop and pee issues from a 6-year-old would cause me so much stress and ruin

family outings. I never knew adoption would mean PTSD for me and my husband.
- I never thought genetics played such a huge role.
- I never thought a small child would try to destroy my family and almost succeed.
- I never imagined I would be divorced and living alone just because I wanted to help a child.
- I never thought I'd help my adopted child through cancer and almost go to prison for it after she manipulated the system.
- If only I had known our bio kids would end up with PTSD.
- **When I adopted, I didn't know we'd have to put alarms on the bedroom doors for fear they would kill us in our sleep.**
- It's not like having bio kids. It is fundamentally different, and any agency or person trying to tell you differently is gas lighting you. Don't buy the lie. EVERY child who is adopted is adopted because they experienced loss. That does something to a child.
- I never thought we'd have to put Plexiglas between the front and rear car seats to keep us safe from her while driving.
- Before I adopted, I never knew that I could provide for a child so long and then worry she would come back and kill me for it later.
- Very close friends who said they would support us are shutting us out. Everyone is so focused on how our daughter will handle everything, I'm feeling forgotten and abandoned. Don't I matter in this equation?
- I never knew I would feel like I'd lost myself by adopting a child. I wonder if I will ever be "me" again.
- I never knew I'd feel like I'd lost my faith and my love for God, feeling like I'd been tortured in my own home for over 11 years, all because I wanted to help and love a hurt child.
- That I would spend my days protecting my bio children from their tormentor and even have to take them into the bathroom with me, so he wouldn't do something to them in the two minutes I was taking care of myself.
- **How is this from God?**

- I never knew that I, the one who loved to be around children before adopting, would feel like running and screaming every time I'd hear a child scream or cry or whine. I never knew I'd want to get away from children all together from then on.
- I never knew the person I'd become is someone I don't recognize anymore. The person who used to love to help others in any way, shape or form, and not this person who wants to be a recluse.
- I never knew we'd lose almost all our friends and family because they couldn't tolerate or understand the child we were trying to help. They couldn't understand why we didn't just give them back right away.
- I never knew people would not believe me but would believe her. People I've known all my life. People who should know the kind of person I am. I have no one. **I'm so alone.**
- Before adopting I thought love was all that was needed to help these poor kids who'd been neglected. Love is not enough. Love is what they hate, and they will destroy your family, one hug at a time.
- When I adopted, I had no clue that **a six-year-old child would become my abuser.** And that other adults around me would blame me or think I was lying.
- Before I adopted, I never had bruises all over my arms; I never had glass jars and Pyrex dishes, or dining room chairs thrown at me; I had never been attacked while simply washing the dishes.
- I never could have seen that one day I would be on vacation with my husband after all the trauma was out of our home and all I did for a solid week was cry. I didn't know how to relax or have fun anymore.
- **Before adoption I never feared for my other kids' safety.**
- When I adopted, I never knew the level of lies and deceit that could come from adults whose job is to help the orphan. They just wanted to make money and/or get my child out of the orphanage. My "happy, developmentally normal" child is anything but.
- I had no idea I was paying a large sum of money we didn't really have to bring someone into my home who completely disrespected women of all ages and would look down at me as his servant. And he is eleven years old.

- When we adopted I had no idea that the person I had been all my life would disappear into this person I don't even know. I don't act like myself, I don't even think like myself anymore. I'm completely lost. How did this happen when all I wanted to do was make a difference to someone's life? How do I find me?
- I didn't know I wouldn't like me very much anymore. **I hate the guilt that I did this to my family.**
- Before adoption I really thought my friends were my friends.
- I couldn't fathom being kicked out of an adoption support group for daring to share some of the problems we were experiencing. No one wanted to hear the bad stuff. They all wanted the fairy tale.
- Before we adopted I had no idea that I would be on first name basis with all the police officers in our town.
- I didn't know the "Touched by Adoption" Facebook® frame would make me physically ill. I hate National Adoption Month and thinking about how many families are setting themselves up for disaster like ours.
- **I never thought I would lose all sense of confidence in my own decisions. I no longer trust myself to make decisions, even little ones.**
- Before I adopted I never realized people lied about their own adoption stories to make them seem better. I wish I had known more of the truth behind the happy pictures on Facebook®. I see them now and don't believe them one bit. And it makes me mad. **If they had told the truth maybe my little girl would not have been raped in her own home** and we as a family would not be broken apart into a million pieces. I hate those who lie about their own adoption stories.
- **I had no clue I would have a true sociopath in my home whose single goal in life is to destroy me and who has no comprehension of consequences.**
- When we adopted, we didn't know how much we would wish for a 'return policy'.
- I never thought I would hate adoption or my child.

- Touched by Adoption! Yes, we have been TOUCHED by adoption. I hate November. (National Adoption Month).
- I never thought I would have such a hard time with following and continuing to trust God.
- I never thought a kid would be so hateful to me, for loving on her.
- When I adopted I believed all children wanted parents.
- When I adopted I didn't have a contact in every department of the police and court system. I certainly didn't have people there that answered the phone and knew my number.
- **When we adopted we never thought we would have to strategize every waking minute to keep our biological children safe.**
- When we adopted we never thought we'd be in a court room again to dissolve the adoption.
- When we adopted, I didn't realize we only needed a one-bedroom house because adopted son sleeps on the couch all day and watches television all night. The other three kids sleep in our room to keep them safe from him.
- I never thought my personal reputation would be dragged through the mud. No people! We are not abusers.
- Before we adopted I had no idea that friends I've had all my life would believe I could abuse a child. That they really believe what he is saying truly boggles my mind. And that after they saw us raising two other children to adulthood. It makes no sense to me.
- **I never thought giving a child a chance would cost me my marriage and family.**
- I didn't know I would read newspaper stories of children and teenagers doing atrocious things and automatically think that they are adopted. Or that I would read of a parent doing something awful to a child and think, I'll bet he was adopted and has RAD.
- I never thought my adoption would cost me friendships and family relationships.
- Before we adopted we truly believed that all teens do stupid things. Oh my God, not like this!! I never imagined! No! All teens do NOT do stuff like this!

- **I never thought I'd be told that I just didn't love my adopted daughter enough.**
- I never thought DCF would be a part of my world this painfully close.
- I never thought I could permanently dislike, but still love a child.
- When I adopted I didn't think I would seriously think about committing a crime, so I could vacation in prison.
- When adopting I never thought I'd always look at the policeman pulled up next to me at a light to see if he'd been to our house.
- **I never thought I'd admit my 7-year-old to a psych hospital for self-harming and aggression toward others and pets.**
- I thought I could handle just about anything a child could do.
- I would never have imagined that the adorable little girl we adopted would self-harm so she could go into school and tell her teacher that I abused her, so she could go to a better mom.
- When we adopted I didn't know something could be harder to go through than losing my dad when I was 7. Whew! Being the victims of a fraudulent adoption agency's scam takes the cake.
- When we adopted I didn't realize the word "adopt" would end up making me break out in hives.
- I never thought the term "damned if you do and damned if you don't" would apply to my life.
- When we adopted I never thought I would spend my 15th anniversary at two different psych wards for two different kids because they both wanted to kill me.
- **Before we adopted I truly didn't know what it was like to be in constant fear for my life and what that would do to my health.**
- That I would no longer have any social life. None!
- I never thought I would dread upcoming holidays, birthdays or any other special times because she makes them so unbearable.
- When I adopted I didn't know those who wrote referral letters and made glowing recommendations that we were great parents based on our bio kids, and who fought to help us bring our daughter home, would be the same people who would later accuse us of being horrific parents.

- How much I would hate the word, "adopted". I flinched the other day when someone posted on Facebook® that they adopted a cat.
- I never thought I would sell the home of my dreams because of so many horrible memories there. My husband and I now live in a tiny apartment because it's all we can afford. We are in debt, probably for the rest of our lives, paying for courts, therapists, hospital bills and more. When we adopted we were told he was the best little guy in the orphanage. He had so many problems I can't list them in this little paragraph. **The boy is in a group home where they have him isolated due to his sexual aggressiveness. He is 10.**
- Before we adopted I didn't know I would spend my days wondering how much trouble I would be in with the government if I just took him back to his country and left him there. And weighing how much better a life sentence in prison would be compared to what I'm living with now.
- I didn't know how humiliated I would feel when I was falsely accused of beating her. How could my friends actually believe I would be capable of that? I'm devastated.
- When I adopted, I had no idea just how much love couldn't fix. I didn't know that nothing could change her core belief that the world is not a safe place.
- I am no longer judgmental of anything I hear or read in the news. After living my own hell, I have more insight to what really might be going on behind the scenes in those stories.
- **I'm so afraid. Every minute. Night and day.**
- I never thought "naked teenage girls" would be the most frequented website of this kid. I also never anticipated how relieved we would ALL be when he finally walked out.
- I never thought when she went to school I would look at her sketch book to find black and white pictures with knives going through body parts with red dripping blood and of her hanging herself. I searched her room and found nothing, then checked her school locker. Inside I found a noose.
- I never thought I could resent a child so much!

- **I never thought trying to make a difference for a child would cost me my job, my health, and my marriage.**
- I never thought that one day I would hear of a murder, a wreck or an overdose and wonder if it is her. And then think it's only a matter of time.
- I never thought I would be an awful, burnt out, cynical person.
- I always thought if I loved enough I could solve all her problems. Nope!
- **I never thought I would realize that "mom" is just another word like house, tree and dog.**
- That when I do actually fall asleep my sleep is filled with nightmares.
- We have five other amazing bio children we raised but somehow our adopted son's issues (who came to us at age 10) are all our fault...ugh. People are so cruel to us.
- I had a countdown clock on my phone and computer. She wasn't 16 yet when I started it. So even though it was over 1200 days, when she was screaming in our faces and generally stressing out our family - it was soothing to watch those seconds fly away.
- **That a six-year-old could be addicted to porn.** And she is a girl!! Oh my God!
- I never imagined thinking about driving off a bridge with him in the car with me, so I didn't have to care for him ONE MORE DAY. My death would have brought me so much peace. Scary thoughts and I hated having them.
- I never imagined having an adopted kid who hates me, wants to kill me, smears fecal matter all over the house, pees in the vents, destroys property, lies incessantly, and on and on.
- I think most of my PTSD is from the non-stop screaming. I think I'm going mad.
- That I would look at typical "bad" behavior from my friend's children and think, "boy, do you have it good", when they complain to me about it. I wish our issues were so tame.
- When I adopted, I didn't know we'd have to put alarms in the bedroom door for fear that they would kill us in our sleep.

- I never thought I would have thoughts like one night when we were in the ER and his oxygen plummeted to 23% that I hoped it wouldn't recover. There was a fleeting moment I thought it was over for all of us. He bounced back. I feigned relief. Then I hated myself for thinking that.
- **That my adopted daughter at age 8 would threaten to kill me and reached for knives in the knife block.**
- I didn't know the true meaning of sleep deprivation. I didn't know someone could live on less than four hours of constantly interrupted sleep every night for more than three years.
- I never imagined when he was late waking up in the morning that both my husband and I would secretly hope he had died peacefully in his sleep. I can hardly live with thinking that I am a horrible person. I hate myself most days.
- That every sharp object in our home was locked away. Can you imagine trying to cook without sharp knives? Or cutting without scissors? Our home is a sterile institution now and I can't tell you how much I hate it.
- I never thought that even though we only had our son for three years that during that time I had gotten to the point that I did not recognize myself! I had no clue that I would need to go on meds to parent my adoptive child.
- I didn't know that when a friend asked if they could find someone to provide a break during the day (aka respite, but I didn't know that term at the time) that I would burst into tears and tell her "no, because they will bring him back". I needed him gone for good.
- **I always thought that if I loved enough I could fix any issue.** What I didn't know was I would have to protect one adopted daughter from killing the other adopted daughter. We had alarms on all the doors, knives and any sort of weapon had to be hidden. I never knew this could almost ruin a marriage, cause PTSD in me and in my adopted daughter who was being abused.

- Before adoption, I never knew the phone numbers for police detectives, the district attorney, the public defender, and the child advocacy center, would all be listed in my phone contact list.
- **Where in the hell does a five-year-old learn to rape a baby?**
- I had no idea that our close and happy family, who had hobbies and traveled, would be so torn apart that we don't even see our older, grown, married children anymore.
- Before I adopted I had no idea that someday I would do everything I could to reverse the adoption after the trauma to our family. My favorite quote is from Nacho Libre. "I hate all the orphans of the world". I know that sounds terrible but try living my hell of a life before you judge me.
- **I never thought I would contemplate suicide.**
- I don't know who I am anymore. I'm a completely different person. And not a good one. Adoption ruined me.
- I never thought I would see a post about adoption on social media and see evil and danger coming into the house that will destroy all the peace and love that is currently there.
- I never thought that leaving children in orphanages would be what they really needed and the only reason they wanted to be adopted was to be able to steal and have more freedom.
- When I adopted I had no idea that loving and devoting myself to a child would destroy me because of that child's inability to reciprocate kindness, love or empathy.
- **Before we adopted I had no clue how isolated we would become.**
- That when you have a RAD child that one day Amazon® will send you more texts than real people because you've lost all your friends.
- **I honestly thought the boy we hosted was exchanged for an evil twin at the orphanage.**
- I didn't know my heart could hurt this much.

What are they thinking?

Before going any further, I want to give you a glimpse of what goes on in the minds of parents and orphans *before* adoption.

Adoptive parents/families

Would be adoptive parents are under the illusion that days and nights are spent living in the orphanage with the orphan dreaming constantly of a forever family. (Think "*Little Orphan Annie®*." Grey, Harold. Print.). That when they are adopted the orphan will come to them with open arms and hearts and be eternally grateful they were "saved" and they now have a family and a future. They will embrace the family, school, and the learning process and one day will become a productive member of society. The family will stand proud they were able to make a difference in the life of an orphan, or two, or more. The adoptive family wholeheartedly believes they are making a difference in the life of an orphan. Don't get me wrong, I know this outcome does happen - sometimes. But not often enough to maintain the current process. Understand, this is **NOT** the way most orphans think.

The orphan

The orphan spends their days and nights dreaming of escaping the orphanage and returning to their biological families. It matters not how horrific the family; the child/teen wants them back. They dream of their mom and dad and brothers and sisters. They dream of being reunited and everything being perfect. And if they don't have a mom or a dad there is most likely some living relative who becomes their dream. If there are no relatives, they dream of escape, reaching the city, finding a good job and being on their own without the daily rules of the orphanage. They are convinced they can make it on their own. This is their dream. It is NOT a dream of adoption. Let me repeat that. It is NOT a dream of being adopted! It is one of escape and autonomy. (THIS is where money needs to be spent. Helping these children/teens transition into real life right in their own country. Helping them get training to find a decent job, helping them find a job and a safe place to live.)

An orphan who has been exposed to the idea of being hosted or adopted

A new plan has been formed. They see America like the comedy shows or movies they've watched on TV. Oh yes, they get TV time in the orphanage! Many of them have some type of phone where they can get on the internet and watch American TV and movies. Imagine watching a family comedy show and being convinced it was reality. You wouldn't. But they do. Absolutely. Unlimited money, their own car and phone, days spent at the mall shopping for anything they want with your credit card, no responsibility and laughter and hugs if they do anything wrong. Who wouldn't want that life?

Disneyland® hosting!

If the child/teen has been hosted, a whole new dynamic is thrown in which I like to call the "Disneyland® effect". That's when a child/teen visits for several weeks and the host family makes the stay like a trip to a theme park. The family showers them with new clothes and with fun trips and outings. The family has the best of intentions. They only want to give the child/teen some fun and happiness. However, a false reality is created and later, when the child/teen is adopted (by either this family or another), the child/teen is under the impression family life resembles a permanent vacation. They are convinced America really is like the T.V. shows. It DOES NOT MATTER if they are told differently. They will only believe what they experienced (or saw on T.V.). This is an immense problem in the adoption world. It raises expectations abnormally high for the future adoptee. Even if the family stays to a "normal" routine during hosting it is so far removed from the orphan's daily orphanage life it can't help but raise false expectations.

Additionally, these children/teens are EXCELLENT at hiding their true nature, for weeks and even months, to achieve their goal. Smoking, drinking, sexual deviance, and other repulsive behaviors, and most especially RAD (Reactive Attachment Disorder). These children/teens can, and do, hide it all, for the sake of one simple goal.

GET OUT OF THE ORPHANAGE – PERIOD!

The child/teen will "fake it until they make it". This is a setup for future failure. I've had parents tell me they hosted for six weeks and saw none of the horrific behaviors which began immediately once they arrived home with the child/teen; post-adoption.

While being hosted the child/teen has thoughts such as, "If I could find a family to adopt me, I could spend a few years in America and become very rich. Then I will come back to my country, find my real family and because I'm so rich from America I will fix everything wrong with them." OR "I can pay for them all to come to America to live with me in my big mansion." THIS is now their dream. Truly. (My jaw literally dropped when I was told this by one of ours and we were told it was quite common in their orphanage. They dream of going back to their country with tens of thousands of dollars, so they can be the one everyone else looks up to. One of ours told us he was going to be "The Man".)

AND THE ADOPTIVE FAMILY HAS NO CLUE THAT THIS IS THE ORPHANS PLAN. NONE. ZERO. ZIP.

When the adopted child/teen arrives in America and real-life hits them, look out! All hell is about to break loose, and the family has no idea an atomic bomb is about to shatter their family. The adoptive family begins to justify the escalating bad behavior like we did.

- Well, he did grow up without his family and in that horrid orphanage. (Remember the urine smell, dirt floors and iron bars on the windows.)
- You must expect some bumps in the road with what she's had to deal with.
- He just needs more love, we must show him our love no matter what.
- She needs therapy. Let's get her with a good therapist to work through all her issues.
- He's just like any other teenager. None of them are perfect. They all do bad things. I know plenty of biological teens who act out and do regretful things.

- She didn't mean to do that or say that. It's just the hurt coming out.

When the adopted child/teen realizes they didn't get the TV family, they think they just got dealt a bad hand. They got a "bad" family. They move into destroy mode and think, "If I can destroy this family then "they" will give me to a better family." Nothing you, or anyone else, says or does will persuade them otherwise. They are convinced. After all, they saw it on all the TV shows. This terrible family is obviously lying to them.

These children/teens will not believe ANYTHING the family or anyone else says contrary to their delusion. In fact, they tend to believe the exact opposite of everything any member of the family says. The adoptees are fantastic liars and they think everyone else lies equally. Normal reasoning is not accepted.

They are convinced you adopted them to get more money from the government. Some believe you get a monthly check from the government for adopting them, and the government paid you to adopt them. Nothing you say will convince them otherwise. You can show them piles of proof in the forms of receipts, letters, bills and reports – they still won't believe you.

Many times, they believe they were adopted into household slavery, otherwise known as family chores. We sat down with pen and paper to show our adoptees that hiring a full-time housekeeper who actually did a good job, without all of the drama, would have been far cheaper than adopting and they still did not believe us. AND, while we were in the orphanages with them, we sat down with each of them and laid out EXACTLY how our family operated. We outlined our expectations of chores, school, fun times, vacations, and responsibilities. We even talked about nightly teeth brushing and daily showers with all body parts being cleaned. Each of them nodded heads and agreed. Then they signed paperwork and testified in court before a judge that they understood and wanted to be adopted. Arriving home all of that flew right out the window.

THEY WILL NEVER BELIEVE YOU ADOPTED THEM TO GIVE THEM A BETTER LIFE!

The adoptee cannot comprehend anyone doing anything so selfless; so, they make up an ulterior motive by the parents to justify bad behavior towards the family. Whatever the ulterior motive is becomes an absolute fact to them. Nothing and no one will sway them. If you say anything different, "you are a liar and you don't want them to be happy."

CHAPTER 2

Who We Were

It was August of 2012 and Tom and I had successfully blended a family of eight; Tom and I and our six children. We were married the summer of 1994, each bringing two children into the marriage. In 1998 we had Garrett and in 2000, Katherine. People often asked us how we successfully blended our families together (from essentially three marriages). The children all behaved as if they were biological brothers and sisters. People suggested we write a book. We laughed. We had simple parenting rules and we stuck to them. It didn't seem like a big deal to us. And we loved having teenagers.

When this adoption story started, we had only two of the six remaining at home, the four older children grown and on their own. Garrett was 13 and Katherine was 11. We were also grandparents to five wonderful grandchildren.

To reflect, we had started home schooling the youngest two when Garrett entered second grade. Tom was a born teacher and loved digging into topics with them. When teaching geography or history many times we would take family field trips to places like Columbus, Ohio to see the replica of the Santa Maria. Everything became a teaching moment for us. In the beginning Tom was the main teacher while I ran our tanning salons. Then I began an Arbonne home based business and Tom went back into the workforce. We sold the salons and I became their main teacher.

Tom is the kindest, gentlest and absolutely funniest man I've ever known. He was constantly coming up with jokes and pranks. When our older children were still at home they came up with a game of "tie me up with a rope to see how fast I can get out of it – Houdini style." If they couldn't, they would come to me to untie them, then they would take the rope right back to Tom to do it again. They would play with him for hours. He now plays the same game with our dog Reagan. Reagan will bring him the rope, Tom will tie him loosely and then Reagan will come right to me to untie him. Then Reagan will take the rope right back to Tom. It's hilarious and exactly what our children used to do.

Tom taught the neighborhood children four-square on the driveway, went on long bike rides with them, and we all had a blast watching him prank their friends who were over with his famous quarter trick. He was "that" dad.

When Hurricane Katrina struck he immediately signed up to help with cleanup efforts, first with Samaritan's Purse, then he organized a second trip with the church we were attending at the time. He's the guy you call when you need anything. No matter what he's doing, he drops it and will be there for you.

We've been married for almost 24 years and even through the insanity of the last five I am more in love with him than ever and I respect him so very much.

Garrett and Katherine. How do I tell you about these two amazing teens? They are two years plus 3 days apart in birth and ever since Katherine was about 6 months old they've been joined at the hip.

They are super smart and born leaders. Garrett is the strong, gentle, stable, can't rattle me guy who kept watch over our little Tornado Girl. He is honorable, dependable, and like his dad, there to help anyone at any time, even if it costs him dearly. Prior to adopting, he showed an interest in computers, so we were looking at transitioning him into our local public high school for more training. He is and always has been a hugger. I used to gratefully say, "I'll never lack for hugs and love as long as Garrett is around." He is planning a career in the Air Force. That's our Garrett, always wanting to serve.

Katherine. The baby of the family. She now stands at 5'10" and is all muscle. Still the Tornado Girl, she runs - FAST. When she was little, she could get anywhere faster than anyone else, and she still can. She started public school in 7th grade and came to me one day to say, "Mom, I want to stop being on the swim team and run cross country at school." That was the beginning of her love of competing. She has been the #1 female distance runner for both cross country and track for her school since that day in 7th grade when she realized she could run fast. She has inner strength (thank Yahweh for that), is beautiful, both inside and out, and has a focus for her future I haven't seen in many teenagers.

She is loving, affectionate and determined. We have spent the last 17 years working to keep her safe without breaking her incredible spirit for adventure and pushing the limits.

Her goal is to run cross country and track in college and go on to the Olympics for distance running. Oh! And her huge life goal is to be the first woman to break the 4-minute mile. She is my mini-me; my heart.

Me. (At this writing I've just turned 60.) Who was I before all of this? It's not easy writing about myself. I was a busy person. I had been running an Arbonne home-based business for more than 15 years, helping to home school Garrett and Katherine, and kept up our home. I had spent a couple of years attending culinary arts school and did an internship at a local restaurant. I loved to cook and bake. I even taught some home school cooking classes for our local home school groups. I enjoyed my life. It was centered on my family.

I loved Yahweh, but really didn't have Him as a priority in my life. He was just "there". I went to church, but that was about it other than listening to Christian music. We had a backyard swimming pool and I loved spending summers poolside in the sun. We took nice family vacations once or twice a year. It was a good life. My business was doing well, my family was happy, and I was content with my life.

We were all pretty satisfied with where we were headed as a family and as individuals. That all changed one summer night at the dinner table.

CHAPTER 3

Our First Adoption

I had gotten an email early in the week. It arrived as a mass email sent to our home school group. A family who was hosting a teen boy from Ukraine had an emergency and needed a place for him to stay his remaining three weeks in the U.S. I deleted the message and moved on. Over the next few days I would think about, then dismiss that email. I was having a great summer with Garrett and Katherine. I worked my business and loved being home with my children. Tom was working for a mortgage company in the city. I didn't even know what hosting was. And why Ukraine of all places? I looked it up on a map.

On Friday night Tom was home for dinner and I mentioned the email. He said, "Why not? We have two almost teens and a backyard pool. Why not give the boy some fun for three weeks? Look into it," he said. I made a call and the following Tuesday I was waiting at arrivals at Detroit Metro to pick up Viktor, who was 15, and who spoke decent English. That was all I knew. That should have been my first clue - not everything you're told in this hosting/adoption business is the truth.

He arrived, and it was true his name was Viktor and he was 15. What was also true was he spoke almost no English and he was angry and sullen. He didn't say anything to me as I took his bag and walked to my car. We drove a very long, silent 45 minutes home. I showed him the room he would be staying in and he waved me away and shut the door. When he was still there several hours later, I knocked and opened the door. He was lying on the bed in the dark. I encouraged him to come downstairs and he finally complied. We ended up having a good evening, even playing a game of Sorry® after dinner. He helped Garrett and Katherine clean up, then returned to his room for the night.

The next three days were more of the same. He would stay in his room unless persuaded to join us for family time. It took a lot of convincing to get him outside and into the pool, but once there he had a great time, even getting out our mini trampoline to do flips into the water. He vacillated between sitting in the dark in his room and then having the time of his life with us. One day Tom suggested going to play putt-putt golf and go-karting. Garrett, Katherine and Viktor laughed so hard trying to beat each other around the race course. Viktor gave the impression he was having fun, but once home I found him back in his room sitting in the dark.

I wondered if there was more to the story of the other family having a family emergency. Was it really that this boy was just difficult, and they couldn't handle him? I brushed the feeling aside. The first of too many times of pushing aside gut feelings.

First recommendation if you are considering adoption

Listen to your gut. Most likely it's Yahweh talking to you. You might want to listen very carefully. My gut warned me on several occasions and I continually brushed it off. I rationalized. I made excuses. I justified behaviors.

Because I wanted to figure this thing out with Viktor, I called and spoke to a woman at the hosting agency who put me in touch with their hosting facilitator in Ukraine. Viktor and I spoke with him via Skype®. I was told by this man that Viktor was very discouraged because he thought he would be adopted by the family in Minnesota, but they had "turned him away" and his time was running out. The facilitator told me all Viktor wanted to do now was go back to Ukraine and put America behind him.

This poor teen! We found out he had been hosted several times prior to that summer and each time went back to Ukraine without having found his "forever family". This is what both the hosting agency and the Ukrainian facilitator told us. Our hearts went out to him. No wonder he was acting out!

I didn't know at the time that it was **absolutely illegal,** according to Ukrainian adoption law, to speak about adoption while a child/teen was being hosted. Ukrainian law is very strict about no pre-selection of children prior to visiting the government operated Department for Family and Children in Kiev, Ukraine (DFC), formerly known as the SDA.

However, Tom and I assumed all this hosting organization and the Ukrainian facilitator said was true. After all, they were the experts! Since the Skype® conversation was entirely in Russian I had no way of knowing what was actually said. I never asked why he had been hosted by several families and not one was interested in adopting him. Was he really discouraged or was this his personality? What were Viktor and the facilitator really saying?

BELIEVING ADULTS IN THE HOSTING/ADOPTION WORLD, MAKING EXCUSES FOR BAD BEHAVIOR ON THE PART OF AN ORPHAN, AND IGNORING THE SIGNS OF BIGGER PROBLEMS LURKING BECAME THE START OF SOME VERY BAD HABITS ON OUR END.

We were terribly naïve. Because we had already raised four grown children to adulthood and still had two teens at home, we thought we knew what we were doing. We had no idea the adoption experience would be all new territory, that disorders such as RAD existed, and we were absolutely clueless about any potential hazards.

After discussing all the hosting agency had told me that night with Tom, we went to bed determined to give Viktor a good time for the rest of his stay with us. The next morning Tom was walking out the door for work when he turned to me and said, "I think we're supposed to adopt Viktor." I nodded my head and told him I would investigate what was involved.

I know many of you who are reading this right now, who are living in your own adoption hell, have your own moments where you would give almost anything for a do-over. This is one of our moments.

I've never been one to want a do-over in life. Even the bad experiences have been lessons of life and I'm grateful for them. However, this is one of those moments where I've thought many times that had I known what I was getting our family into, I would have adamantly said, "**NO!**"

As I promised Tom, I called the hosting agency and told the woman we might be interested in adopting Viktor. I inquired about the cost and was told $10,000 to $12,000. HA! (If you're parent, who has adopted internationally, you are laughing at that one.) A bold-faced lie if there ever was one. The actual sum was just over $25,000! The hosting agency was well aware of the costs of international adoption. They also know once you're in the process and have money spent, it's near impossible to give up on your investment, especially since you are so heavily committed emotionally. You just keep shoveling the money out.

Long afterwards, I mentioned to her it was quite a bit more, in fact more than double, what she had told me. Her response was she just told me about the fees. I call B.S. She knew full well we had zero clue on adoption costs and she knew quite well what the approximate costs were. The right thing to do would have been to give us a full picture. Fees plus travel plus costs plus more travel plus and plus and plus.

Oh! And don't forget money for bribes. HA! That's right. Bribes!

And there was no mention made of how costly it would be once we brought Viktor home. You expect clothing and food costs, costs for sports and extracurricular activities, etc. We were not made aware of the "other" potential liabilities.

If only I had known – Financially...

- When I adopted I didn't know we would go into massive debt with therapy, psychiatric hospitals, and residential treatment facilities before eventually turning her over to the state for help and respite.

- Before we adopted we didn't know we would pay so much money and go into huge debt just to be physically and emotionally abused and there was no way out of it.
- I wrote a check for this? To constantly fight for my own survival and that of my biological children and to have paid so much money to live in this situation is mind-blowing. Not only are we all at risk from him, we owe so much money I can't see being debt-free again in my lifetime.
- I didn't anticipate three years post disruption selling even our dining room table to continue to work out from under the massive debt of medical bills left in the wake of an adoption where we weren't told the whole story of his medical conditions.
- The amount of breakage in our home has been incredible. Our debt continues to escalate.
- I never thought that two years after he was gone from our home I would break down sobbing after glancing at my old broken furniture. Furniture he destroyed and due to the costs of adoption and post-adoption debt, we can't afford to replace. I don't know how to live like this.
- I didn't know we were obligating ourselves to pay for child support, psychologists, lawyers, court fees, damages and replacement costs, hospital and ambulance costs, etc. And those are just the financial losses. Just to be hated and disrespected by ungrateful children.
- **I didn't know that if we could barely afford the adoption expense, we sure couldn't afford the needs that followed.**

Hosting Agencies

I'm going to pause here for a moment to talk about hosting agencies and adoption. This was another area where we were sadly lacking in knowledge. Knowing what we know now there were several irregularities which should have warned us we were heading into troubled waters. We went based on the assumption that this agency (and other hosting/adoption organizations) was reputable, honest, and reliable. We expected they had the best interests of both the adoptee and adoptive parents at heart. Boy, were we wrong.

On the surface, helping orphans find families sounds good. I do believe that some who work for these agencies have the best intentions. I know several people who have left hosting organizations because they realized just how many families were being led down the same path we traveled, and they couldn't stomach being a part of it anymore. One admitted to me she could barely function because she lives with so much guilt from the adoptions for which she'd advocated. She said most of those adoptions had caused severe trauma for those families and she was having a hard time living with the knowledge that she participated in making those adoptions happen. Her own family was living with the devastation of a RAD adoption. The sad part is many of these hosting organizations pass themselves off as Christian. On the outside, it makes them seem more credible - believable.

Missed Red Flags

We were able to pick Viktor up from the airport and NO ONE CHECKED US OUT FIRST! I had one short conversation with the woman at the hosting agency and a short conversation with the woman who was currently hosting him in Minnesota. They sent this 15-year-old boy on a plane from one state to another, to a home of complete strangers, with zero background checks. Not one person asked for references or verification. This agency was willing to do anything to find hosts without regard for the children/teens safety. We had no home study, no references, no criminal background checks, nada. We didn't even submit our ID's. In hindsight this was scary, but because we were pretty cool people, I just figured everyone knew we were cool people. Gah!

As I mentioned, hosting agencies and potential adoptive families are forbidden to talk about adoption with these teens because Ukrainian law does not allow for pre-selection of adopted children/teens. The basis for bringing these teens to America is simply to host and give them a taste of American life – a vacation. Compliance with Ukrainian law went right out the window with regards to Viktor. Agencies have a monetary interest in finding permanent homes for orphans and we bought into that "forever family" jargon hook, line and sinker. We were given unsubstantiated statistics like the postcard I shared: At age 16 they are thrown out of the orphanage onto the streets without anything. Most of them will end up in prostitution or dead.

What is not told potential adoptive families is many of the orphans are not true orphans at all but are "social orphans" who have living family members. After graduation the orphan will naturally gravitate towards those family members. Are those families perfect? Nope. Many of them are alcoholics and out of work. But, nonetheless they are family.

And family trumps America almost every time!

I also wonder now how much good it does for the orphan to be hosted in America simply for the "taste of America" aspect. I've been to Ukraine. It's not like America in the slightest. Should the orphan not be adopted but continue to live in Ukraine (or whichever country they are from), wouldn't the massive cultural difference between the typical Ukrainian and typical American make it just that much harder for them? They've now gotten a taste of Filet Mignon, but their future is ground beef. How is that helping them?

I believe any person or organization who has a vested interest (they make money) from adoptions should be scrutinized **very** closely before making any financial arrangements with them. These are businesses with payrolls and overhead to meet. They present themselves as selfless, and many who work there are. Bottom line: they are in the business of finding homes for orphans and running their operation whether it be a for-profit or non-profit.

Honestly – and I'm going to be very blunt here - which is probably going to make a lot of people really mad – I believe this is a form of *legal human trafficking*. I don't quite know how we all got to this point to begin with. Really. Who thought it would be a good idea to take children and teens from one country and culture to a completely different one while charging a whole lot of money? Who is profiting here? Just sayin'.

The orphans **CANNOT** possibly understand the ramifications of moving to an entirely different culture and family structure or understand the emotional and mental effects of such a decision. They may say otherwise, but they simply do not. They cannot. This is not their fault. They have no way of comprehending the challenges they will face. They have no way of knowing how much of an alternate universe they will be part of after the adoption. They are completely unprepared for the enormous shock to their system. In the resources section there are "The Four Stages of Cultural Adjustment". You will read how incredibly difficult it is to change cultures – and this was written for adults who move from one country to another – not children and teens who have never developed emotionally or mentally. It takes the difficulty of adjustment to a whole new level of "almost impossible". And this only addresses culture, not the fact the orphan now has to learn how to live within a family structure with parents and siblings when they never have before. I wonder how many adults could handle this level of stress and trauma.

Additionally, many of the children/teens don't have a voice in the matter. I know, I know. They must sign a written document in Ukraine and go to court and give their buy-in if they are over a certain age. I personally know several cases where these children/teens were coerced by orphanage workers. The child/teen is told to agree "or else!" How is this business of adoption <u>not</u> a form of legalized human trafficking?

THIS HAS GOT TO STOP!!!

Now, you're already thinking WHOA she's crazy! HA! Just keep reading. Hang in there with me!

Family X. When we adopted we didn't realize we would be active participants in legalized human trafficking.

Legalized Human Trafficking

My definition of human trafficking, for the purposes of this book, varies slightly from the common definition. I am advocating for expanding the illegality of human trafficking to include the "legalized" version.

Legalized human trafficking is when a teen or child is transported from one country to another and one or more people make a profit based on the transfer under the guise of adoption.

Back to our story. "Oh no", we thought. Viktor was going to be 16 in April. We couldn't let him age out onto the cold streets of Ukraine! There became a sense of urgency, almost panic, for the adoption process to begin. Our entire family went into high gear adoption mode. We needed to get Viktor home with us as soon as possible before he turned 16! We all bought into the looming doom of aging out. We worked hard on mountains of paperwork, an invasive home study and held fundraisers to help with the costs, which were quickly accruing. We were told, "Everyone does fundraisers so the money you need will be there." (At this writing we are still well over $80,000 in debt.)

Fundraising is incredibly hard and is a full-time job on top of whatever else you are doing in your life. The funds generated are usually only a drop in the bucket. Most families are left with crushing debt from the adoption alone. The huge costs once these children/teens are brought home from medical bills, counseling which is not covered by insurance, court costs, home repairs, and much more are staggering. One friend spent over $150,000 to clear her name from abuse charges alleged by her adopted children, who falsified the complaint just to get her into trouble because she wouldn't let them have their phones to look up porn websites. (Very common.)

The adoption process for Viktor required two trips to Ukraine. Tom was unable to travel because of his job, so I went alone. The travel was brutal in January, staying first one week, then going back for three more weeks.

The adoption process was grueling. I spent money like water. I missed my family. At the same time my heart was breaking because there were so many more orphans just like Viktor and I could only bring one orphan home.

I was so moved with compassion I became an *Advocate* for those left behind. Typing that word "Advocate" made my stomach turn. I want to throw up. I'm sick at how many teens were adopted and are now living in this country due to my influence. And how many of those families (almost 100% of them) are living in turmoil because of their adoption. Sometimes the weight of my involvement makes it hard to function. I see a post on Facebook® from one of the adoptive parents who I influenced, and I know they are going through hell thanks, in part, to me. I spread my ignorance about adoption far and wide and there are many casualties. To those families, I am deeply sorry. This is one of those times I truly would turn back the hands of time and keep my big mouth shut. When so many of these adoptions fail in one way or another I am convinced there must be a better way. And I'm determined to find it.

Family X. There was a boy in Viktor's orphanage who told me one day he really wanted a family. Could I please find him a family in America? I took a picture of him smiling and posted it on social media. In just a few days someone reached out to me to inquire about him. I told her everything I knew. They adopted him. The boy was happy he was finally adopted and was so thankful to me for finding him a family. He was relieved he would not age out and be tossed into the streets in Ukraine. He walked around that orphanage as if he had won the lottery and was so excited. After he was adopted, and we were still in country he couldn't stop thanking me and hugging me because he loved his new family so much.

After coming to America things spiraled downhill fast. The lies and manipulations began. After counseling (paid for out of pocket by the family) he was put on anti-depressants. Soon, he was caught selling those prescription drugs at school. He suffered from depression and was selling his own meds! He began telling everyone in their very small community his family did not love him, and he couldn't live with them anymore. He claimed he never really wanted to be adopted and he was forced by them to leave his country. His adoptive mom would call me sobbing because they loved him so much and he was not bonding with them at all. She was at a total loss. Since I was there at the start and through the process I know for a fact he wanted to be adopted and he loved his new parents. But to everyone else he tells the tale of a victim.

Orphans are always believed by outsiders. <u>Always</u>.

At this writing this boy is now living with another family in town. The adoptive family is devastated by the lies told about them in their small town. They are working hard to recover. They wonder if all they sacrificed to give the boy a future was worth it.

A common thought among us who have adopted.

In this boy's case I truly believe his mind could not make the transition from Ukrainian to American culture. I spent several weeks with him in Ukraine where he was one of the happiest boys I'd met. He always had a huge smile on his face and he was full of love and laughter. Moving to America changed him. Something snapped. I saw him a few months after the adoption in his new home and he was nothing like the boy in the orphanage. Adoption ruined his life, and the lives of his adoptive family. None of them were at fault. None of them had any way of knowing the effect this culture change would have on him.

My story of cultural adjustment. During the second adoption I spent eleven weeks in Ukraine. I was in my late 50's, educated and I loved to travel. I had traveled around the world several times, but by the fifth week in Ukraine my stress level had increased ten-fold. Just going to the corner grocery story was challenging. I craved tuna fish but couldn't figure out which can contained what type of meat. No one could help me because of the language barrier. There was no peanut butter and no Mexican restaurants or even the ingredients to prepare Mexican food. Restaurants served drinks without ice cubes. My ears hurt from constantly hearing another language. Toilets were holes in the ground. Try squatting wearing pants with nothing to hold onto for balance. HA! I missed everything I was used to having and being around.

Ukraine is a beautiful country and the people were friendly. But it was not America. It was not home. By eight weeks Tom and I were strained to the point we were snapping at every little stupid thing. By ten weeks I thought I was losing my mind. All I could think of was being home. I told friends that I needed to get home NOW, or I was going to lose it. At the time we didn't make the connection that our adopted teens would have it much worse. Only hindsight has given us that perspective.

Family X. After writing on my blog one day, I got a message from an adoptive mom asking to call and talk with me. We talked for two hours. She explained they were from a very small town out west and their local law enforcement agency was not empathetic to their situation. She and her husband had several biological children and they had decided to adopt a teen girl for the same reasons as Tom and me. They wanted to save one girl from likely prostitution. She and her husband were both in the mental health field and were familiar with terms such as Fetal Alcohol Spectrum Disorders (FASD) and Reactive Attachment Disorder (RAD). They thought they were more prepared than most. They weren't.

Fetal Alcohol Spectrum Disorders (FASD)

FASD is an umbrella term describing the range of effects that can occur in an individual whose mother drank alcohol during pregnancy. These effects may include physical, mental, behavioral, and/or learning disabilities with possible lifelong implications.
(https://depts.washington.edu/fasdpn/htmls/fasd-fas.htm)

Reactive attachment disorder (RAD)

RAD is described in clinical literature as a severe and relatively *uncommon disorder* which can affect children. RAD is characterized by markedly disturbed and developmentally inappropriate ways of relating socially in most contexts.

>(https://www.mayoclinic.org/diseases-conditions/reactive-attachment-disorder/symptoms-causes/syc-20352939)

(My opinion is RAD may be uncommon in "normal" situations, but when it comes to adopted children/teens it is far more widespread than anyone in the mental health field will admit.)

> "If a child is not attached – does not form a loving bond with the mother – he does not develop an attachment to the rest of mankind. The unattached child literally does not have a stake in humanity" (Magid & McKelvey 1988).

> "At the core of the unattached, is a deep-seeded rage, far beyond normal anger. This rage is suppressed in their psyche. Now, we all have some degree of rage, but the rage of psychopaths is that, born of unfulfilled needs as infants. Incomprehensible pain is forever locked in their souls, because of the abandonment they felt as infants." (Magid & McKelvey 1988)

RAD is **VERY** dangerous. The RAD teen/child attaches to one of the adoptive parents, usually the one they see rescuing them, typically the mom. As soon as the RAD teen/child feels they have control over the relationship and situation, they turn on the parent they attached to and that parent become enemy #1. The change may be gradual at first, from hugging and loving to obstinate and argumentative. The progression from there to vindictiveness, manipulating others to turn against the parent(s), exaggerating stories from the orphanage to cast themselves into the role of the victim, running to authorities to "turn in" the parent or parents for fabricated abuses (verbal, emotional, mental and/or physical/sexual), abusing the parent(s) and other family members, and much more.

To the RAD, the enemy needs to be destroyed in whatever way possible. In the meantime, they are continually on the lookout for their next "savior". Someone to rescue them from their "terrible situation". It is a never-ending quest to be attached to someone. They never find what they are missing unless the RAD teen/child is willing to understand and accept their diagnosis, which is uncommon, especially in teenagers. Treatment requires years of therapy and RAD trained therapists are scarce. The older the child/teen is when adopted, the less likely they are to agree to treatment. Instead, in many cases RAD teen/child simply moves on to another savior family who feels sorry for them until the same cycle repeats. The new family becomes the enemy with the RAD teen/child seeking yet another savior/caregiver.

Back to the mental health professionals who adopted: This couple felt they were very capable of raising an adopted teen, even if she was diagnosed with either of these disorders, however, they were told this girl did not have any physical or mental issues; a typical tactic of orphanage personnel.

This mom was raw emotion when I spoke with her. Their home was a war zone. They all lived in fear. The adopted girl talked brazenly about what she wanted to do their family. She wanted them dead. She told them her dream was to burn down their home at night while they were all sleeping and watch them all die. She told them that she would stand there laughing at the burning house. She would laugh to hear them all screaming. She explained how she and her husband took turns on watch. They never slept together or at the same time. They had no sharp objects in the home and had even removed all cooking utensils. The adopted teen urinated on the floors of the home whenever she could. She smeared feces everywhere.

The family had a small one-bedroom cottage on their property where the biological children were living. The family spent most of their time in the cottage. Hostages. They reached out to their adoption agency who refused to help them. Social services wanted to blame them and had opened an investigation. They were threatened with removal of their biological children. Local law enforcement treated them like criminals. When law enforcement and social services spoke to the adopted teen, they saw a sweet, good-natured, smiling, adorable teenager who was at a loss as to why her family, whom she loved so much, was saying such bad things about her.

When the parents told officers some of the things the girl had done, she told officers she was being blamed for things the biological children had done, so they could get rid of her. She had always dreamt of a forever family, she said, and she was so sad all they did was abuse her, only fed her small amounts of food and kept her locked in her room. Law enforcement/SS never questioned the fact there were no locks on the adopted girl's bedroom door or windows. This same story can be told repeatedly. There was never any true investigation, but automatic judgement and guilt for the parent(s).

Family X...If only I had known...RAD.

- My RAD was non-verbal until almost three. Not long after he turned 3 he started talking about how he was going to kill me. I was shocked as he had very little TV and no internet exposure. Just shy of age 4 he took a knife from the sink and tried to stab his younger brother. I watched him look at the knife and I could see him process how he could use the knife to kill his brother. I stopped him before he could do any harm.

    He would throw such fits of rage the house would be destroyed. I'd have bruises from trying to stop him, our puppy would go into hiding, and I would have my younger child hide, too, until RAD's rage subsided.

    I took RAD to the hospital to try and get help for him and they reported me to OCS/CPS who told me the only help they could offer was to remove him from my home. Even a one-month respite for us would take at least two to three years to regain custody. I said, "No, that isn't what we need," I was told an investigation would be opened because a child of his age is incapable of having a mental illness and this behavior stemmed from abuse.

    For four months we were investigated with RAD interviewed alone three times. They made two home visits and implied my husband had PTSD from his military deployment. They threatened to remove my younger child.

This is what happens when we parents ask for HELP. We are immediately vilified. WE are NOT the enemy! We are simply trying to seek help and treatment for our children.

As I continued to fight for my child, I was reported for abuse again. This time by our pediatrician who reported me for "Exaggeration of symptoms with intent to hospitalize the child unnecessarily." I was simply asking for my child to be seen by a psychiatrist because our family doctor couldn't renew the medications he needed. Medications my RAD had already been prescribed during his SECOND inpatient hospital stay that transpired because he was deemed dangerous to others.

The American justice system and child and family services is flawed. OCS/DCF/CPS is a joke. They are NOT out to help parents or children but have their own agenda. Medical professionals are not educated in RAD or other attachment trauma issues. We parents are seeing this trauma play out daily and we need to be believed when we ask for help for our children. Before more tragedies take place.

Our story. Viktor. The weeks spent in Ukraine adopting Viktor made my heart hurt. I would wake up in the morning, eat breakfast, and then walk one mile to the grocery store. I loaded two bags as full as I could and still be able to carry them with fruit, protein bars, nuts and other snack foods. After walking back to the hotel, I would wait until noon, then a car would pick me up to take me to Viktor's orphanage where I would have two hours to spend with him. I exited the car, looked at the 12-foot-tall iron fence with a grimace, then walked through the heavy iron gate and up the sidewalk to the entrance where a stone-faced woman unlocked the door to let me enter. I would smile at her and say good afternoon. She glared back at me. (My goal was to coax a smile from her before we left the final time – it never happened.)

I walked past her and breathed in the smell of sewer. It was nasty. The first time I almost gagged, but after a few days, became accustomed to holding my breath until I got further into the building where the stench wasn't as bad. Viktor would be waiting in the entry way with two or three friends and I would hand the bags to him to distribute. Their favorites were bananas, jerky and sunflower seeds. Viktor enjoyed handing out the snacks to the others and I emailed Tom, telling him Viktor only kept one banana and a small package of sunflower seeds for himself. He gave all the rest away; dividing it up fairly between everyone else, including the little ones. His selflessness was a positive sign for us. Truthfully, it was his way of being "the man."

Of the two hours we spent the first 30 minutes in the teachers' lounge where he played games on my iPad with his friends. Then we would walk through the orphanage, down the stairs to the lower level, then down a long hallway to the gym where I would watch him and his friends play basketball. He always had friends with him. One day he took me on a tour both inside and outside. A pack of orphans followed us everywhere we went, hungry for any attention I would give them. Outside were some ancient, broken playground structures where they did Parkour (outdoor extreme gymnastics). Inside he showed off a room next to the gym where three homemade ping pong tables were set up. He told me he was champion. One day while walking in the main hallway he pointed out a large sign. He stopped and pointed to it. It was concerning the dangers of smoking – of course written in Russian, but through the pictures I understood the meaning. He said to me, "I no smoke. Smoke bad. I athlete." Another good sign, which I passed along to Tom via email.

Viktor led me down a narrow, dark hallway where we walked on dirt floors to another section of the building, then up the stairs to the dorms. There were several sections, each unisex "home" to ten to twelve orphans. The girls' bedrooms were separated from the boys by a small TV room, small dining area and bathroom, which had a squatty potty (hole in the floor), one open shower and a small sink. Everything was very sparse. The bedrooms had nothing on the walls, twin beds with a blanket, no pillow, and a large empty cabinet. Outside the dining room was a wall with summer camp type pictures of orphans participating in various activities. There were also pictures of graduated orphans. Underneath was a long row of shoes. I asked Viktor about them and he told me they all shared. If the size fit they wore it. They all shared clothing, too. He would wear the same outfit for a full week, then on wash day he would choose a different outfit. No one owned anything of value. He had a few pictures and some wooden figurines he had been given by the local church.

After the visit I would take a taxi back to the hotel. The rest of the day was spent thinking about everything I had experienced that day. When I fell asleep I had nightmares about orphans left behind. I was determined to do something about this enormous problem. Children of the world deserved better than this! I was angry. I was upset. I felt I had a Yahweh-given mission to help these orphans find families.

I spent far more money in Ukraine than planned. The "gift" of $1,000 to the orphanage director. After observing the orphanage smelling of sewer, walking on nasty dirt floors, and seeing how the children shared clothing and shoes, I wondered where the "gift" went. Was it "pocketed" by the director wearing her full-length fur coat and carrying her designer bag? Hundreds of dollars were spent to ensure paperwork was completed in a timely manner (otherwise known as bribes). Many times, I'd walk up to a window in a government office and was told, "Well, this will take three weeks, but if you pay an extra $50 or $100 American you can have it later today." Then I'd return later in the day and maybe it was done. Maybe it was not. I saw too many shrugged shoulders and heard, "Nothing I can do". I'd paid the extortion fees because the alternative was three more weeks of incurred expenses, which was not affordable – relationally, emotionally or financially. I'd go back the next day and hope. And time dragged on and costs and frustration mounted.

I kept a detailed log of our expenses. It cost just over $25,000 to adopt Viktor. It included coming back to America to find out, since my husband had not traveled and gone to court in Ukraine, we now needed to file for an American birth certificate, and U.S. Citizenship was not automatic. Another surprise. Another $1,000 we weren't prepared for. "Oh, we thought you knew that", or "we thought so and so would have told you that". More frustration with the process.

Some may wonder why we didn't ask. In this adoption process you don't even know there are questions you should ask. You are walking blind, following the advice of those who stand to make the most money from the transaction. I'd never tried to get citizenship for someone before so there were questions I had no idea should even be asked.

CHAPTER 4

Orphan Alcoholics

We finally brought Viktor home. The first few weeks were good. We later learned about something called a "honeymoon period". At the time we felt relieved all seemed to be going well in our home. Viktor was getting along well with Garrett and Katherine and there were no signs of the sullen, angry teen we hosted. Viktor seemed content and other than some odd food inclinations, appeared to be adjusting well.

The first month we let a lot of our "normal" activities go, including home schooling and family chores, to have some good bonding time. Once we made the decision to get back to some structure, and to start school again, including teaching Viktor English, things started sliding downhill very quickly. The honeymoon was over. The angry, sullen, withdrawn teen we had seen off and on during hosting reappeared instantly. He seemed mad all the time. He became extremely picky with food and spent as much time in his room as we would allow.

The food issue was very frustrating. I can't count how many times I would make dishes he requested, meals which took hours to prepare, only for him to take one look and turn to me as if to say, what is this crap? "I no eat that!" he'd snarl. And walk away. Four hours prior he'd told me he wanted potato varenyky! One time Tom spent two days making Kholodets Z Ptytsy (poultry aspic), a Ukrainian delicacy which Viktor said he wanted. The dish turned out perfect and looked exactly like the picture in the Ukrainian/English cookbook I had picked up at the street market in Kiev.

Viktor took one bite, stood up from the table, and walked away without a word.

We would spend hours coaxing him to the dinner table to enjoy family time. Then we would pay the price of having a sullen or argumentative teen to deal with. This was quite something when we spoke no Russian and he spoke almost no English. The stress level in our home started rising, but we shrugged it off telling ourselves it was an adjustment period. I spoke with a fellow adoptive mama who suggested we check out our local school ESL offerings and perhaps enroll him in public school.

We did, and it changed things somewhat for the better, at least for a short time. Our local high school had an amazing ESL program and teachers. Viktor took a liking to one teacher in particular, so we enrolled him in 10th grade. It was the lowest grade we could put him in due to his age and graduation requirements. Having him at school and out of the house during most of the day took some pressure off us and appeared to give him an outlet for his moodiness. He came home upbeat most days, leading us to believe there was progress.

Institutionalization

Living in an institution changes a person. Orphans become institutionalized. This was a reality we never contemplated. Viktor was used to living an institutionalized life. He never had anyone in the role of a parent and this drastic adjustment to having involved parents would inevitably lead to confrontations. In the orphanage, the director had little to do with the children/teens. There were "caretakers" who came and went, as well as teachers who came during the day to teach. The children and teens lived 24/7 in the orphanage, rarely leaving except possibly to go to church services on Sundays. There was little bonding with caretakers or teachers, who, like anyplace else, would come in, do their job, and leave to be with their own families. Or leave permanently, in search of better employment. There was no stability or consistency in personnel. The days were very structured, with meals, school, and free time planned down to the minute.

Imagine being someplace where each hour of the day and night there was a ringing bell telling you to shower, eat, play, go to class, study, sleep. Day after day the same routine. As they grew into teens, the orphans' only objective was to escape their confinement. Period. Viktor's orphanage was more like a prison, surrounded by that intimidating 12-foot-tall iron fence. Every door was either guarded by someone or locked. The windows had iron bars and couldn't be opened. The orphans spent their days sneaking off to a certain spot in the yard, out of view of the windows, climbing the fence and running away, then routinely being picked up by local police and returned to the orphanage where certain punishment by the director awaited them.

I was horrified by what I witnessed. That iron fence and gate still live in my memory. I was devastated to think of any child or teen suffering there in that stinking hole.

Certainly there must be a solution to this atrocity!

However, the solution for Viktor (or any other orphan) was not to bring him to America. Uprooting him to another country, within a family structure he could not connect with, or they him, forcing him to learn a new language and culture, was too overwhelming. He simply had no concept how a family should operate. It was a situation destined for failure. Our family was ill-prepared for such a transition and Viktor most certainly was not prepared, or even capable of adapting.

For many orphans the new home simply turns into another orphanage and biological children, if any, become part of the disaster.

I know there are going to be people who disagree. (No way, you say. Your children live in a nice home in America, with plenty of food, opportunities and parents who care.) Just keep reading. Garrett and Katherine now know what it's like to live in a dysfunctional Ukrainian orphanage. Our home eventually morphed into one with Tom and I viewed as the caretakers.

It became the only way for our family to survive.

Time passed with Viktor in school. He began struggling, then stopped trying. He began spending most of his time in the neighborhood park doing parkour. One day Tom realized all the liquor we had in the house was gone. The bottles were still there, but there was nothing in them. My cooking liquors were gone, too. Who drinks cooking sherry? Our homemade cough medicine and elderberry elixirs were gone, leaving only the berries at the bottom of the jars.

I sat down with Viktor late one night to talk with him. The empty bottles sat on the table in front of us. Communication was extremely difficult and now we had to address the serious issue of the missing alcohol through a translation app on my phone.

"So Viktor, tell me about all of this." Pointing to the empty bottles.

"What!" He replied angrily with his heavy Russian accent and broken English. It sounded more like "Vut!"

"These empty bottles Dad found. Why are you drinking?"

"Me no drink. I am athlete. I do Parkour. Drinking bad for athletes. I no drink alcohol."

"Viktor, I know you have been drinking. You can deny it, but I know this was you. There was no one else it could be. I also know you are smoking cigarettes."

"Me no drink. Me no smoke. I am athlete. I do Parkour. Drinking and smoking bad for athletes. I no drink alcohol or smoke."

"Viktor, please tell me the truth. I just want to help you."

This went on for more than an hour. He stood his ground.

Finally, he caved and told me, "I six my father make me sit at table with bottle of vodka and pack of cigarettes and told me it time to be a man. He made me smoke and drink." In that moment my heart was broken for that poor little six-year-old he had been and the teenager he was now who had to live with that memory.

I gently told him, "Go to bed and we will make a fresh start tomorrow." Later, I learned this was all part of a lie to get himself out of trouble. A pattern was forming in which Viktor would say anything he had to so he could keep doing whatever he wanted. He'd make up stories, we would feel sorry for him, and we would let him off the hook. We never knew what was true or a made-up story.

He wanted to keep drinking and smoking so was just sneakier. He would drink some and then fill up the balance with water. When we removed all the alcohol from the house all of the cold medicine disappeared. Then we removed the cold medicine. Then he creatively started making his own moonshine.

One day an entire bag of apples disappeared. He told me he was so hungry, and he never got apples in the orphanage. I felt sorry for him and bought more apples. They disappeared. I bought more. A couple weeks later I had the urge to go into the playhouse in the back yard. (Mostly, it was where we kept pool stuff since Garrett and Katherine had grown out of playing in it.) I reached my hand above the door. (To this day I don't know why I went out there or why I put my hand up there. I honestly felt the need to go out there. I wasn't looking for anything in particular. I can't explain it.) I touched glass. There were four-quart mason jars full of apple moonshine. So that's where all the apples went! I called Viktor out to the clubhouse and in front of him I poured the hooch out onto the compost. He was livid. The look on his face was priceless!

He screamed at me, "It take me weeks to make that! It a lot work to do that! Why you throw it all out?"

Before I even had a chance to answer he ran back into the house and then out the front door. We didn't see him until late that night. He was mad for days.

He didn't get it. At all. It was a game to him. Fool us any way he could so he could do whatever he wanted. He was so good at saying "I'm sorry". And I guess we wanted to believe him. We wanted to think he was getting better or making better choices. We just wanted the best for him.

We wanted what our family sacrificed for him to mean something.

Family X...If only I had known...Alcoholics

- I look back to when we brought the two boys home and remember how excited and happy we all were. We were a family of four with our bio son and daughter, 15 and 13, and so excited to have two more brothers in the family. We were told they were the best boys in the orphanage and everyone there would miss them very much. The two brothers were nine and seven and had been in the orphanage since they were toddlers. They seemed cheerful and full of smiles when we met them at the orphanage. They kept asking us to play game after game with them while we were there. We asked about any problems we should be aware of and were told by the director that these were good boys who never got into trouble. They did well on their school work and got along well with the other kids. We felt it was a perfect match.

Once home it all changed very quickly. My husband came to me one afternoon and asked if I had drunk any beer. I'm not a beer drinker and reminded him of that. He said he had put six cans of beer in the refrigerator and now there were two. He said he was sure because he had put six in to chill the night before because he had a friend coming over to watch the game later that afternoon. We couldn't explain. Later I was putting away clothes in the boys' dressers and in the bottom drawer I found four empty beer cans under some jeans. I called my husband to check it out. We looked at each other in shock. And here we thought things were going really well. Our eyes were opened in that instant.

The past two years have been absolute hell. We have two alcoholics living with us. We have long since rid our home of any alcohol and never bring any in the house. Somehow, and we can't figure out how, no matter what restrictions we put on them (at ages eleven and nine), they find alcohol.

The boys are augmentative, demeaning to others both at school and home, are not doing well learning English since they constantly speak only Russian to each other. They are verbally and

physically abusive to anyone in authority. They have gotten suspended from school several times for hitting and twice for being caught with alcohol. They don't deny their actions and they refuse to tell us where they are getting the alcohol. I never thought children this age could be so resourceful. Our home is hell. I can tell you that everyone in that orphanage lied to us about these boys. I hate that we brought them into our peaceful home. I hate that we adopted. I would like to help them, but they don't think they are doing anything wrong.
I feel like I'm in prison.

- Recently we found a stash of empty vodka bottles at the back of our property under a large pine tree. We are guessing they somehow stole the liquor from a local store. Seriously, there were more than twenty bottles – the liter size. Cheap vodka. And hundreds of cigarette butts.

Viktor. During this time, we were still convinced, as difficult as it was, we had done the right thing and we should keep advocating for other orphans. I had come home with Viktor in early February 2013 and that summer, we hosted two more boys from the same country who we were told needed to find forever families. We were "successful" finding homes for both. And during that summer we advocated for several more orphans and were "successful" finding them families, too. My summer of shame. The summer I thought I was doing so much good only to find out later how dreadful it turned out to be for those forever families.

Family X. Lies, lies, lies. One of the boys we hosted was full of vinegar we liked to say. He had spirit. He loved playing practical jokes on us. As soon hosting began I started passionately advocating for him. I posted on social media and a friend shared my post. I got a call asking if I would bring the boy to a church outing to meet with a family who was interested. They bonded instantly at that outing and the family made the decision to move forward with adoption. (PLEASE NO MORE INSTANT BONDING. It's not healthy. It's not normal. It's a BAD sign.)

What none of us knew at the time is this boy had a plan. And he manipulated all of us. He came across as sweet, funny and loveable. He seemed to fall in love with his "forever family". In fact, it was made mention by several people how much the boy looked like his new "dad". The family went all out fundraising to make the adoption happen fast. In country the mom spent weeks by herself. The boy became argumentative with the mom. More of those red flags which are glossed over with platitudes like:

- He is scared of the future
- He is just acting out
- There are a lot of changes happening in his life
- Everything will be fine once we get home.

Like many of us, this mother spent her time in country justifying his bad behavior and reminding herself they were adopting to rescue an orphan.

By and by they came home and surprise, surprise, things didn't get better. In fact, they got a whole lot worse. Especially when the boy actually told the parents his real reason for being adopted. His goal was to get a lot of money in America and bring his biological mother here to live with him. When the parents learned this, they told the boy he wouldn't be able to bring his biological mother to America because, legally, she was no longer his mother. He went ballistic and overnight turned into a monster.

He then had one goal in life. To destroy the mom who took him away from his biological mother and Ukraine. It did not matter one whit that it was his idea to be adopted by this family. It only mattered that his plan, the plan he formulated way back in the orphanage, way back before being hosted and then adopted, had been dashed. And the one who dashed it? His adoptive mom.

So now mom is his target.

She and everything she holds dear will now be destroyed. That is his mission. He falsely accused her of abusing him to the point he dug his fingers into his own neck to bruise himself. Fortunately for her, at the time he said it happened, she was not even in the same city and had an alibi. He eventually admitted to the lie. Although he has since been taken out of the family home he has continued to harass the family through social media posts and hanging around their neighborhood. He has been blatant about his plans to destroy the family through whatever means possible. They have since moved out of state to protect themselves from this boy. They were afraid he would follow them, so they've completely dropped off of social media and isolated themselves from friends and family who might inadvertently tell him where they've gone.

Summer passed with several more families entwined in the adoption process of orphans for whom we had advocated. School began, and we struggled to find a successful routine for Viktor, who hated being a part of a family. Independence was his only motivation, just like in the orphanage, and it manifested through relentless rebellion. We were busy with work, schooling the teens and our business, and didn't realize we were all sinking deeper into a pit. Money started to come up missing, but we brushed it off thinking we misplaced it, or didn't remember spending it.

Looking back, we were clueless. I hate to admit it because I know I'm a smart person; but in this realm, I was just about as stupid as they come. This boy played me every day and I let him. Maybe I let him because it was easier that way. Most likely a part of me knew what he was up to, but I chose not to deal with it. I had a list of justifications for him, some of them I've already told you. I've never tolerated so much bad behavior in my life! Maybe part of the reason was if I admitted the truth, then everything we had done up to that point was wrong; something I wasn't prepared to admit. I had a mission from Yahweh, I knew, to help get these teens adopted before they aged out. If I admitted to myself adopting him was a big farce, what was my mission then? I had invested so much, and I was too prideful to acknowledge the truth and walk away from adoption and advocacy.

The greatest Book in the world tells us pride goes before a fall. My family was about to be dropped from pride's skyscraper. Garrett and Katherine were slipping through the cracks and we didn't realize that either. I guess it is natural whenever you have anything out of the ordinary in your life, you're going to concentrate on the abnormality and let other things go.

Having Viktor was like having a special needs child in our home and most of the focus was on him. And because we were allowing Viktor to get away with so much, it affected how we parented our bio teens. The drinking, the smoking, the defiant attitude were all things we would never have tolerated in our two biological teens. And they both knew it. We didn't realize Garrett and Katherine began to feel unworthy.

We made a HUGE MISTAKE here. **HUGE!** I'm going to try to get through this next part without bawling. My throat is closed up right now just thinking about it.

We **ASSUMED** since Garrett and Katherine were strong, wonderful, loving, kind, dependable and independent teens and they had both worked very hard to make this adoption happen, that they were okay through this period of adjustment. **THEY WERE NOT!!!** They felt unloved, unappreciated and forgotten. They felt unworthy of our time and attention. They felt Viktor could do anything and get away with it, which was mostly true. Viktor was like a vacuum, sucking up all the attention, albeit mostly negative attention. Our bio teens started to withdraw. And we didn't notice. We were so into handling issues surrounding Viktor and advocating for orphans and then the next adoption, we didn't even notice. And it was almost fatal, and I mean that literally. **WE DID NOT NOTICE** and we nearly lost our babies.

Looking back over this adoption journey made me realize during that time I was a total failure as a mother to Garrett and Katherine. I didn't realize until it was almost too late. I had bought into all the adoption hype and that's all I was focused on. How many teens could we get adopted before they aged out? Even though Viktor stretched us, we were so good at justifying his behavior and honestly, we thought, "If this is as bad as it gets, then we will be okay." Another mistake. Thinking he was the worst it could be. If you could see me now you'd see me shaking my head with my eyes closed. Teeth clenched. Trying to stop the tears.

IT CAN GET SO MUCH WORSE!

CHAPTER 5

Piling More On

Biological Children/Teens

I'm just going to come out and say this. Unless something is done in the adoption business to protect families, if you have biological children/teens in the home, **DO NOT THINK ABOUT BRINGING AN ORPHAN INTO YOUR HOME!** Under **ANY** circumstances. It **WILL** have a negative effect on them. Unless you are willing to sacrifice your precious children/teens on the altar of adoption like I did, STOP thinking about adoption NOW.

Both of my bio teens contemplated suicide as a way out of the horror they were living.

And before the adoption these were healthy, smart, well-adjusted, caring, loving, selfless teens who were committed to adoption. They held fundraisers to raise money for Viktor's adoption. They gave their savings. They were willing to sacrifice and make room in our home, in their lives and to share their parents. They were excited to have Viktor as their new brother. Can you even image how we felt when we discovered the depth of their pain? How devastating it was to hear our precious baby boy and girl talk about ending their lives? Imagine how you would feel. **IT WAS NOT WORTH IT!** Find another way to help orphans. Any other way which doesn't involve bringing them into your home. Subjecting Garrett and

Katherine to the trauma of adopting these unstable orphans is my biggest life regret.

I've probably said this a hundred times to people online, in my blog and privately. IF YOU HAVE BIO'S AT HOME DO NOT ADOPT. DO NOT ADOPT. DO NOT ADOPT. Unless you are willing to surrender your bios to the god of adoption, DO NOT ADOPT. I'm writing this almost two years after our experience, and Garrett and Katherine are still working hard to recover. It is a daily undertaking. We all have a long way to go to heal. IT WAS NOT WORTH IT! To try and "save" an orphan and damage another child/teen in the process IS NOT WORTH IT!! Please hear me on this.

Glass Children

At first glance this would seem to mean children who are fragile and breakable. Actually, they are children/teens who appear strong and capable; the good kids who go out of their way to not disappoint. Glass children/teens are those growing up in a home with a sibling who takes up a disproportionate amount of parental energy such as; obvious physical or emotional disability, child with addiction, serious illness or significant behavioral issues such as RAD. These siblings are called glass children because their overwhelmed parents, instead of looking at them and seeing their needs, look right through them at the fire they are currently fighting with the troubled child/teen. Glass children are seen as the child who needs less parental attention because they are so responsible, and this is an answer to prayer for the parents who are already completely overwhelmed. It is completely destructive to the "strong" child/teen.

I strongly recommend watching the fantastic TedX San Antonio by Alicia Arenes; Recognizing Glass Children.

(https://www.youtube.com/watch?v=MSwqo-g2Tbk)

When you have a RAD child/teen, in addition to being essentially ignored, glass children are commonly abused by the sibling with RAD. Glass children may exhibit similar symptoms of a child growing up in a domestic abuse household such as:

- Trouble focusing in school
- Flashbacks
- Memory avoidance
- Fear of death
- Low self-esteem
- Intrusive memories
- Emotional numbing
- Loss of interest and motivation in previously enjoyed activities
- Nightmares
- Trouble sleeping
- Altered brain function
- Hyper-vigilance
- Prone to depression, anxiety, suicidal thoughts
- ADHD due to PTSD
- PTSD
- High emotional outbursts over minor incidents
- Quick to anger and/or tears

(Thank you to Julia MacMonagle at wwwthemotherranch.com for the information on glass children. Thank you for the work you are doing for all of our glass children. You can follow her blog at http://themotherranch.blogspot.com.)

Fall came and went, and we were muddling through with Viktor. Then December. I was sitting at my computer one evening when my phone rang. A woman from a hosting agency with which I wasn't familiar said she heard I was good at advocating and finding homes for orphans. Would I help them with two teens they had coming over winter break? The fees were all covered and all I had to do was drive to Atlanta to pick up and then drop off again a few weeks later. I talked to Tom and we agreed. The next week I drove to Atlanta, picked up the two teen boys and drove home. The very next day I went to work to find them families. They were both seemingly good boys and we didn't see any signs of trouble. We had zero intention of ever adopting again.

Within a week we had found an interested family for one of them. They contacted the hosting agency and it was approved that J. would spend the rest of break with the prospective family to see if they bonded. Tom drove J. to meet with the other family and dropped him off. They ended up adopting J. It has not been an easy journey for them.

However, we were not having success with the other boy, Sasha. He was somewhat shy but personable and nice looking. No matter what I wrote about him on social media, no one was interested. Time was counting down and I was frustrated. Why could I find homes for all the children/teens except this one? He was helpful around the house and he and Viktor seemed to bond well. He attached himself to Tom and followed him around. Sasha would constantly ask Tom if he needed help with chopping wood or ask me if I needed help cleaning the kitchen after meals. He was a very helpful young man.

A few days before I was to leave to take him to Atlanta, Tom and I talked and decided to ask Sasha if he wanted to be a part of our family. As much as neither of us wanted to go through that process again and although we had no money set aside, we felt it was the right thing to do. This boy was turning 16 the next spring so there was no time to mess around waiting for someone else to step up.

We hopped on the adoption roller coaster again. Not much time passed when I got a message from a friend on social media. She knew of a girl from the same orphanage as our Viktor, and the girl was wonderful. Would we possibly consider her, too? We spoke to our home study agency and they decided to approve us for up to three additional teens.

OKAY now that we know what we know, this was totally INSANE!!!! They said we could have up to three more!!! And they could be **unrelated!!!!!** We told ourselves we could do this. We were good at this parenting thing. We never actually stopped to ask Yahweh for his opinion on any of this, but we were sure this must be from Him. We thought we knew what He wanted. It FELT right! Right?

Wrong!

If anyone ever asks me if they should bring four adopted children/teens home – unrelated to each other and especially with biological children/teens in the home - I would shout from the rooftops **NO NO NO NO NO NO NO!!** It is literally the most insane thing a family could think of to do. But there we were!

We told ourselves we would leave it in Yahweh's hands and we would bring home whomever He wanted. We honestly believed we were following His guidance. I still wrestle with this aspect. In hindsight, I wonder to whom we were really listening.

Yahweh

Our family follows the Bible and Yahweh is the Name of God so that is how we refer to Him.

> *Ezekiel 39:7 "So will I make My holy Name known in the midst of My people Israel and I will not let them pollute My holy Name anymore."*

We do our best to live our lives according to His will, although we messed up royally getting into this adoption nightmare.

Christianity teaches, and rightly so, that the Bible says to take care of the widows and the orphans.

> *James 1:27: "Pure and undefiled religion in the sight of Yahweh our Father is this: to visit orphans and widows in their distress, and to keep oneself unstained by the world."*

To Christians that means adoption or fostering. Giving children/teens without a family, a family. That's what we believed. That's what our decisions to adopt were based upon.

When we fail to actually study the Word as instructed to do, we miss important details like He NEVER told us to bring orphans into our homes.

> *2 Timothy 2:15: "Be diligent to present yourself approved to Yahweh as a workman who does not need to be ashamed, accurately handling the word of truth."*

He said to care for them. He never said to bring them to a different country, culture, language, family setting, etc. which would be a complete shock to their system. He said to care for them; provide food, clothing, schooling, shelter, and a possible future. We Christians have misinterpreted His Word. Badly. The result of not seeking His guidance and working to help a child/teen in their own environment to have a real future, has been painful consequences to ourselves and our bio children, without having much of a positive impact on the adoptees at all. In fact, it has left everyone, including the adoptees themselves, damaged.

I was reading my Bible and came across the parable Yahshua (Jesus) told about the Samaritan man.

> *Luke 10:33: "But a Samaritan, as he journeyed, came to where he was, and when he saw him, he had compassion. He went to him and bound up his wounds, pouring on oil and wine. Then he set him on his own animal and brought him to an inn and took care of him. And the next day he took out two denarii and gave them to the innkeeper, saying, 'Take care of him, and whatever more you spend, I will repay you when I come back.' Which of these three, do you think, proved to be a neighbor to the man who fell among the robbers?" He said, "The one who showed him mercy." And Yahshua said to him, "You go, and do likewise."*

Please note the Samaritan man did not take the man into his own home. He used his resources to help him right where the man was. That is a great lesson for all of us, especially in the adoption world.

When we thought we were following Yahweh's will, we were forcing our own. We thought we were doing it for Him, but we were doing it to make ourselves feel godlier. I sometimes wonder which god we were really serving.

As I said, I still wrestle with this daily. On one hand I think maybe He did tell us to adopt. Thousands of families before ours have gone through adoption hell and not much at all had been reported. I looked for books written about adoptions like ours and couldn't find many. I believe I was meant to peel back the cover of these "unscrupulous adoptions" and expose them and those responsible.

People are harassed, worn out, afraid to speak out, or just plain feel humiliated they failed at something so important. My opinion is Yahweh knew I would obey Him and speak out. (At least after some prodding. Hey, even Moses balked at going back to Egypt and Jonah ran the other way instead of doing what Yahweh wanted right away. At least I didn't end up in the belly of a fish. Wow! I think I might be getting my sense of humor back.)

January/February 2014. Well, we did it. We went through the entire paperwork process all over again. Home study, medicals, apostille documents to send to Ukraine and then lo and behold a war started there. We found out adopting the girl from Viktor's orphanage would most likely not be possible. After our home study was completed and we were approved for three, we made another huge mistake.

We decided since we were approved for three it was our duty to bring three home.

What in the world were we thinking? (We weren't.) As I said, we honestly figured if what we were dealing with in Viktor was the worst of it, then we could handle whatever else came our way. Boy, were we wrong. And we were PRIDEFUL. That word. That word is at the root of this whole mess. Pride.

I'm just going to go all raw and real here and put this mess out there. It was nice being "that" person. Well-liked, admired, doing life for Yahweh. Following His Word, His example. I think many of us go through life looking for approval for all sorts of reasons and some of us end up in the adoption world where we think we've found it. And it feels good to feel like you are on a mission for God. Like you have real purpose and a reason for being on this planet. You feel like you're doing what He wants you do and that feels great. You hear things like:

"You're such a good person".

"I could never do what you're doing".

"I always wanted to adopt, but blah blah blah."
"I'm so honored to know you and that you're really doing it".

You respond, "I'm not really, I'm just following Yahweh's guidance", or some other humble remark. Blech! Honestly, I should have said, "I'm just doing this so I feel worthy in my life". UGH! It really did feel good "knowing" I was doing something God wanted me to do. I confused worthiness with pride.

I sacrificed my family on the altar of my pride. Period. There you go.

Proverbs 16:18 Pride goes before destruction, and a haughty spirit before a fall.

Now, please hear me. Not everyone who adopts does it for the same reason I did. Everyone has their own reasons. I've just decided that I'm going to be brutally honest about everything, including my own inadequacies. Because those inadequacies only *added* to the entire fiasco. The reason for adopting, whether it was like mine or altruism, or wanting to grow a family, really wouldn't have mattered. It was a recipe for disaster.

During this time, I put feelers out to hosting groups I knew and posted on social media that if anyone knew of any girls who were aging out, to let me know. We decided on a girl due to the *fear* of a life of prostitution she might be subjected to.

Fear

This word. I have henceforth decided that I will never, ever again in my life do something, or not do something, based on fear. Fear is a liar and a thief. Fear is the opposite of trust. Fear is evil. Fear causes so many problems. Fear is from the pit of hell. Fear is from the devil himself.

Our fear was a girl was going to age out (turn 16), get kicked out of the orphanage, find herself in prostitution, and then be killed.

Fear drove our entire decision-making process on behalf of the girl we adopted.

And I hate that it did. I was never a fearful person before this experience. I was the charge up the hill. I can do it. Never give up. Never fear. A "no matter what" person. Many times through this process I've wondered how people manage who were not so bold starting out. Who didn't have my kind of inner strength? If I could be brought so low through this, what about them? Then I looked closer at the casualties. Divorces, bio children taken away and put into foster care, parents in jail, and more. I am so grateful to Yahweh for His strength in me through this time. We were still driven by fear. And it began with fearing for these orphans.

What would happen to them if we did nothing?

CHAPTER 6

Our Second Adoption

Someone reached out to us about a girl they had wanted to adopt but couldn't. We did some checking and found she wasn't available, so we continued our search. Then another person reached out with information on a girl, Arina, who was about to turn 16 that summer. Perfect. The woman had information from someone who had personally met Arina and would be happy to send me information about the girl. First, she emailed Arina's bio to me:

> "A" is a pleasant girl with a big smile. She is calm and focused, and easy to be around. She enjoys drawing, knitting, art, and writing in her free time. She is a "B" student with biology, language and literature as favorite subjects. She has seen her friends hosted and prays that this summer she will be picked, too. She would like to be a hairdresser when she grows up. This girl chooses to actively participate in church related activities offered to children at her orphanage. At age 15, "A" is a last chance child. (Paper ready with summer birth month.)

The next day I received another message about Arina from the sponsoring hosting organization.

> Good morning Kathe. I received the following answers to my question that I sent to my friend, the pastor's wife, who knows Arina. It is their church that Arina attends. Each

> *weekend, the pastor and his wife bring several kids to stay in their home for the weekend and attend church, and last weekend was Arina's turn. Arina volunteers to participate in all the church activities that the pastor and his wife do at the orphanage for the kids. They say that Arina is the "real deal" as far as loving the Lord!*

Arina's answers to the questions:

> *She likes light colors. She likes a large family. She likes children. She likes to play outside, she likes to ride a bicycle very much! She likes to help you if you need her help. Just say to her and she will be a good helper! Everywhere! On the kitchen, in the garden. She is a quiet girl. But if she will know that she can trust you, she will speak and talk to you and share with you all her things.*

I thought to myself that this girl sounds so sweet and wonderful and we had a pastor, and his wife, and this other woman vouching for her! This sounded like the experience would be so much better than the one we had with Viktor.

Our hearts were set on adopting Sasha, the girl from Mariupol (Viktor's orphanage), that is, if war there didn't prevent it, and this new girl, Arina. Travel arrangements were made, and Tom and I flew to Kiev on June 24, 2014. Just before departing I opened a private group on social media to keep everyone appraised of our journey. This outlet became a private blog where I would record our progress. We looked forward to the adventure very much.

Tom and I were determined to spend the Ukraine summer enjoying ourselves. The country was absolutely stunning, with huge fields of sunflowers everywhere. There was so much history in the city of Kiev and we drank it all in. We were upbeat, and we knew our teens at home were in good hands, with their older, adult siblings.

We spent some time hanging out in Kiev, waiting for our appointment and meeting several other families who were also on an adoption journey.

Finally, the day for our appointment at the SDA arrived. We met up with our facilitator, then walked up to the second floor for our appointment.

Our facilitator sat in a chair, Tom and I, a couch. The woman in charge of adoptions was young, pretty and very friendly. She greeted us with a big smile and then brought out the file on the girl in Mariupol. Although everything was in order, adoptions were currently on hold in her region due to the conflict with Russia. Americans were refused entry due to the increased risk. We would not be allowed to proceed with her adoption at that time. We were told if things changed before we left the country, we could come back then.

We were very disappointed but asked to see the file on Arina. Filing for her first was urgent since she was aging out in just a few days. Her birthday was quickly approaching, and we needed to meet her and decide if she was a good fit for our family. To our surprise, we learned Arina had a brother, who had just turned 17.

Unexpected Decisions!

A new twist developed. In order to adopt Arina, one of two things were necessary: This brother needed to give consent to the adoption, or alternatively we could adopt him alongside Arina. Though he was past the American adoption cutoff of 16 years old, because he had a younger sibling who was being adopted, we were told an exception could be made.

Had we been told about this brother ahead of time, we could have thought this through, talked to some others who had been down this road, and made an informed decision. But we had exactly five minutes to decide about these two teens whom we had never met and with whom we had never spoken. And we hadn't even gotten any information about the brother prior to traveling like we had with Arina. Should we adopt Arina's brother, our three slots would be filled, so even if the war ended, we would not be able to adopt the girl in Mariupol, with whom we had already corresponded and were looking forward to having in our family. We were completely unprepared for this new development. Tom and I talked it over best we could with our facilitator in those five minutes, and decided to meet Arina and her brother, Dima. Perhaps the brother would allow a separation and that would fit with our plans.

The next day, after getting the approval documentation from the SDA, we traveled to the region by a six-hour train ride and stayed overnight in a local hotel. In the morning, we hired a car and driver and traveled to the orphanage to meet Arina and Dima. We walked onto the grounds and up to the door. I told Tom I was pleasantly surprised. It was pretty with flowers everywhere and was obviously well-kept. We saw painters rolling bright yellow paint on the walls and gardeners tending huge flower beds. The interior of the building was spotless. This orphanage was a stark contrast to Viktor's cold dark grey orphanage.

As we walked in, several teens were sitting quietly on a bench just inside the door. We walked past them and were led to the director's office. We had brought her a small gift of good coffee and a scarf. She graciously accepted them, thanked us, and then went to a locked cabinet. She took out a ring of keys and locked her gifts away.

It was then we noticed there were locks everywhere. Doors, cabinets, drawers. All locked. We glanced at each other. Knowing how Viktor liked taking things that weren't his, this didn't really surprise us, but I couldn't imagine having to carry jailer-like keys everywhere.

This director was quite different than the director at Viktor's orphanage. She was friendly and pleasant. She hugged both Tom and me and talked quite excitedly about Arina and Dima. She was thrilled they would at last have a family. She told us they had been orphaned since the girl was 7, the boy 8. They were good kids, she said, two of the best in the orphanage. She was very proud of them. She told us their mother had died but didn't say how. They had a younger brother, although he was adopted when he quite young and since then Arina and Dima had no contact with him. They also had several older siblings and a father, but since arriving at the orphanage, had zero contact even though the relatives lived less than 30 minutes away.

We were so sad for them. So much family and not one cared about these two! Our hearts hurt for them.

The director recommended we meet Arina and Dima then spend some time with them; talking with them to decide on their possible adoption. We did. They were two of the teens who had been sitting on the bench when we first came into the building. The Director introduced us to Arina and

Dima and told us that Arina had woken at 5:00 a.m. to start getting ready for our 10:00 a.m. appointment. All of the girls had helped her so she would look her best for us. Her hair was in a beautiful braid and she wore a pretty dress. Dima was wearing a nice shirt and pants.

EMOTION

I want to stop here for a moment and talk about emotion. We had been on an emotional roller coaster since the December before when we decided to adopt Sasha. I call it the *Adoption High*. You are really on a "high". You're doing Yahweh's work. Your feet are on the ground - working. You're making a difference. It is crazy emotional. You are totally focused on saving teens from certain destruction. That's all you think about. Dream about. Talk about. There is no talk of sense. No wisdom. No time to think it through. It is pure emotion. You make really bad decisions when you decide based upon emotions and not facts. Especially when you assume Yahweh is automatically for it so you don't stop and ask His opinion.

From the moment we walked up to those two teens and realized who they were, we were 100 percent emotionally invested. We were told Dima, were we not to adopt him, would most likely be snapped up into the Ukrainian military. After all, they were at war with big bad Russia! We'd seen the evidence first hand! When we drove around the region, we were stopped several times at checkpoints and had to show our papers because we were very close to Russian occupied territory.

We simply couldn't allow Dima to go into the military, which is far different from our American military. There was no discussion of Dima allowing Arina to be separated and adopted without him after hearing about the military. We found out much later orphans are exempt from military duty unless they enlist.

We were invited by Arina and Dima to visit the room where Arina slept. There were five twin beds in the clean, but sparsely furnished room. Each bed had a cubby underneath. There was nothing in Arina's cubby. She held everything she owned in this world in a small, light blue backpack. We sat on the ends of the beds, while Arina and Dima stood, one leaning against the wall and the other standing near our facilitator. This was our first interaction with them and we spoke with the help of our facilitator, who translated for us.

I began by asking them to tell us about themselves. Arina spoke first. "We have been here in the orphanage for many years. We were hosted once to America and it was good. We have wanted a family for a long time, but no one hosted us or came for us. We have no family and we are happy you are here now, and we hope you will be our family."

I glanced at Tom who nodded and then I said, "We would like to tell you how things are in our family." They both nodded, and I continued, "We have Garrett who is 15 and Katherine who is 13, and we adopted Viktor from Mariupol last year, and he is 16. They all attend the high school near our home and that is where you will go to school, too." They nodded yes. "We all work together to do family chores; do you understand what that means?" There was some back and forth with our facilitator and then they both nodded yes.

"We want both of you to understand that we all work together to be sure the house is always clean and you will have to do your part. We eat family meals together most nights, unless someone is working their job or have something at school, like robotics or sports. Do you have any questions?" They went back and forth with our facilitator to understand what things like robotics meant then they both turned to us and said, "Nyet". They chattered to the facilitator who told us, "They understand and are good with all of it and they have no questions."

I continued, "We expect you to work hard in school and learn English because that is the only way you will do well in America. We want you to understand that this is going to be very hard for you. It will be the hardest thing you've ever done. You must learn another language and learn how to live in another country. It is going to take a lot of time and hard work for you. Do you understand?"

They both nodded yes.

"Do you have questions for us?" Tom asked.

Dima held out a book he was holding. I took it and looked; it was an English translation Bible. Through the translator he said, "I am trying to learn English and would like you to help me learn it better." I was thrilled! He wanted to learn English, and was trying on his own, using a Bible of all things!

Through the translator they told us, "We love going to church and we love Jesus." We asked Arina and Dima to tell us what they wanted out of life in America. Between the two of them they said they wanted to live a good life and go to school and learn and maybe college. Their answers made us smile.

After spending an hour with them, describing life in our home, we finally asked the question, "Do you want us to adopt you?" They both exclaimed, "Yes, yes!" And they both had huge smiles on their faces. Tom and I stood up and Arina stepped forward to hug me, then Dima. Then both teens hugged Tom. We were all smiling and happy. It was an exciting time! We spent time figuring out what they'd like their American names to be. Sometimes adopted children want to keep their names and sometimes they want American names. It didn't matter to us, we said. We told them Viktor had kept his name but changed his middle name to his Ukrainian last name, then added our last name. Dima decided to keep his name but added an American middle name. Arina decided to keep her first name and also added an American middle name.

Finally, we walked back to the front door and left our new babies there.

The Sales Pitch

Coaching by orphanage staff.

We didn't know at the time but have since learned this is very common. The children/teens are told stories about how life in America is going to be and a beautiful picture is painted. They are coached how to answer appealing ways to prospective parents. The orphans may be threatened with harm, to act the right way and say the right things. Because these children/teens are already expert liars, the sales pitch comes naturally to them. We didn't find out until we were home that Arina and Dima had both been coached on what to say and how to behave with us. Later, upon arriving home and hearing their confession we were shocked to learn the entire scene in that room of empty cubbies and the English Bible was staged.

In hindsight, one thing that stands out as a HUGE red flag was Arina's instant attachment to me. We had no knowledge of RAD at the time and was just taken in by this exceedingly affectionate girl. She was so happy to finally have a mom again, I rationalized. She was like Velcro, hugging me every chance she got and making it clear she couldn't wait for us all to be a family. She didn't leave my side any time we were at the orphanage.

We spent all of July bouncing back and forth between Kiev, the orphanage in Zaporozhye and the orphanage in Romny, and by the first week of August we had picked Arina and Dima up from their orphanage and driven with them to our apartment in Kiev. (Finalizing their adoption in the region had taken several trips via train and one by car, which was an adventure all by itself. There was an issue with Arina's original birth certificate which cost us an extra trip to the region and several hundred dollars which we hadn't been prepared to spend.)

When the day arrived to pick Arina and Dima up from the orphanage, where they said good-bye to their friends, it was highly emotional for Tom and me. However, as we drove away I noticed neither Arina nor Dima so much as glanced back at the only home they had known for many years. There was absolutely no emotion on their faces. We then drove our rental car from the Zaporozhye region to Kiev, without navigation, at an average speed of 15 miles per hour, down crazy roads peppered with potholes the size of craters, and with headlamps that barely worked. Exhausted, we finally arrived in Kiev at 4 a.m., but had the two of the three teens. Now it was time to finish up the adoption of Sasha.

Sasha's adoption was simpler, but far costlier as there was much bribing of officials in the orphanage and in Romny city. We had no choice but to pay the bribes unless we wanted to spend several more weeks in Ukraine or give up on the adoption. We found out later that the assistant director went to jail for demanding too many bribes.

We were exhausted, frustrated, terribly homesick and we soon began seeing signs of unrest with Arina and Dima.

The sweet, innocent, affectionate teens we spent time with in the orphanage disappeared overnight. They became argumentative, disrespectful, and very distant. They wanted nothing to do with us and had to be bribed to spend any time engaged in family activities like playing cards or going for walks around Kiev. Unless it was their idea to do something, they'd refuse. We never saw another smile from them unless they were getting something they wanted. Arina shut herself up into one of the bedrooms and refused to come out.

STOP!

Seeing these signs, knowing what we know now, should have caused us to stop right there, call our facilitator and tell him in no uncertain terms the adoption of Arina and Dima was not going any further and to do whatever was necessary to stop and reverse it. No debate. No negotiation.

Instead, we made excuses for them. In hindsight we should have taken both of them immediately back to their orphanage. We should have done whatever paperwork was necessary, at whatever cost, to make them Ukrainian citizens again and put things right back where we started.

Then moved on with our lives without them, never looking back.

We didn't have a clue we were seeing signs of RAD. That their behavior meant something was dangerously wrong. Their behavior meant we were not told the full story about them in the orphanage or by those who knew them. I write them here as a warning to those in the adoption process. Learn from our mistakes. You can stop the adoption all the way until you board that plane for the USA. Just go to the embassy and tell them there has been a mistake. Then tell your facilitator to reverse the adoption.

Whatever cost you might incur at this point is NOTHING compared to what you will be forced to deal with once home in America. Do not allow your PRIDE to convince you to continue. Do not concern yourself with people who helped you, who gave you money, who ran bake sales for you. If they are truly friends, they will understand. Be humble and stand firm against anyone who tries to convince you to just go home with your adopted child/teen and everything will be fine.

Remember, NONE of those people will have to live with your adopted child/teen. You do. Your family does. You can reverse the adoption before you leave the country. What you cannot undo is the damage they will cause once you get them home. AND most likely if someone is trying to convince you to stay the course, they will NOT stand by you when things go to hell in a handbasket. They will be the first to abandon you. Listen to your gut.

Pay attention to the signs

Arina spent every minute in Kiev in her bedroom unless we forced her to come out. There was no hanging around me anymore. It was as if she was a completely different teen than the one in the orphanage. No hugs, no Velcro, no wanting to help me in the kitchen. She had a phone she brought from the orphanage, and she was constantly talking with friends from the orphanage, she said. She never wanted to do anything with us. She didn't even want to explore Kiev, even though she had never been there. She wouldn't come out of her room. She was angry. She was spiteful. She was belligerent. She was antagonistic. She was defiant. It was like Dr. Jekyll and Mr. Hyde. This was not the same girl. It's like there were twins and we got the evil twin by mistake. That the good twin was left in the orphanage. Tom and I were mystified. She point blank refused to do anything.

This was a daily conversation while in the apartment in Kiev. All through the translate app.

Me: "Arina, we're going to go explore around the city today. It's going to be fun and we'll stop at Domino's pizza to pick up dinner. Get dressed so we can leave in ten minutes."

Arina: "No, I stay here. I no walk today. I tired." This from a girl who spent all her time lying on her bed and sleeping.

Me: "We are all going, Arina. We're going to walk around those underground shops where we bought that shirt for you. Maybe you'll see something else you like."

Arina: "No, I stay here. You no make me go."

Me: "Arina, please let's go. After the underground shops we're taking the metro to Ocean Plaza, then we're walking back and will get our pizza on the way for dinner. We are going to be gone several hours and you cannot stay here in the apartment by yourself."

Arina: "Yes, I stay here. I no baby."

Me: "Arina, you are going with us. We are going to be gone all day, we'll eat lunch at Ocean Plaza, and you cannot stay here. Get dressed. We are leaving in 5 minutes."

Arina: "I no go. I stay here. You no make me."

Me: (by now completely exasperated by this exchange) "Arina, we are leaving in 5 minutes. You will be ready to leave with us or I will take your phone away for the rest of the day." I walk out of the room toward the front of the apartment. She is screaming at me in Russian. (Why in the world did I not call our facilitator right then I don't know. I have replayed these scenes many times and beat myself up over not making that call.)

Minutes later Tom, Dima, and I were all standing at the front door ready to walk out when Arina came out of her room to leave with us. The threat of losing the phone did it.

I should have made the phone disappear. Her behavior would have most likely escalated to the point where I would have had to get others involved and perhaps that might have caused things to turn out differently.

Instead of waking up to the truth, we began to justify more on her behalf; she's going to miss her friends, let her have this time to adjust, it will be better once we are in America, etc.

Days later, Tom and I decided to take them to the Dnieper River where there was an amazing zip line 500 meters high over the river. Tom and I had ridden it with some new friends several weeks before we picked up the teens, and we were excited to be able to take the teens. Arina stubbornly refused to leave the apartment. Nothing we could say made a difference. She was sullen, moody, angry and adamant she was staying put. She threw a temper tantrum and told us she threw her SIM card for her phone from her third story window. We all spent time looking for it in the pouring rain. Later she mysteriously found it in her room. I threatened to take the phone away, she shrugged. We finally left without her.

I kept saying once we were on that plane to America everything would be better. I wrote in my group on social media how I couldn't wait to get on that plane. I said Arina and Dima would be fine once we were out of Ukraine.

Dima was silently rebellious. He simply refused to do anything we asked and just sat on the couch as if no one was talking to him. He completely ignored us. It was like talking to a wall.

I had taken my laptop so I could work my Arbonne business in between adoption tasks. I had loaded an English language learning program for Arina, Dima and Sasha, once he arrived. Arina and Dima refused to spend any time learning, even though when we talked at the orphanage we had agreed to start English lessons right away. The boy who showed us his Bible and asked us to help him learn English completely disappeared. Now that we were in Kiev they said, "When we get to America."

By mid-August, we had been in Ukraine eight weeks and Tom had to get back home. Our teens needed to get ready for the new school year. I was left alone in the apartment in Kiev, just two blocks from the city square where much of the Ukrainian revolution had taken place, with two newly adopted teens who were being difficult and rebellious. I was working hard to finish up the adoption of Sasha so we could all go home. It was a huge task and now I was alone.

My daily routine was to make a good breakfast, then we would go on long walks to get out of the apartment. Every day I had to coerce them to go with me by threatening no T.V. and no phone. They would walk like snails; so slow I knew they were purposely trying to frustrate me. I had bought some cards and a few simple games at the market and would try to engage with them, but they continually refused. Dima just sat on the couch watching T.V. and Arina on the bed in her room talking on her phone.

A few days after Tom left for the States I found out Arina was talking with a 19-year-old male friend who she said was from her town and was now in the military. "Army Guy" was currently in Kiev. She tried sneaking out to see him. We were on the third floor and the one door to the stairs locked only with a key. I kept the door locked and the key with me always. When we went out walking she tried to ditch me for him. It was exhausting keeping track of this 16-year-old who was becoming more and more defiant every day. And all while I was still traveling back and forth to the Sumy region to finish up Sasha's paperwork.

One day "Army Guy" came to the apartment and I made us all breakfast before our daily walk. "Army Guy" announced he was going with us on the walk. "Army Guy" was in dress clothes (no sign of army in his clothing by the way) and shiny, pointed dress shoes. I silently laughed as I walked to my bedroom to get my shoes.

When Tom was still in Kiev we had so much fun walking around the city. We didn't just stay to the sidewalks but ventured into parks and deep, dark wooded areas and would hike for no less than eight miles. We made our walks into adventures and learned so much about the city by walking it. I continued the adventures with the teens, taking them to places Tom and I had discovered. I thought it would interest them as it was part of their country and history. And I would rather be outside walking than cooped up in that small apartment with two sullen teens. They were never interested and constantly complained.

That day the four of us took off walking. We hadn't gone two miles when we passed a metro (subway) stop and "Army Guy" disappeared. (This grandma in her late 50's, outwalked some "Army Guy" who really just wanted to hang with Arina.) Arina was ticked at me for making her walk, and then mad "Army Guy" had left her.

I guess I was fortunate (or not) she didn't disappear with him on the metro. I was so far ahead of the three of them, she could have ducked on the train with him and I never would have found her in that huge city. I admit many times in the past few years I wished she would have done exactly that. I know how horrid it sounds. It's the truth and I'll bet there are several hundred adoptive parents thinking the same thing about their adoptees.

Much later, long after we came home to America, we learned the truth. "Army Guy" was not some friend from her home town, but someone she had just "met" on an internet site on her phone. Merely days after we arrived in Kiev, she was already looking for her next savior.

Looking back, it is obvious this adoption was a complete fraud. But at the time, I was someone who looked on the bright side, the positive. Who looked for the good in everything and person. I justified their bad behavior. Exactly as we had done with Viktor. I constantly rationalized with "poor orphan" victim mentality. I excused them time and time again.

FRAUD

Nasty word. Fraud. Fraud has many faces in the adoption industry.

- **Fraud by the hosting agency.** Bringing children/teens to America, effectively modeling them with the best sides showing. They use cute pictures and write appealing life stories. There should be an award for whomever is writing those bios. Seriously. "He is a smart, excellent student, loves sports and is looking for a family who loves the outdoors." Or how about this one. "Loves music and wants to learn to play the piano. Loves little children and pets." (Watch out for this one. Your pet is going to come up missing and your little child is going to be molested.) Or, "He is very smart, friendly, confident, good-natured and intelligent boy. He is also artistic, likes singing and dancing, likes sports, gymnastics most of all. He does well at school." Or this one, "She is a very easy going and sweet girl, she is artistic, likes dancing and singing, very active, she likes embroidery, reading and playing with her friends. She likes school and does well at school, favorite subject is math." Who wouldn't want one of these amazing children/teens as part of their family? It's kind of like seeing a bio on a dating site and showing up for a blind date to meet a tall, dark, fit, and handsome doctor. Instead you find out he is 20 years older than advertised, a protruding gut, balding and works in a doctor's office…as the janitor.
- **Fraud by the orphanage.** The orphanage administrators know which children/teens are trouble. While I can't prove this, after reading hundreds of stories and experiencing our own there seems to be a common thread – written bios which don't match up to the child/teen who was adopted. In our case, three of the four were

exactly opposite of their stories. It's almost as if someone ignored every negative attribute and wrote pure fiction. I look back on the "ad" for Arina and realize not one thing supported who she really was. "A real heart for the Lord!" That girl never once, while in Kiev or in our home, acted like she loved Yahweh. In fact, anytime we did anything resembling church, even praying at dinner, she became snotty and disruptive.

For centuries, countries have been cleaning house by getting rid of their undesirables. Adoption seems like a viable way for these countries to "clean house". Not only that, there is blatant misrepresentation concerning biological families. In our case, we were told there was no family interaction at all, or at least not for many years. There are many cases where the adoptive family is told there is no biological family when the child was fraudulently taken from the birth parents or sold by the birth parents to the adoption agency or orphanage.

Many will say "fraud" is too harsh a word. They will say most of these people just want to help these poor orphans find families. I call B.S. I would believe that if there wasn't an ungodly amount of money changing hands. Too many people have a vested interest in keeping this industry viable, especially in a country where the local currency is 25 or more to $1 American dollar. Anyone who specializes in an industry where they are raking in hundreds of thousands of American dollars can consider himself or herself extremely wealthy. When the facilitators involved make anywhere from $9,000 to $25,000 American dollars **per** adoptee and they generate just five or six adoptions a year that is an enormous salary in a country where the average *monthly* wage is $200 to $400 U.S. dollars. There are little to no expenses for the facilitator either, because the families pay ALL expenses.

No, I don't really believe anything anyone says about doing it for the "right" reasons anymore. Not if there is money involved.

Chapter 7

Love and Abuse

Finally I finished Sasha's paperwork and picked him up from his orphanage. Now all we had was about two weeks in Kiev to process the medicals and U.S. Embassy paperwork. Two more weeks of killing time and trying to get Arina and Dima to engage. More getting out the apartment for walks around the city. I realized the only time Arina and Dima were friendly or said they were sorry for something they did was when they wanted something from me. They would apologize but never change their behavior. This was the beginning of the abusive relationship.

There was a sense of entitlement and never any gratitude. They both expected when they saw something they wanted, I would buy it for them. When I explained they could use their own money, they became belligerent and would throw temper tantrums. When I did buy them something there was never any thanks. It was as if they were owed everything.

Sasha, on the other hand, was very grateful. The day I picked him up from his orphanage I took him to get a new pair of shoes because his were falling apart. He thanked me continually for the next three days. I couldn't do anything for him without profuse thanks.

Initially when Tom and I returned to Kiev with Arina and Dima, we took them shopping. They had left the orphanage with the clothes they were wearing and little else. We bought them each several articles of clothing, new shoes and socks, and their own toiletries. Arina had one pair of ragged undies that was shared between several girls in the orphanage. She saw some pretty ones at the mall, so we bought her ten pair. I did get a genuine smile for that purchase. In one day they owned more new clothing than they ever had in their entire lives. They didn't say a word to us all the way back to the apartment, though. Instead, they took their new things into their rooms and closed the doors.

Orphan savings accounts

We were told when an orphan goes into the orphanage in Ukraine and they still have living family members, the family must pay a monthly sum which is supposed to be deposited into a savings account for the orphan to use once they leave the orphanage. We were told if there was no family, the government put money in the account.

In Arina and Dima's case, the director handed me a sealed envelope for each of them. Once arriving in Kiev, I submitted those envelopes to the local bank and they each received just over $1,000 in U.S. dollars. It was a huge sum for them! We allowed Arina and Dima to spend a small part of their savings in Kiev for souvenirs then took the balance back to America and opened their new savings accounts. Sasha, even though he had been in the orphanage much longer, had no account. We were told by the assistant director, Irena, there was none for him. We found out later she stole from his account until it was gone. The director at Viktor's orphanage in Mariupol told our facilitator there was no savings account for Viktor. We now know that was a lie as well.

All I wanted was to be home. I missed Garrett and Katherine terribly. I missed my husband who had left the week before. I was tired of being in Ukraine where I couldn't speak the language and where even going to the grocery store was frustrating because I couldn't read the labels. One time I thought I was buying baking powder to make pancakes, and once back at the apartment realized it was corn starch. Hmmmm...that's why the pancakes turned out so flat.

I was convinced as difficult as Arina and Dima were, once home it would all change.

Orphans Biological Family

The last night in Kiev I had taken the three teens to see the fireworks over the river. Instead of watching the impressive show, Arina spent the entire time with her face down talking into her phone. I finally asked Dima who she was talking to, thinking it was her friends from the orphanage. He said, "My father." "WHAT? I thought you didn't have any communication with your father?" Communication was almost impossible as I spoke no Russian and they spoke almost no English. I was trying to communicate through the translate app, which wasn't working due to poor Wi-Fi signal. Dima shrugged, which I was realizing was his way of shutting down the conversation. Right then I should have picked up the phone and called my facilitator. Instead I was just relieved we were leaving at 4 a.m. the next day for the airport. I ignored another gut check.

If I had gotten translation, I would have found out that they not only spoke with their bio father, but all four older siblings on a weekly basis, sometimes more often. They saw them on a regular basis, too. Once I found out Arina was talking to her father I should have stomped on the adoption brakes and investigated the situation. Remember, we were told they had not heard from their bio family since they arrived at the orphanage more than 9 years before. Part of our decision to adopt them was based on the fabrication they had no family relationships to turn to once they were out of the orphanage.

Again, for those of you in process, until you get on that plane to America it is not too late to annul the adoption. I could have called foul and stopped everything, undone all paperwork and moved on. One simple phone call would have changed everything for our family.

Now we've learned had they stayed in Ukraine after getting out of the orphanage, they would have migrated right to their bio family. They only reason they stayed so long at the orphanage was because it was more economical for their family. All the adults there knew this. No one informed us. We now believe everyone also knew Arina and Dima were trouble and how better to solve the problem than to send them away to America. After hearing many horror stories from other adoptive parents, I believe this is common. Ship the trouble to another country. It's been done for thousands of years. (Within two days of arriving home they asked to Skype® with their bio family. That's when, using Viktor as a translator, we found out all of the above. Too little, too late.)

I finished up the paperwork in Kiev and finally boarded a plane for America the first week of September 2014. I'd spent eleven weeks away from my family. Going through immigration at the Kiev airport was freaky. So many questions by the customs officials there. "Why was I taking three teenagers to America?" I submitted to them all my documentation. Everywhere in the airport, and even at the American Embassy, there are posters warning against human trafficking. (Now I wonder about human trafficking. Is it always about forced labor or sex? Or is adoption a form of legalized human trafficking? I now believe we were unknowing partners in trafficking.) We four finally made it through customs and into the waiting area. Once boarded I sighed with relief to finally be on the plane heading home. I had no clue everything was about to change, and my family was about to go to all-out war with four teenagers from Ukraine.

Family X was a family of five. Dad, mom and three littles. All under the age of 5. Dad and mom have a heart for orphans and for years have supported different agencies. One day at their church a hosting agency representative is the guest speaker. Dad and mom turn to each other and smile. Yes! This is their heart. A heart for orphans. They talk after church with the representative from the agency to find out more. There is such a need for teens who are aging out. They say they will talk and pray. They did. Although they had no experience with teenagers and had littles at home there was no objection from their social worker who did their home study. They were approved. (WHAT THE HELL IS WRONG WITH THESE SOCIAL WORKERS??????) They decide on a boy because their three little ones are boys and they felt they were more comfortable with boys than girls. They brought their 13-year-old boy home a year later and a bomb went off in their family.

A year later the family was shattered. All three littles have been sexually and physically abused by the adopted teen. Although vigilant, the parents were not prepared for this possibility so did not know to protect the littles. When bruising started showing up in private areas, the mom took the littles to the doctor who then reported them to the local social services (SS) organization. After an invasive and accusatory investigation, when first the dad, then the mom was accused, finally the now 14-year-old adopted son was found to be the assailant. DUH! By this time all three littles were removed from the parents and were in foster care, with no counseling. The dad, after spending several weeks in jail for abuse, was let out and moved out, not being able to handle the destruction to his family. The mom was left in the home with the adopted son who was now physically abusing her. She was told by the authorities there was nothing they could do.

At this writing she is in an apartment, divorced, no access to her littles and stuck with a now 16-year-old who has told her in no uncertain terms that he is going to kill her then find her littles and kill them, too.

Family X. If only I had known...safety

- I didn't know my bio kids would not ever feel safe within the walls of their own home because their adopted brother only feels relief by hurting them.
- I didn't realize that even after our adopted was gone from the house that two years later my daughter would still lock her bedroom door to feel safe.
- When we adopted I didn't realize my darling thirteen-year-old daughter would be molested and raped by our ten year old adopted son and we would end up losing her to foster care for neglect. I will never recover from the regret of this adoption. I miss my daughter every minute. I want to die. All because we wanted to help another child have a future.
- I never thought I would be living alone while the love of my life, my husband, moved out due to the stress and accusations against us by the one we adopted. We are now divorced and never speak. He is broken. So am I.
- **I never thought my adopted daughters would physically and sexually abuse my biological sons.**

- That even three years after he was gone from our home that my bio daughter would wake up screaming in the middle of the night thinking he was in the room with her trying to rape her.
- When we adopted our two host children we had no idea the bombshell it would be on our bio children. We never would have done it had we known.
- **When I adopted, I never knew that my biological daughter would end up suicidal after being relentlessly bullied by her adopted brother.**

Abuse by an adoptee against an adoptive parent

Family X. I received a private message from a woman who told me her story could be the one above except her husband was still in the home with her. They were fighting to get their adopted son out of the house and get their bio children back. The day before, their adopted son had beat up her husband. Brutally. Blood all over his face. Just attacked him out of nowhere. Why? Because the adopted son was not allowed to use his phone to get on a porn website. Yup. Normal parenting action resulted in the parent being beaten.

And you might ask, "Why didn't the dad fight back?"

Are you crazy?

No way. If there was even one bruise on that adopted son, the dad would have been hauled off to jail for child abuse. He had no choice but to just take it and run from the assault best he could.

Self-defense is NOT an option. In the eyes of the authorities the children/teens are **always** right, and the parents are **always** wrong. Once authorities realize the child/teen really committed the crime, that child/teen is released right back into the home. There are no repercussions for them and they are free to continue the abuse. And they will. Because now they know they can get away with it.

THEY JUST NEED MORE LOVE!

Family X. I was on social media. Someone was telling the story of their adopted son who was raging constantly, hitting them, breaking things in the home and undressing, then urinating all over the home. She was broken, completely broken. She had given everything she had to this boy for more than three years. Expensive therapies, a laundry list of "try this, try that" approaches, and more love than you can imagine. And by the way, no one does this, for this long, if they don't have deep love and commitment. This boy was just eleven so this had been going on since he was eight.

This child HATES her. With a passion that goes far beyond anything you or I can imagine. This child spends every waking moment figuring out more ways to HURT her, destroy her, and destroy everything she holds dear. This child sees her as the person who took him away from everything he knew up to the point of the adoption. And it matters not one bit that he said he wanted to be adopted and have a family. She does not dare show any affection to anyone or anything because he will instantly target it for destruction. If she has a special object he will break it simply because she likes it. If she has a special day planned he will ruin it just because he can. If she gives the dog a toy he will torment the dog.

This woman has watched this child not only destroy her home, but her family. Her bio daughter is in therapy, diagnosed with PTSD. Yeah, that thing soldiers in battle have. All the bio daughter wants is to be out of the house, away from the daily drama/trauma. This woman has watched her husband fall away from her and he is now the defender of the adopted teen. Yup! Happens more than you think. It's called **TRIANGULATION!** And RAD (Reactive Attachment Disorder) children/teens are experts. Unless you've lived it, you'll think it's made up. Nothing can be *that bad*, you think.

A "friend" on her page told her to just hold on because...

"He just needs more love."

TRIANGULATION

When the adopted child/teen is allowed to come between the married parents. They show their worst side only to one parent, typically the mom who they see as the enemy, and never, ever show that side to the other parent. To the other parent they are loving, gentle, and sweet as can be. Triangulation is also common with the adoptive parent or parents and someone outside of the family such as a family friend, relative of the family such as a grandparent or aunt/uncle or even a family that the teen comes to know through school, work or friends.

In one recent instance, the father moved out into an apartment with the adopted daughter leaving both the mother and two bio children in the home. The father was convinced the mother was crazy and making everything up. Even after being shown pictures the father believed the adopted daughter when she said the mother did it all to get the adopted daughter in trouble with him. He is fighting for custody of the bio children, but bio children refuse to go to the apartment with adopted daughter because they know the truth. This is common. Way too common.

Triangulation Advice

I'm going to give two pieces of advice here. First, if you are the husband in an adoption scenario where your wife is telling you horror stories of what's going on behind your back BELIEVE HER!!! Research triangulation. You MUST show a united front with your wife to the adopted child/teen. Every single time. Do NOT let one teensy crack show in your unity because I guarantee you the RAD child/teen will see it and use it against your wife. I know you don't want to believe that the sweet, affectionate girl/boy is a terror, but they are. And they are bent on destroying your family, however they can. I showed my husband a picture of a little boy on social media. He was the sweetest looking little guy you've ever seen. My husband agreed. I said, "He has just spent the last four hours brutally terrorizing his teachers and his adoptive mom and now is being held in a psych ward at the hospital. And he is six years old."

And second, if you are a friend of someone going through adoption hell, please listen to me. Do NOT tell them any of the following:

- You just need to give them more time.
- You just need to give them more love.
- Remember you are doing this for God.
- Would you want this child re-homed, or in an institution if he/she were your bio child/teen?
- You just need to try this. Or this. Or this. Or this. AS IF those things and a hundred more weren't already tried. Do you think we are that uneducated? Really?

AND...DO **NOT** under **ANY** circumstances, try to befriend the child/teen. You will then be a part of a triangulation situation and you WILL make matters MUCH worse! And if you are truly a friend you will just love on your friend, BELIEVE her and don't do anything unless she has given her permission. Do NOT buy things for the child/teen. In fact, do not even acknowledge that they exist if you are around them. I know that sounds mean, but these are NOT normal children/teens and if you insert yourself into the situation you WILL cause more harm.

Do not offer to have them over to your house. Do not offer to drive them anywhere. Do not offer to fix their plate at a church function. Do not go up to them in a store, restaurant, church, etc. and ask them if they are alright after they have been disciplined. Do not act like you feel sorry for them – ever! You have no idea of the damage that you are doing to the entire family when you do this!

Attachment damaged children/teens need specific parenting and when you interfere you are actually setting them back in their progress and completely undermining the one person who really does give a damn and has invested more than you will ever know in them – their mom.

AND....if there are bio children/teens LOVE on them! As much as you can. Give them your time, attention, take them out for lunch or an adventure. Just love on them. Don't think you have to treat the adopted and bios the same. You don't. They are not the same. And those bio children/teens need all the love and support they can get.

Please Don't Correct Me Correcting My Kids

Here is an excerpt from an amazing blog post on this very subject from **"The Pirtle Family."** (https://pirtles.blogspot.com/2015/12/please-dont-correct-me-correcting-my.html)

I am normally very open to criticism. As I flounder through this world of parenting I need all the help I can get. I am constantly seeking the advice of those who have done this thing right, as well as those who haven't, but wish they had. If I'm seriously doing something to mess up my kids, I'd like to be the first to know about it so I can change it before it's too late.

However, when it comes to my Haitian children, unless you have walked in my shoes or have professional experience I more than likely will withhold asking your opinion on how to handle them. This is in no way intended to be rude, but you simply don't understand and you will make the wrong call almost every time because you will want to parent them as you would a child who hasn't endured the trauma and issues with attachment they have. Despite how long you have been a parent, I more than likely know more about what is best in any given situation regarding them than you do. So…unless you have put hours and hours into studying the effects of trauma on the infant and childhood brain, I don't want to hear it. Unless you have endured daily meltdowns from my children and sweated, talked, hugged and worked through it with them for hours, I don't want to hear it. Unless you have already tried the traditional parenting strategies over and over to see them fail and worsen the issues, I don't want to hear it.

4 simple things you DON'T understand about my children.

1. **His need to manipulate and control is insatiable.** And you will not see him doing it…I do. So when you see me correcting how slow he is in getting into the car, or putting his shoes on, please don't ask me to be patient with him. Everything must be on his time so as to show HE is in control, not others. Allow me to correct him in a way that shows I love him, I am in control and he is truly better off that way.

2. **He wants YOU to be his mother.** When my child wants a play date at your house, I will more than likely decline. My son wants desperately to be a part of your family (whoever you are) so as not to have to do the hard work of trusting his own family to love and care for him. This sounds crazy to you, but it is so very true...please trust me. There are some people who are a threat to our bonding as a family and some who aren't. Time spent with certain people will throw him into a tizzy that takes a great deal of time, love, and patience to work through to bring him back to a place where he wants me to be his mom again. Please trust me to decide what is best regarding with who and how he spends his time.

3. **He doesn't trust adults. Any of them. Ever. Not you, not me.** My children truly think they know more than you or I do about everything. So when his soccer coach tells him how to play his position, he won't do it. He truly believes he knows more than the coach and what is best so he is in CONTROL. As a young child, adults around him rarely had his best interest at heart. He has learned to rely on himself as they proved unreliable at almost every turn. He is slowly learning what he never learned as a young child; God intended for adults to protect, love and nurture him. He now lives in a world where adults being in control is what is best for him because they are reliable and he can depend on them.

4. **Issues with food are real, difficult, and irrational.** When you see me correcting what you may perceive as the nit pickiest little thing about how and what they eat, it's because I have a wealth of information you are not privy to. You haven't seen the true fear in their eyes when they find out a meal might be delayed or when others are helping themselves to pizza and quantities are diminishing. You haven't seen the obsession with food that, without intervention, would quickly take over their lives in a truly dysfunctional way. My children have suffered true hunger in a way your children never have. Food will incite their survival instinct faster than anything else. I am using food to teach them to trust. Lest you think I write this post in vain, let me share one of many experiences with you. People, strangers even, feel the need to correct my parenting of these two on a regular basis and feel the need to intervene in ways they never would have regarding my biological children. For example, after my 10 year old son

deliberately and harshly splashed a toddler in the face at a public pool, I gave him a stern talking to and had him sit out of the pool in the shade for a while. He later pointed out a lady who came to him while he was sitting down and asked him if I was his mother, if he was alright, and if he needed help. This lady has no idea that she played right into his manipulative, controlling, little hand. His hand of wanting to manipulate any given situation where he is in control, appearing as a victim of undue parental aggression in his life, and bonding with strangers instead of his family. She had NO idea the damage she incurred that I spent the next however long undoing. I've stopped trying to explain to people. I'm tired of being brushed off as an over-thinking, over-analytical, over-protective, irrational mother who is blowing things out of proportion. When I say I need to be the one to fix his plate at potluck, I do. When I say he can't ride in your car with you to the store, he can't. When I say he needs to sit by me instead of you or your child, he does. I'm not being over-anything, I am simply trying to help our family survive and teach my children how to love and be loved. I'm simply trying to avoid a meltdown that you won't be there to deal with the next day.

If only I had known...Triangulation

- I never could have imagined losing my mom and my sister when they believed what adopted daughter 13 said about me and took her side against me. Seriously I'm broken because they don't know me better than that after 50 years!
- I didn't know that by adopting I would lose almost all of my closest friends and some of my family from lies told about me and my family by our adopted daughter.
- That my own brother would turn against me and take the side of the girl who was abusing me daily.
- That one day out of the blue my parents would serve me with court papers for custody of my adopted son who is 14 because they believed his lies that I am abusing him. He turned them against me. They raised me. They've known me for over 45 years. They watched me raise two other children to adulthood. Now they

believe him???? I would never have believed this level of manipulation exists. I find it hard to trust what anyone says anymore.

- Living the brokenness right now! And "well-meaning" people just make our situation exponentially harder. **I had no idea how people would turn against us and believe them and not us.**
- I never realized that I would have strangers walking up to my child asking if he was okay after I disciplined him (gave him a talking to and a time-out after he spit in a bowl of food on a church buffet) and that would cause our family three days of abuse from him. What gives people the right to insert themselves into our lives?
- Before we adopted I could never imagine my best friend of more than 20 years believing our adopted son that I molested him and turning me into CPS without even talking to me about it first. And she knew some of the stuff we were dealing with in regard to him. **I spent 12 days in jail before the truth finally came out** and she hasn't even reached out to me to apologize. My trust in humans is gone.
- Before we adopted I didn't know that our RAD kids would use every outing, every church service, school, etc. as an opportunity to win people over to them to use against us. And use them they did. We have no one anymore. We've lost all of our friends and family.
- Before we adopted I never knew that a child could manipulate adults to the degree our RAD's have in our extended family, friends, their schools and our church. **Who teaches an 8-year-old to manipulate like that?** How do they know how do to that?
- Before I adopted I would never have thought that my own brother would judge me and turn away from me after I spent seven years doing everything under the sun to help our adopted daughter before putting her in respite. And the fact is that we still tried to help her after being lied to by everyone who worked on our adoption. They knew she was trouble and never said anything until it was too late.

- I had no idea that someday I would be physically, emotionally, and mentally exhausted trying to defend myself from her lies.

I hope this message about triangulation gets across the fact that someone inserting themselves into a family who has adopted, thinking they can help, without permission from the parents, is a disaster in the making. I realize most people have good hearts, especially when it comes to children. We all want to protect children. But as much as any of us would like, these children and teens are NOT normal. They are broken. And YOU can't fix them. Certainly not by taking their side of things against the one person who has invested the most to help them heal.

Spend your time, money, and energy to support the parents of the adopted child/teen. Ask them what they need and then do that and only that.

That's my 25 cents on triangulation. I hope you listen if you know someone who has adopted.

CHAPTER 8

Finally Arrived Home

Emotions ran wild. I was so relieved to be back in my home, with my family, hugging my children who I hadn't seen in almost eleven weeks. We had to think about getting everyone settled in and all I wanted to do was cry, and sleep. I was exhausted. But happy to be in my own home.

By the time we arrived home all of the teens at home had started school for the year. We decided to keep the three new teens at home to give them an adjustment period before introducing them to a school routine. (Looking back I don't think it would have mattered if we had enrolled them immediately. Having them sitting around all day with not much to do didn't help.) Just like in the apartment in Kiev I set up the laptop for them to work on their English. Sasha complied, and he already had some decent English skills. Arina and Dima were completely obstinate. When I reminded them what they committed to while in Ukraine, they just shrugged. (I was reminded of the shrugged shoulders by government employees when they didn't provide the service requested and paid for.) Arina and Dima did that a lot. Just sat and shrugged their shoulders while looking at me with a blank stare. I was confused. What happened to the happy, smiling teens we had spent time with in the orphanage? The teens I thought would materialize once we were home? I never saw them again. Not even for one minute.

We couldn't force Arina and Dima to cooperate, so we resorted to trades. They wanted to get on the internet to talk to their friends, so we traded internet time for English learning time. For every half hour they spent learning, they would get time to talk with their friends. That lasted two days then we realized they were not just talking to their friends in Ukraine but setting up new accounts to "friend" people they didn't even know. People from not only Ukraine, but America, Russia, and the Middle East. ACK! What were they thinking? It was nothing new for them, we found out. THEN the first of many bombs were dropped. One day they were Skyping® with someone when I walked by and asked who it was. A brother. Then another brother. Then a sister. Then their father. With Viktor translating we found out the truth. They had ongoing relationships with all their older siblings, an aunt and their bio father.

The Lies Came Out

When this information materialized I asked a question. The answer was like a punch in the gut. "Why did you want to be adopted and come to America if you had family you could have lived with?" Arina looked straight at me (with Viktor translating) and with venom in her voice and eyes so hateful I actually took a step backwards, she replied, "I no want to be adopted. I want to be back in Ukraine now. I hate America. I hate you. I only say I want to be adopted so Dima would be adopted. He only want to be adopted so he no go in army and be killed in war. I want to run away from you in Kiev, but you watch me too much. I hate you. You ruin my life when you bring me to America away from my friends. I hate you."

I didn't even know how to respond. In horror I looked at Viktor and he said, "She is stupid and a bad girl. You made a big mistake to bring her here. She is big trouble." This observation from another Ukrainian who wasn't all that impressive himself. I looked at Dima and he just shrugged. As if to say, "Well, it worked. We fooled you, didn't we?"

Family X. "My husband and I adopted a sibling group of five children in November of 2013 from western Ukraine.

One adopted daughter told us she was "forced" to go with us. She has strangled my bio daughter and smeared feces on clothing and through the house, cut clothing, and sawed through my kitchen cabinet drawers with a steak knife. She kicked my bio son in the crotch so hard he threw up for an hour. She rubbed soap in her disabled sibling's eyes, and she has hit him in the face with shoes so hard we thought she broke his nose. She bites, hits, kicks, and ripped the skin from my arms. Her aggression is not limited to our family or home. She consistently behaves the same at school. She pulls hair out of kids' heads at school, punching and kicking other children. We have provided her with intensive in-home therapy, individual therapy, psychologists, and accepted medication to calm her aggression and given it consistently, we have spent countless hours trying to help her over the last twenty months, with no success. She has been diagnosed with a multitude of psychological disorders, including PTSD, associative disorders, personality disorders, etc. A recently translated document explains she was not the "healthy" child we were told she was, and that all her psychotic behaviors did not simply appear post adoption.

One adopted son has been violent and aggressive toward his younger siblings, and older brothers, and his adoptive father. He was hitting his youngest sibling with special needs when no one was around, putting porn in the younger kid's faces and punching our dog in the face, which a neighbor saw and reported to us. He refused to follow even the simplest of rules. He lied to make others feel sorry for him. He took things we bought for him and sold them at school, then lied and said he lost them. He told us he knew we were not told the truth by the people in Ukraine. He said he only agreed to be adopted so he could escape the school he was in and come to America. He thought it would be a nice "vacation" and he planned to come to America for only a short time. "Now send me home."

And those are only two of the five children.

Things started spiraling downhill fast once the truth about Arina and Dima's biological relationships came to light. They didn't have to hide anything any longer about who they were or their true motives.

We stopped allowing them on the internet access without our direct supervision. We were careful to monitor who they spoke with and made sure it was someone they actually knew and not some random stranger.

They soon discovered our local public library where free, unlimited and unsupervised internet access was available, and it was a convenient five-minute walk from our home. We couldn't force them to stay home and we quickly realized we had two teens in our home, who after being home just a couple of weeks, were in complete control of our household. It was as if they had educated themselves on the laws in our state and knew what they could get away with, what we could do and not do, and how far they could go without getting into trouble. That's when the second bomb dropped.

VK – VKontakte

Definition: VK (VKontakte; Russian: ВКонта́кте, meaning In Contact) is a Russian-based online social media and social networking service. It is available in several languages, but it is especially popular among Russian-speaking users.

This is a Russian run social media source like Facebook®, except it's not. It's full of porn, and other indecencies. It's a place where the lowest of low people hang out online. Ukrainian teens love VK. It's their place to keep in touch with all their friends, and connect with other adopted children/teens, as well as their friends still in Ukraine. There is a huge amount of education about America, adoption and about how to take advantage of "stupid" Americans who adopt. They can watch pirated T.V. shows and movies. They learn to navigate our social services system and learn how to skirt the local laws. There is an entire educational network for adoptees.

Our adopted teens found out within a week that living in Michigan they could come and go as they pleased as early as age 16, which they all were, except for Sasha. We could not force them to do anything. Not one thing. And because they were under 18, we had to report them missing if they didn't come home by a certain time, but there was nothing the police could actually do. That two-year gap between ages 16 and 18 in Michigan set us up for a two-year battle with Viktor, Arina, Dima and with our own justice system.

We found ourselves in a dreadful cycle of telling them to do a chore, or to work on their English, to have Arina and Dima shrug their shoulders and walk out of the house to go to the library. There, they would go online with VK until they "met" someone who was local. They would tell the sad story of being adopted by horrible people and being forced to live at the library. They claimed to have no food and barely any clothing. The sucker would show up, take them shopping, out to eat and back to their home for a night, or two, or even weeks. We would report them missing to our local police and keep an eye out for them when driving around or online. We were constantly on edge thinking at some point they would meet someone who was bad news and something terrible would happen to them. We were scared for them and hoped they would change.

From time to time I would get a private message via Facebook® from a man who had picked them up asking for more information about Arina and Dima. A few times I got the impression they were honestly concerned, but most times I deduced that Arina was trading "favors" for things they were being given. They were looking for them to "connect" with her again.

After we had been home about a month we enrolled them in school. We hoped a daily routine would be better for them and they would start learning something since they absolutely refused to learn English or anything else at home. At first school went well, or so it seemed. They gave the impression they were happy to be in classes and the disrespectful behavior at home alleviated somewhat. Then one day I received a phone call from one of the counselors at school. She had given Arina $5 because Arina had forgotten her lunch. Really?

I'm a good cook and I love cooking. I went to culinary school. Every morning I was up by 6 a.m. to cook a hot breakfast and make lunches for all my teens. Sandwiches on homemade bread, homemade cookies, etc. These were gourmet lunches. I told the counselor Arina had left with her lunch that morning and I was confused. When they got home from school, I asked about it. Arina shrugged. Then Viktor told me every day, as soon as she got to school, Arina threw her lunch in the trash and then begged lunch money from other students and teachers. She had been doing this since the first day of school.

I immediately called both her teacher and the counselor.

Her teacher informed me, "I have given her money for lunch. I know her counselor has, too. Even some of the other students."

I told her, "Please stop. Please tell everyone to stop. I make her a homemade breakfast every morning and send her with a lunch every day. She is only doing this to try and control the situation and me."

When Arina came home I sat her down and said, "I talked with your teacher and counselor today and I know you are throwing your lunch in the trash and telling everyone that I am not feeding you so they will give you money. They are not going to give you money anymore. If you throw away your lunch you will go hungry."

Running Away

She stood up and ran out of the house. She came home about 11:00 p.m. and went straight to bed without a word.

The next day she acted as if nothing happened.

That night after dinner, as usual, everyone was expected to help clean up. (That's the deal. I make a great dinner. The six teens work together to clean up.) Arina decided she shouldn't have to do anything to help, so she complained to Garrett to hurry so she could leave and go to the library before it closed. He told her to calm down, that he was doing a good job cleaning and she needed to be patient. His mild-mannered answer sent her flying out the door. About 9:30 p.m. Dima, Sasha and Viktor left to search for her. Sasha and Viktor came back an hour later with no sign of Dima. "Where is Dima?" I asked. Shrugged shoulders were the answer.

It was early November. We'd been home about two months. I was still very concerned and protective. I was worried almost daily something might to happen to Arina. She was so petite and seemed so fragile. I was still making excuses for her; for all of them. I wanted them to have a better life, to make better choices. I jumped in my car and drove around looking for my missing teens for more than two hours.

At 12:30 a.m. Dima finally showed up at the house just a few minutes after I had returned. I asked if he saw Arina. He said, "She is coming". 20

minutes later she sauntered in the front door. The three of us were standing in the kitchen and I simply said, "Arina, I was very worried about you and don't want anything to happen to you. Please stop doing this, just walking out the door and being gone for hours." She turned around and stormed right back out the door again. I tossed and turned on the couch all night waiting for her. At 5:30 a.m. I finally got up to start making breakfast and lunches. She strolled in the door at 6:10 a.m. as if nothing happened.

I took her into my office with Viktor to translate. I told her she could not do that anymore. We are a family and when she leaves like that her family worries about her safety. I implored her to talk to me if she was upset about anything. She just sat there with her arms folded, then got up, walked into the kitchen, grabbed her lunch, and walked out again, without a single word.

Control

We still didn't know what we were dealing with. She was in full blown RAD mode and we had no clue. None of us did. Nothing I said or did would be worth anything from this point onward. Caring. Talking. Concern. Love. Support. Nada. I was now in a war with a very real enemy but only one side knew it and it wasn't me. In fact, the more I showed concern or love, the more control she felt she had and she used that control to her advantage. It took a few more months for me to realize showing any emotion at all just empowered her. She wanted to hurt me any way she could. I had to learn to stay in strict control of my emotions any time I was with her. The extended forced emotional suppression was dangerous in that it created insurmountable emotional barriers in me. Before long, nothing could get through my wall. My two bio teens reacted similarly. Even today we are all still working on breaking through our walls of self-protection.

NORMAL PARENTING DOES NOT WORK!

Loving, caring, talking, hugging and empathy are irrelevant to RAD children/teens and will cause more damage and <u>will</u> be used against you. All it takes is someone to buy into RAD's storyline and the RAD child/teen has that person to use. YES, they are using you. Your kindness. Your generosity. Your good heart. They are using you to get back at me, using you to get what they want, using you to get CPS involved, and using you to get out of responsibilities. They will use you until you can't do anything more for them and they will move on to someone else. All the while we are judged for keeping their world small and controlled. We will be called terrible parents and told we need parenting classes. Told we just need to love them more. Told to just let them be kids. To let them have internet time, or T.V. time. Or whatever the heck else they want.

One night at 4:00 a.m. the police called me to come and pick up Arina and Dima. They had both been gone most of the night and the police had them at the high school, also a five-minute walk from our home. They had been in there since lock up at 10 pm, and employing their orphanage-taught skills, they somehow kept out of sight of the custodians who worked there all night. They finally got caught about 4:00 a.m. by the custodians, who called the police.

When I arrived at the school, Arina and Dima refused to leave with me. The officers, the two teens and I stood in the atrium of the school trying to convince the two teens to get into my car and go home. I reached out to someone who spoke Russian and who was familiar with adoptees. After another 20 minutes he talked them into getting in my car. Once home they both said, "I'm sorry mom", which I learned quickly was only used to smooth things over with no consequences. Sorry was a tool to be used to manipulate Tom and me. Because there were no serious consequences from the legal system, Arina and Dima soon lost all fear of law enforcement and the "I'm sorry" platitude was gone for good.

Family X arrived in Ukraine to adopt a teen girl they had hosted twice. She had spent several weeks in their home over two different hosting periods; a summer and a winter. She never made mention of any biological family, especially a younger sister. She was fun and engaging during hosting and they couldn't wait to make her a member of their family.

When they went to their appointment it was much like ours, only the girl had a younger sister, aged 9, that no one had said anything about. The sister was in a different orphanage than the teen girl. The prospective family was told to adopt both, or neither. (Another couple forced to make an instant decision.) Being the amazing people they are, they agreed to adopt both, even though they had never met the younger sister.

Once home the older girl started acting out. The teen was constantly on the internet and it was found she was visiting porn sites. This girl started running away, then both girls ran away. It was discovered that the older girl had "met" a local man on VK who promised them the world. The girls met up with him at a local coffee shop. The family found them a few weeks later when one of them finally posted on social media. The parents alerted police, who picked them up and brought them home.

The girls were furious with the mom for taking them away from their "real" family. This man and his girlfriend. After threatening to stab the mom with knives until she was dead – in front of the police officer who brought the girls home – the older girl was taken away into custody to see if anything could be done to help her. Nothing happened. The girl was instead returned to the family. The child repeated the threat a few weeks later in front of their therapist, who recommended a residential treatment center. This girl is now living there at a cost of over $6,000 a month. The younger daughter is exhibiting similar behaviors and has attempted running away several times.

Family X. If I only had known...Child Protective Services (CPS)

- I didn't know we would have abandonment charges filed against us.
- I didn't think other professional adults would choose to believe the stories of a confirmed liar over the parents. Over and over and over, even after the previous lies were disproven.

- I never imagined being investigated by CPS and put through their hell…twice in one year.
- I never thought CPS would accuse us of abuse because we "isolated" our adopted teens by not giving them personal iPhones. "Isolated?" Our attorney asked. "Yes," said CPS. "You are isolating them because they can't text their friends before and after school."
- That the adoption world aftermath is very disjointed, and the courts don't know what DSHS/CPS knows and DSHS/CPS doesn't know what mental health knows and parents don't know all the resources and trying to stitch it all together is a nightmare. AND no one is trained to deal with RAD. One officer had never heard the term RAD.
- We had 5 CPS investigations in less than 2 years and they were all multiple allegations. There were no apologies when it all came out the children were lying just because we said no to unlimited internet.
- We had 5 CPS investigations over 18 months. All were found to be based on lies to get what our adopted boys wanted out of us. Not one person in our situation had ever heard of RAD. They told us we were crazy.
- **I never thought adopting and just trying to help a child would cost me $70,000 in attorney fees to clear my name of false allegations.**
- I never thought I'd have CPS knocking on my door accusing me of not feeding my adopted daughter, when I'd spent mornings making lunches and all day cooking home cooked meals so she would feel loved.

CHAPTER 9

24 Hours
One Day in Our Life

December 2-3, 2014
Three Months Home with Four Ukrainian Teens

2 pm – all four Ukrainians came home from school. I made homemade borscht. This is a traditional Ukrainian soup with chicken, beets, tomatoes, potatoes, carrots, etc. It is labor intensive, takes about six hours to make, and entails major chopping of fresh vegetables. It's absolutely delicious and I made it frequently as it was one thing I could count on all four Ukrainians eating without complaint. I wanted them to feel loved and welcome in their new home. I also baked fresh Ciabatta bread. The house smelled heavenly. They all ate except Dima who immediately headed upstairs saying, "no hungry". Two bowls each. Arina ate three. No complaints. No appreciation, but no complaints, so I took it as a win.

3 pm – Viktor left for work at a local restaurant. Sasha finished his English homework and asked to go to the library. "Yes." Arina was gone. She left the house and never said a word. There was no hint anything was wrong. She never did her homework. Dima was up in his room. He was hiding something. I could always tell. I didn't know what yet. He said he didn't know where Arina went.

5 pm – I made dinner for all of teens. Tom and I were going out for our weekly "keep our sanity" dinner date. Viktor and Sasha both came home to eat. They had just eaten the borsch and fresh bread three hours earlier and now another full meal of roast chicken, potatoes and roasted vegetables was waiting.

Marriage

A friend asked me if Tom and I had ever thought of divorce during all the craziness. I answered, "No." There were some pretty rough spots, but we never got to that point. Three pieces of advice are (1) Keep your spouse #1 in your home. No matter what the drama of the day might be, hug them and love on them. Set aside time alone with them on a regular basis. A time to recharge the marriage batteries. (2) No blaming your spouse. Period. And (3) the best marriage is a marriage of three. The two of you plus Yahweh. Pray together. Spend time in the Word together.

> *Ecclesiastes 4:12: And though a man might prevail against one who is alone, two will withstand him - a threefold cord is not quickly broken.*

There were definitely some terrible days and weeks between us. We argued. We were both stressed far beyond what any normal married couple dealt with and it was 24/7 for years. Many times we held our tongues when what we really wanted to do was lash out at the other person. To blame, screaming at the other, "This is all your fault" would have been an easy out and maybe for a few minutes letting the anger spill out onto someone else, instead of where it really belonged, would have made us feel better. But that's the easy road, the wide path. The hard road, the narrow path was to take responsibility, no matter how hard it got. To just dig in and get through the day, or the hour. And we both did that, with the help of Yahweh. Another thing on my "Grateful to Yahweh" list.

7 pm – Tom and I walked in to find Viktor and Sasha and Katherine doing their homework. The kitchen was a disaster with food still left out. The three told me Arina was at the library and refused to come home – again. Dima was still up in his room, had refused to come down, and never ate.

8 pm – Katherine came to us upset because money is missing. Two weeks previous the money she had hidden in her room went missing, so she found a new place in another part of the house to hide her treasure. It was about $6 in coins, plus two Canadian dollar coins. We had a crying 14-year-old who had been robbed. We had a 17-year-old boy who was hiding something in his room and a 16-year-old girl who was not coming home – again.

Viktor said, "Arina took Katherine's money. She had it at school today and she gave me one of the Canadian dollars." He took it out of his pocket and handed it to me. That girl can find money and valuables like no one else. She should go into detective work, I thought. I see a flashback to the orphanage and the director with her keys, locking up even her coffee.

9 pm - The library was closing so I drove there and waited outside for Arina to emerge. She came out, took one look at me and headed across the lawn towards the high school. I got out of the car and said, "Come home and have dinner and let's talk about whatever is bothering you." She took off running towards the school. I drove next door to the police station and filed another report.

The police were becoming aware we had an escalating situation with two of our newly adopted teens. This was now several runaway reports filed and they realized Arina and Dima were trouble. The officer told me if Arina and Dima kept running away and causing problems for us, the city would get the county involved. After I left the station, I drove past the library on my way home and saw Arina standing inside the vestibule, which was never locked. It was somewhat warm there so it seemed it was where she intended to stay for the night. I called the police officer to let him know.

20 minutes later the doorbell rang. Officer B. stood there. Arina was in the police car, refusing to get out. We took Viktor outside to help translate. She refused to budge. She would not say why she left the house or why she wouldn't come home. (I was concluding she was going to do the opposite of whatever she thought I wanted her to do.) Officer B. said, "Get out of this car and into your house or I will drag you there." Arina replied, in very snotty Russian translated by Viktor, "I hate this family. They are bad family. I no go in house."

Viktor got very angry with her and said, "What is wrong with this family? They are good family to you. They take care of you. Mom makes you food you like and you eat and you run away. You make mom cry. Mom wants to help you and you run away." Then he repeated what he said in English so we would understand what he told Arina.

This was good for the officer to hear from another Ukrainian adoptee, I thought. Finally, Sasha came out of the house and reasoned with her, "Arina, it is better you come in by yourself instead of the police dragging you." She complied, finally. Officer B. shook his head, got into his car, and drove away.

10 pm - For the next three hours, through a translation app, I found out she was mad because I wouldn't let her talk on the phone all night long. I wouldn't let her stay up and be so tired she would sleep in school all the next day. She was mad because Viktor had been letting her use his phone and I made him stop giving it to her. She was mad because I locked up the house phones at 9:00 p.m. because she stayed up all night, three nights in a row, and then slept in school. She was mad because her teachers called me to tell about her sleeping in class. She wouldn't tell me who she was talking to those long nights. She had no friends here, so it must have been local people she met online. I finally convinced her to go to bed.

At last I was able to stumble upstairs, exhausted. I couldn't wait to be in my bed. I'd been awake since 5:00 a.m.

1 am - As I walked up the stairs I heard music coming from the boys' room. Garrett was still downstairs studying so I knew it wasn't him. All music was to be off by 10:00 p.m. so everyone could get good sleep. Before I could even think about climbing into my bed, I had to see what was going on. I walked into the boys' bedroom to see Sasha asleep. Dima had some electronic gadget which he quickly tried to hide. Great! Another problem. He was not supposed to have electronics. He decided to curl up in a ball and turn away from me, clutching his gadget. This is why he had spent the last two days up here alone and not eating. Where did this gizmo come from? I sat down on the bed and asked, "Where did you get it?" "A friend." He muttered.

This was the start of all things being laid upon some random friend. We learned anytime any one of the adoptees showed up with something new; clothing, gadgets, shoes, food, whatever, it was always from "a friend." Sometimes the friends had names like "John the Chinese guy".

I prodded, "Did your friend let you borrow it?"

Dima: "No, he gave it to me."

I finally got a look at it. It was a brand-new phone.

Me: "I'm not sure you know anyone here that would give you a brand-new phone. Who is this friend?"

Dima: "Nobody."

Now we have a "nobody friend" who bought him a phone. Right! I suspected he had lifted it at the local drug store. I reached over and took the charger and earbuds which were lying there. I wasn't going to wrestle him for the phone. He got mad and stormed downstairs where Arina had already gotten back out of bed and was throwing things around and making tons of noise. All I wanted to do was get some sleep. I was dead tired.

We'd been home three months and we knew Arina and Dima were not the teens we were led to believe they were by all those people in Ukraine. A girl who just wanted a mama to help her cook and garden and sew. Oh no! This girl wanted nothing to do with any of those things – especially a mama. And this boy, Dima! That Bible he was holding onto so tightly in Ukraine. He had carried it around with him everywhere we went. If there was any waiting time he sat down and read it. We were bamboozled. Not one time since arriving at the apartment in Kiev did that boy touch that Bible. In fact, when he finally left home for good, he left it behind. It meant nothing to him. It was a tool to show us he was a good boy. We were left wondering who put him up to that one. Could it be that nice pastor or his wife? I don't know. He didn't seem smart enough to think of it all by himself.

3 am - I finally got Arina to stay in her room. I gave up on Dima and crawled into bed after I locked my bedroom door - something I'd never done before that night. Why? I couldn't tell you. Just unsettled. And I was tired and just wanted to sleep. I ended up getting up and going downstairs three more times during the next three hours because of excessive noise.

Dima was still up walking around, opening kitchen drawers and slamming them shut. He was deliberately trying to keep everyone in the house awake.

4:30 am - I walked into the kitchen to see him standing there in just underwear with his junk hanging out of the front opening. Now this was December. We kept our heat at 62 degrees at night. It was cold outside and a bit chilly inside and this 17-year-old was standing there almost stark naked in the middle of my kitchen. I looked away and told him get to his room immediately. The tone of my voice must have done something because he went upstairs and slammed the door. I felt sick. I wished I could un-see what I saw. I fell into bed and hoped to get an hour of sleep. It never happened. The constant noise of banging continued. I just laid there until my alarm went off. (It would be more than two years before I would be able to get a full night of sleep again.)

6 am - The alarm went off and I groaned. No sleep – again. I went down to start breakfast. That day was homemade sausage and egg rollups, a green's drink and vitamins. Arina would get an Arbonne protein shake because her stomach had been bothering her and it digested better than eggs. Then it started. Arina refused to get out of bed. "I'm tired", she said. "Yeah, I know. Me, too. I'm sorry you stayed up most of the night, but you're getting up and going to school." I replied.

Tom was done with this behavior and so was I. This girl had taken complete control of our home and we were just done. He took a Dixie cup of water and said, "Either you get out of bed this instant, get dressed for school and downstairs for breakfast or this water is going on you." She rolled away from us toward the wall. He poured it on her. The look on her face as she turned towards us was priceless. She was spitting mad.

She jumped off her bed (top bunk – Katherine slept on the bottom bunk) and started throwing things around the room. She pulled dresser drawers out and threw them across the room, breaking one of them and spilling the contents all over the room.

Katherine came in from the bathroom and started crying. This was her room, too. She had just worked the night before to clean up from the last bout of Arina's temper tantrums. Katherine had some of her things on her dresser and those went flying and broke. Katherine was trying to get into the room to stop Arina from destroying any more of her things. Instead I took her into my room to calm her down.

Viktor and Sasha had been standing in the doorway with me when Tom poured the water. I came out of our bedroom to find Tom, Viktor and Sasha standing in the hall outside the room. I asked the boys to try and get her to stop throwing things and screaming. Arina slammed the bedroom door on them and we could hear things being thrown and broken in the room. The boys tried to talk to her through the door, but it made no difference. The noise went on for almost 15 minutes. Then quiet.

She came down ten minutes later dressed in new clothes, new coat, and new boots and stormed out the front door screaming she was going to the police.

The room was completely destroyed. We took pictures of the damage. The police told us we should have filed charges against Arina for malicious destruction of property, but at that point we were still hoping time would work things out. Hindsight we should have followed the police recommendation. Perhaps it would have prevented some of the things that happened later and honestly, I think had we done so, Garrett and Katherine would have felt better about the entire mess. To them it seemed like we allowed the adopted teens to keep getting away with horrible things. We definitely did.

ROOMS

Advice: if after all you've read, you are still set on adopting and you have bio children/teens. Your bio children/teens MUST be allowed to stay in their own rooms without bunking up with ANY of the adopted children/teens. Install good solid locks on their doors which can't be easily picked. Your bios MUST have a place where they can find peace and safety. Under NO circumstances should bios be put in with adopted – at least for a long, long time and once you know, for a fact, those adopted will not cause harm to your bios, or their property. No exceptions.

Katherine was devastated about her room. Many of her things were destroyed and had been tossed about the room. She asked that we make a room in the basement and move her down there, away from Arina. Looking back, we should have moved Arina and left Katherine in the room. Why did we move Katherine and not Arina? Although our basement is nice and finished and has finished rooms we could see how Arina would spin a move to the basement to others. We didn't want to take the risk of a potential CPS investigation. Katherine told us she never wanted to go into that bedroom again after watching Arina destroy it so many times. (To this day she refuses to go in there. We should have moved Arina anyway and re-done the room for Katherine. The move did not serve Katherine and Arina kept trashing that once beautiful room.)

7 am - We finally got Katherine settled and off to school. The entire morning was chaotic. Everyone was upset. Garrett left without breakfast and without even a hug – a behavior most unlike him. Arina was gone. Where? It was anyone's guess. Dima announced he was not going to school. What was it with these teens thinking they could make the rules? Oh yeah, they could. It was the law.

(Have I mentioned that I'm pretty sure Satan hated me, and he had a talk with Yahweh and Yahweh said, "Sure, I'll let you have a go at her, but I'll pray for her." Yup! It just kept coming.)

> *Luke 22:31-32:* *"Simon, Simon, behold, Satan has demanded permission to sift you like wheat, but I have prayed for you, that your faith may not fail, and you, when once have turned again, strengthen your brothers."*

Tom and I both went up to the boys' room with Viktor and Sasha, who would now be late for school. In just three short months we had already learned to have witnesses with us. (That is ADVICE I give to anyone in this situation. Witnesses who told the truth were invaluable in our defense, time after time. Honestly, I will tell you if we hadn't had witnesses, instead of writing this book while sitting in my home, I would probably be writing from jail. Tom, too.)

Dima was curled up on his bed flatly refusing to get up.

Me: "Dima get up. You need to go to school."

Dima: "I'm tired."

Me: "I'll bet you are. You were up walking around mostly naked and banging cabinets in my kitchen most of the night. You have to get up and go to school right now."

Dima: "No!"

Tom picked up the side of the mattress which was on a low to the floor frame and flipped it over. Dima sprang to his feet as the mattress was going over and instantly changed. Wow! Have you ever seen a mild-mannered person change right in front of your eyes? This meek and soft boy became someone else in an instant. There was pure venom in his eyes. Russian spewed out of his mouth a mile a minute. He yelled, "I go police". Viktor and Sasha stood there and looked at him in disbelief. Sasha turned to us and said, "He is crazy!"

I said, "OK, go ahead and go to the police. And tell them what? That you refused to get out of bed and go to school?" This now became the new threat Arina and Dima would throw at us. Later we realized they both said it for the first time on the same morning. So, who did they talk to that told them that they just need to go to the police? Remember what I said about VK? Yup! Their nice adoption network on VK educated them.

I used the translator app and told him that he had three choices. The police had told me two nights before that at 17 he could make his own decision on where to live.

Me: "Dima, the police told me that you have three choices. You can get dressed and go to school, you can get dressed and go find a job or third, I will contact the county prosecutor to have you removed to a home for incorrigible teenagers. Dima, Dad and I want you to choose to get dressed and go to school, get an education, live with our family and be a part of it, but we can't force you. You have to decide which of these three things you will do. Right now."

Our local Novi police department

This is one area even today I think back and am thankful to Yahweh for His provision. From the first encounter with our local police department, they "got it" concerning Arina and Dima. They saw them for who they really were. This is NOT the case for most people in our situation. Arina and Dima didn't get the memo they were supposed to be sweet and nice in front of the police like most adopted children/teens are. They were belligerent and disrespectful. They showed their true selves. I'm not sure why they did except that they weren't educated about it before it was too late for them.

7:30 am - Dima stormed out of the house promising to go to the police. Viktor and Sasha followed him out the door for school - late. I shook my head and went to clean up the kitchen. After they all left I confessed on my private Facebook® group I'm pretty sure we were sold a bill of goods. This was the boy in Ukraine carrying around his Bible, acting so pious, sitting with me trying to learn English while we were waiting in the orphanage, and he wouldn't even practice for five minutes now without a huge argument. We were deceived. Big time!

Journal entry. December 3, 2014. This is the boy who has horrible teeth and refuses to go to the dentist. Who has trauma issues and refuses to go to counseling because he doesn't think there is anything wrong with him. I can't even make him take a regular shower or brush his teeth. He smells so bad most of the time that no one wants to be around him. His teachers call and ask me to have him wear deodorant. I tell them I would be happy if I could get him to take a shower and actually use soap and shampoo. Seriously, this boy rarely takes a shower and then he just steps in and gets right back out again. He refuses to use soap or get his hair wet. It's not like he is three and I can go in there with him. I don't know what to do!!"

9 am - Tom and I left for a quick trip to the grocery store, locking the house up tight. We came home to find Dima in his bedroom on his phone. We asked him how he got into the house and he ignored us. Later, we realized somehow he had climbed up to the second story where a window had been unlatched by him earlier.

Dima decided he was not going to the police and was not going to school. Tom and I were going to go to the local mall and walk for a couple of miles for some peace and exercise. (One of our "marriage "recharge the batteries" activities.) Not anymore. We couldn't leave Dima home alone. Our trust was eroded. We didn't even like being with him without one of the other teens around as a witness. Tom and I stayed together all day. If I went upstairs for something, Tom went with me. We were not quitters. We still wanted to do everything in our power to make these adoptions work and we were hopeful, given enough love and time, it would work out.

2 pm – After school everyone came home, even Arina, who had gone to school after all. She never said a word to anyone. She just ate her after school snack and went to her room.

This 24-hour period would be repeated over and over again.

A "Friend"

I had many conversations with Arina, Dima and Viktor concerning "friends". Just a few days before the Dima conversation I had this conversation with Arina when she came walking in the house wearing a new outfit.

I inquired, "Where did you get that new outfit?"
Arina: "A friend."
Me: "A friend? Which friend? What is your friends' name?"
Arina: "John."
Me: "John? John who?"
Arina: "John Chinese man."
Me: "Oh! Where did you meet John the Chinese man?"
Arina: "The library."
Me: "And why did John the Chinese man buy you a new outfit?"
Arina: "Because he want to."
Me: "And what did you do for John the Chinese man?"
Arina: "Nothing."
Uh huh – yeah right.
Every. Single. Time. At the library.
Beware of "A Friend."

Family X. Another email from a distraught parent. It started with a dream. Maybe of a daughter with golden pigtails. Maybe of a son with a bright smile. Yet, it ends as a nightmare. We didn't choose for it to be this way. We fought like hell to make sure it wouldn't end this way. Yet, here we are.

When I'm asked to list our issues, I basically write every word I never thought would happen in my life. Theft, jail, lying, sexual craziness, porn, physical violence, pregnancy tests, fugitive task forces, suicide attempts, in-patient treatment, residential drug programs, meth, heroin, naked preaching, wrecked cars, impounded cars, broken window screens, cigarettes in socks, computer locks, broken computers, screaming, yelling, crying, ugliness.

My family told us not to adopt. They told us we wouldn't want someone else's problem. We told them "they are children who want a family". But, they didn't want a family at all. They had a family when they were born. That family did not do anything kind for them. They learned that family sucks. Yes, sucks. So, we sucked before they even met us.

My marriage has survived. I'm shocked to say that. My oldest bio has survived. Survival is great…if you are on a T.V. show where you win a million dollars. Survival is great if you beat cancer. Survival is not great if it's the best thing you can say about the last thirteen years of your life.

My bio son, my husband and I carry scars and still-bleeding wounds. Festering things that just won't leave. Remembering the moment the children we wanted to help so badly told us they hope we go to jail. The moment we finally understood that our adopted children will never love us and even more they actually hate us. But even bigger than that the realization that OUR LOVE CAN'T FIX THEM. There isn't enough love to heal the trauma. Butterflies and unicorns and rainbows aren't going to ever solve this issue.

I live without any of my children now. Bio is in college, adopted son in jail, adopted daughter in denial. Away from me. My heart may never heal, but I go on. Every day I'm one day further away from that life. I work to regain relationships with everyone I lost. YES…ME…I LOST ALL MY TRIBE. Everyone that I cared about abandoned me through this ordeal. I'm so alone now. How do I face the rest of my life so alone? All because we tried to do the right thing by two orphans who didn't want anything I tried to give to them.

All because of lies.

Family X...

- I never thought I'd be triggered by seeing anything "panda"; she begged us to decorate her room in panda. She wanted everything to be panda and once done she completely destroyed her beautiful room.
- I didn't know I would become someone I wouldn't even recognize.
- We met him when he was almost 4 years old. At 12 he became a physical, sexual, and emotional danger to everyone in our home. We tried therapy, medication, love, structure, discipline, encouragement, vitamins, organic food, essential oils, exercise, and massage. He still victimized EVERYONE who came close to him. I was so sure we could save him.
- When I adopted I didn't know I would be mentally tortured by the child I so desperately wanted, loved and cared for.
- When I adopted I didn't know I would have to sign papers to have my daughter committed.
- When I adopted I didn't know Reactive Attachment Disorder (RAD) existed and that it would be a lifelong prison for both the child and our family.

CHAPTER 10

Escalation

Just like the zip line fiasco in Kiev, there were many special fun family times that were ruined by one or more of our adoptees. It was almost guaranteed if we planned something special for the family, one of the adoptees would do their best to ruin it.

One Saturday we decided to take them all to a local indoor trampoline park. I had found half price tickets on the internet. We wanted to surprise them and do something fun; to just get out of the house and away from the drama and maybe blow off a little steam. I made a good breakfast, then asked everyone to pitch in and clean up so we could get going. Tom and I told them we had a fun surprise and wanted to leave by 11:30 a.m. Of course, Arina went right up to her room, refusing to help clean up and as an added bonus, announced to us she would not go with us. Viktor and Sasha talked with her, trying to convince her to come along with us. They told her it would be fun, but it was more important to her to have her own agenda. I went upstairs to talk with her.

Me: "Arina. Remember in the orphanage when dad and I told you and Dima that we have family meals and then everyone cleans up the kitchen? It's not right that you eat with everyone, then you walk away and don't help clean up."

She sat there with arms folded.

Me: "We are leaving in ten minutes. You cannot stay in the house by yourself. We all want you to go with us. We are going to have a lot of fun. Get your coat and let's go."

She threw her pillow across the room, grabbed her new coat (we still had no idea where she was acquiring the new clothing) and stormed out of the house, running down the street. We left without her.

We spent the afternoon having a blast. The activity actually produced smiles and laughter, chatter and bonding. I thought it was good for everyone, including Tom and me. It felt good to laugh. Our time expired and we returned home, but Arina had not. I sent Viktor and Sasha to the library to check for her since she had been MIA for several hours. The library had closed at 5:00 p.m. and there was no sign of her. I received a private message via social media from another adoptive mom that Arina, while at the library earlier in the day, had emailed her adopted daughter.

Arina's entitlement behavior was so difficult on all of us. When she didn't get her way she just walked out. Tom and I had zero recourse. She came and went as she pleased, with no accountability and no responsibility. She had no regard for anyone other than herself. She treated our home like a flop house – a place to eat and sleep. Tom and I were simply "caretakers – providers."

I decided I wouldn't wait up all night again. I needed sleep. Only a few days before this I had spoken to her again about going to counseling. Again, she refused. She said, "Nothing wrong with me. You bad mom. You need counsel so you good mom."

Counseling

Therapy for RAD children/teens is very specialized. You cannot go to a "normal" family therapist. Such professionals are not typically trained in trauma/attachment issues such as RAD, and quite honestly, can and do make matters much worse. There are many stories of unsuspecting therapists being manipulated by the RAD child/teen and the therapist unwittingly becoming part of a triangulation scenario. Since the therapist hasn't been trained in trauma issues, they do not recognize the deceit. They place the blame for the adoptees bad behavior on the adoptive family's inadequacies.

Adoption related traumas and attachment disorders are not the customary family dysfunction. Even RAD trained therapists are a waste of time and money in most cases, since the RAD children/teens are convinced if there is a problem, it does not lie with them, but with their "new" family. Sadly, after thousands of dollars and hours in therapy most families are no better off than when they began.

Family X. "I was not to let my adopted daughter hurt herself or my other children, but then I was told to provide her a room just like the other children, with toys like theirs. Then when she would use those toys to hurt herself I was the one held accountable. When I gave her toys that were more appropriate and safe, those same workers told me I was wrong for treating her different than my other children. We purchased safety gear then were told we shouldn't use it because it made her feel different. I was told not to restrain her but at the same time I was responsible for protecting the other children. I was forced by social services to take several parenting classes. During one class I asked a question about a particular scenario that I was dealing with regularly. They had no answer so instead told me, "Well, that would never happen" and "a child would never do that." The parenting scenarios that were a daily part of our lives completely stumped the parenting teachers. They had zero knowledge or experience with RAD, trauma/attachment issues. They were a complete waste of time and money.

Grateful

I'm going to stop here and give much-deserved praise to Yahweh. I honestly don't know if I can use words to describe how much I grew to utterly depend on Him through these months and years. I'm pretty sure I'm a functioning person because of Him. There are days I talked with Him non-stop. A continuous stream of conversation in my head. The Bible says to pray without ceasing and I can tell you it made all the difference in my life. As bad as the situation became, He protected us from how much worse things could have been. He always provided witnesses. One night while on my knees I could physically feel His presence and I felt, despite the chaos, completely calm. I knew He was right there with me. I knew everything would probably become even more challenging, but He would be there with me through it. He gave me a Holy comfort despite the problems.

Perhaps the ashes of adoption would result in a beautiful opportunity to help others, who, for one reason or another, couldn't voice their horrors. So their information stays hidden. Yahweh knew I would shout it from the rooftops, even if it took some prodding from Him. He knew being raw and real on paper would become my battleground – my weapon to fight back, not only for me, but for all the traumatized voices who are unable to speak for themselves. And for my own children.

I was listening to an online sermon one morning while getting everyone started on their day. It was "It's All Part of the Plan" by Steven Furtick of Elevation Church. In it he said that sometimes Yahweh uses Satan to deliver something that Yahweh means to use for good. When I heard it I exclaimed, "YEAH!" That's what this was! Satan pushed this adoption thing, hoping it would destroy our family, but instead, Yahweh would use it to shed light upon the horrors. He was calling us to educate families, so adoption doesn't destroy hundreds more. Go Yahweh!! And I'm grateful He has given me this opportunity. More than that, I'm grateful my family, while even still recovering, is nonetheless intact, healthy, and we are emerging from the darkest of days.

More Running Away

Dima ran away...again! After a few decent days we were at it again. That night, our rule of all electronics having to be turned in to either Tom or me by 9:00 p.m. was being challenged once again by Dima. Tom, who was a mentor for the high school robotics team, was at the high school and I wanted to go to bed. I had collected everyone's devices except Dima's. I looked for him to try and collect the phone and to remind him he needed take his shower and get ready for bed. I found him weirdly hiding, crouched behind the couch in the family room. (This was the same phone I believed he had stolen and I'd been trying to get from him since I caught him with it days earlier. It had been nothing but destructive for him. His teacher had called to tell me all he did was sit in class with his head in his phone with earbuds. He refused to give it to her.)

Dima stomped up the stairs with the phone, shoved some clothes into his backpack, and stormed out the door. Not a word to any of us. I was bewildered. I couldn't keep doing this. He was 17 and the police told me if he left they couldn't do anything, so don't bother to call them.

It was December in Michigan and very cold. I couldn't stop him. Dima made a choice we didn't agree with but had no control over. It's not like we could physically restrain him. We couldn't even make him turn over the dang phone! I called Tom at the high school to let him know Dima had left again.

The phone he most likely purchased with stolen funds in the first place (we were missing another $100). For the past several days, instead of doing school work, and every moment while home, he played on that stupid phone. He even refused to eat snacks or dinner, because he didn't want to put the phone away. I turned the internet completely off and he still used the phone to play a mindless game. His teacher asked that I keep the phone at home. I told her I wished I could. It was so frustrating to realize we had so little power.

So instead of surrendering the phone for the night, he made a drastic decision. He chose to be outside on his own in the dark and cold.

I was spent. I had five other teens to care for, and a business to run. I made the decision to go to bed.

I didn't even know what to pray for anymore. I was angry and fed up. Arina, Dima and Viktor were badly broken, but they didn't see how desperately so! And certainly, they didn't want to fix anything. And we couldn't force them. Their brokenness was breaking our family. Garrett and Katherine were breaking, even though they weren't showing just how badly yet. Tom and I were trying to muddle through. I had been averaging only three hours of interrupted sleep a night for months. That's all. THREE – BROKEN – HOURS.

The next morning, Dima was still absent. Tom and I were running errands when my cell phone rang. It was a police officer from a department several towns away. Dima had been hanging out in a gas station which also had a fast food restaurant. The owner called the police because they thought he was a runaway. The officers looked in his backpack and found something with the name of our high school. After calling the school to help identify him, they were given my number. I dropped Tom off at home and drove the 30 minutes to pick up Dima. 30 minutes by car!!! He had ridden the distance of about 20 miles on the new bike we had just bought for him, in the middle of the freezing cold night!!

Another two hours lost chasing after one of these teens. I was incredibly frustrated, constantly having to drive all over to pick them up. I learned he had ridden his bike to a nearby 24-hour big box store and hung around there most of the night until they kicked him out. He kept riding until he reached the gas station. The manager said he felt sorry for him and gave him some chicken and fries. He was very concerned until I told him some back story. I was just done. I didn't care who knew what anymore. I was done with pretenses. I paid the manager for Dima's food and walked over to the booth where Dima sat, looking miserable.

We sat across from each other in the booth and I put my hand out for his phone telling him, "Give it to me or I'm leaving you here." He gave it to me without a fuss. Miracle. That showed his level of desperation. All the conversations I had with Dima and Arina were still either through translation by Viktor or Sasha or through a "speak and translate" app on my phone. Arina and Dima knew almost no English even though they had been home for over three months. They made absolutely zero effort to learn.

Me: "What did you do all night long Dima?"

Dima: "Rode my bike. Went to store to get warm."

Me: "Why did you leave? You know dad and I only want you to be safe and go to school and do well, so you can have a good life, right?"

Dima: "Yes."

Me: "Why did you leave?"

Dima: "You want take my phone."

Me: "Dima, you know if you take your phone to bed you will play on it all night, then you will be tired and not do well in school the next day. You know I take your phone, so you will sleep."

Dima: "Yes, I know."

Me: "Dad and I want you to do well. Remember when we talked in Ukraine about going to school and learning English and having a good life?"

Dima: "Yes, I remember."

Me: "Dima. No more phones. They are not good for you. No more phones. Do you understand?"

Dima: "Yes, I understand."

Me: "OK, we are going home. You are going to tell dad that you are sorry, take a shower and then you're going to help me make dinner. Tonight after dinner you're going to go to bed and get good sleep, then go to school tomorrow and tell Miss Shannon you are sorry for how you've been in her class. Do you understand?"

Dima: "Yes, I understand."

The weather was still freezing cold. I think the only reason he got in the car and gave me his phone was because he was exhausted and cold and didn't know what else to do.

I was not happy I would have to put a wet, filthy bike in my car and drive both him and the bike home. In retrospect I should have just left the bike. I don't know why I still cared so much. Probably because we had just bought it and I hate waste. The same reason I kept trying to help.

After all our conversation in the restaurant about not having a phone anymore all he kept asking on the way home is when could he have his phone. I just shook my head no.

We walked into the house and Tom was standing in the kitchen. Tom asked Dima, "Well, Dima...how was your ride? A little cold out there?" The dad thing. Dima glared at him.

Tom and I sat him down to talk about riding aimlessly. Tom said, "You know Dima, 20 miles east instead of southwest would have put you right in the worst area of Detroit and chances are you would be dead right now." Tom pointed in the direction of Detroit. He showed him on a map how close he was to a very dangerous area. Dima didn't respond and sat there staring at the table while Tom talked. When Tom finished talking, Dima cocked his head slightly towards Tom and glared with hatred out of one eye. Whatever plan he had was ruined and now we had his phone. He was home and safe and the repentant demeanor disappeared. We sent him to shower and get ready for dinner. We hoped we had gotten through to him. We found out soon enough our warnings fell on deaf ears.

Electronics

Most adoptive teens are addicted. Horribly addicted. They don't have the ability to tear themselves away from phones, tablets, or computers. ADVICE. If you are bringing a child/teen home do not give them access to any electronics until they have been home many months, or even years. They find a way to get passwords and they go on sites adults shouldn't visit. Many of these adopted children/teens are addicted to porn, as young as age 4, girls and boys, which I had a hard time believing until it was in my own home. To have a 16-year-old girl in my home who would go on porn sites anytime she could was heart breaking.

Journal entry after Dima's running away incident - December 17, 2014. I'm changing. Changing into a person I don't know anymore. A person with a short temper, who is always upset. This is not me. I'm normally positive, upbeat, looking at the bright side of things. I cheer others. I encourage. Now I go to bed with a heavy heart (and seriously I never knew what that phrase meant until the last few months). My heart weighs a ton, and it hurts. I'm a naturally hopeful person. I believe the best in people until they prove me wrong and typically they must prove it several times before I take them seriously. I give chance after chance. My spirit is worn out. I continually do for these four adopted teens with no respect or gratitude from them and who, at the slightest perceived grievance, get angry and either destroy things in my home or walk out not to be seen again for hours and/or days. The hurt I'm feeling is also being felt by Tom and Garrett and Katherine. They are snappish and angry over stupid things now. My beautiful family is so hurt. I feel like I'm carrying around a hundred-pound weight everywhere I go. I was driving someplace the other day and had to pull over and just sob for ten minutes. The least little thing makes me jumpy or the tears start pouring out.

Journal Entry - December 29, 2014. Viktor is regressing. Dynamics in our home have changed once again. The three Ukrainian boys have a pack mentality now. It is them against us. Viktor is more like the boy he was when we first brought him home. He is the ring-leader. Sullen, angry and secretive. Sasha has regressed, too, and is following Viktor around like a little puppy dog and doing everything he is told by him. Dima is just hanging on for the ride. Viktor feels powerful having the other two boys following him around, doing his bidding. Last night it was three hours just to get them all showered and ready for bed. Viktor undermined everything I was trying to get them to do. It's like having a bunch of toddlers. At this point I don't care if any of them shower ever again. Except I'll get more calls from the school about their foul odors.

There is this culture thing going on, which on one hand I get. I really do. They are all Ukrainian. They all speak Russian. They are naturally going to gravitate towards each other. In the beginning, when we first arrived home, Viktor pulled me aside and asked me why we adopted Dima and Arina. He said they were "собаки". I asked what that meant. He said, "In orphanage there different levels for kids. собаки are dogs. Dogs are lowest level, they are bad people. They worst in orphanage." It makes Viktor feel empowered to have the two other boys follow his every word and do whatever he tells them to do.

We've been home almost four months and I know we will get through this. I have no doubt of that. At the very least we have four teens who aren't on the streets in Ukraine right now fending for themselves. Sasha told me the other day when he graduated from the orphanage he was going to be a bum on the streets and beg from people. UGH! Yet now he has all this and there is such entitlement. Wow!

I know there are many of you going through similar trials with your newly adopted children/teens. Every day I pray for all of you. That we stay strong in this battle for these teens. That we are given the wisdom to train them up in the way they should go. That we stay peaceful in our spirits and let Yahweh guide us and keep us. There are so many of us fighting this good fight. And we will win! (I was still so positive and hopeful then.)

GUILT

Oh, how I hate you! Guilt takes a close second to FEAR in this adoption journey. First fear pulls you into adopting and then guilt keeps you there. You feel guilty that you didn't do enough, didn't love enough, or didn't try hard enough to get them into counseling, or try harder in school. It goes on and on. Are you using the right parenting style? You second guess every single thing you do. Guilt keeps you trying long after a sane person would give up. I think this is one reason when someone tells you that you just need to love them more you go ballistic – at least on the inside – because you know deep down that you've invested way beyond what a normal person would. Partly because of guilt.

That same guilt tells you how you must keep quiet because so many people helped you with this adoption and what would they think of you? What about the people who contributed to your fundraiser? What will they think? Guilt tells you to keep the craziness to yourself because no one would believe you because you hardly believe it yourself. Guilt that if you just did a little bit more maybe, just maybe, you could catch a glimpse of that sweet girl you saw in the orphanage. Guilt because you don't want to think later down the road that maybe you could have done something more, or different and things would turn out better. Guilt. It's completely destructive. And keeps you in hell.

Journal entry February 11, 2015. We are at the USCIS office in Detroit for Dima, Arina and Sasha to have their citizenship ceremony. Can I just be dead honest and say that I HATE that we are taking them to this? I know that it's just a formality and they are already citizens, but to me being an American is such a privilege and these teens just don't deserve it. They deceived us. This makes me ill. I want to cry. This should not be happening. They shouldn't get citizenship this easily. They haven't earned it and it means nothing to them. This isn't right.

I'm so sorry, my beloved America.

PROBATIONARY PERIOD!

This is my goal for future adoptions. A probationary period in which either adoptee or adoptive parents can reverse the adoption. These changes would solve several problems we face as adoptive families. I would like the following changes instituted in our immigration law:

- **No immediate citizenship for international adoptees**. As of now, the moment they set foot on American soil they are Americans. Becoming an American should be much more of a privilege. Adoptees should retain the citizenship of their birth country until <u>**at least**</u> one year has passed and the adoptive parents agree they have earned American citizenship. I would be more in favor of two years.
- If adoptee exhibits any of the destructive behavior which our teens and many others do, the adoptive parents can, at any time in that first year (or better two years) reverse the adoption and pay to have the child/teen sent back to their birth country. A full reversal of all aspects of the adoption, including name changes, birth certificates, citizenship, etc. An adoption annulment. With no negative repercussions on the parents.

If these suggestions had been law, or options, we would have reversed three of our four adoptions. I would guess thousands of adoptions would be reversed and this entire adoption process would long ago have been repaired or banned. At the very least we wouldn't have deceitful people becoming automatic Americans and wrecking good families.

Family X. If only we had known...Pain!

- Before adoption I never knew there was such a thing as adoption dissolution and that I would empathize with those who made that choice.
- I asked my oldest daughter what her one sentence or thought would be. She said she didn't know the depth of pain it would cause when well-meaning people ask how her adopted brother is doing in his new home.
- I never thought by trying to help a child and adopting them, that their screaming behaviors would affect my biological children so much that it affected their grades and made them depressed and cause them to lose their hair.
- I never thought having an adopted child in my home would cause my biological children to be embarrassed to have other kids to their home. They were embarrassed by the peeing, the screaming, the lewd behavior and the stealing.
- When we adopted we never thought the very social workers who claimed would help us would blame us for his problems.
- My bio daughter said that she didn't realize that years after he was out of the house that specific screams from kids in stores, or church, or any public place would trigger her and she would just want to hide from it.
- As a formerly bubbly, positive and happy person I now feel like a complete failure at life.
- **Before adoption I didn't know I would just want to cry. Every day. All day long. I've given up. I am no longer a person. I'm just a sobbing machine.**
- When I adopted, I had no idea how much I would begin to doubt and second guess, heck, constantly question my every thought, decision and action. My self-confidence dropped to zero.
- I never knew I could cry this much.

CHAPTER 11

A Snowstorm and Rejection

As I had journaled, the three Ukrainian boys had formed a pack. Sasha had an anger problem which had become more pronounced. His was the quiet sort of anger which would build until he would explode. His face would get very tense and his jaw would clench, and he would get very quiet. Then he would either run off or explode in anger. Anything you told him, he already knew. It would be one thing if he really did know what he was talking about, but he didn't. Tom and I were very frustrated with him because, of the four, he had the absolute best potential and he was blowing it. He was the only one with no signs of RAD and had aspirations for the future. Viktor was a terrible influence on him and Sasha was a follower. He began to blow off his school work and was failing. He was told if he wants to graduate, he would have to go to summer school and repeat two of his classes. He refused to ask us for help and instead asked Viktor, who knew even less than he did.

Sasha turned out to be horribly lazy in direct opposition to his "helpful" behavior during hosting. I don't know if I'd ever been around anyone so lazy. He wouldn't do anything unless I was standing right over him. I found out by talking with Viktor that it was common in the orphanage. The caretakers were busy and soon forgot if they asked one of the orphans to do something. The orphans knew it and learned to walk away and ignore requests. Even in the orphanage no one really had authority over the orphans Now home, if I walked away they disappeared, Sasha most of all.

I talked to him a few days before about the easy vs. the hard road and the outcomes from both. The conversation began with me asking Sasha, "What do you think you would like to do after high school? Do you want to go to college, or learn how to do something like car mechanic, or get a job?"

He replied, "I don't know."

"What are some things you like to do?" I asked.

Sasha: "I like to do things like we do in robotics." He was on the robotics team with Garrett; the same one that Tom was mentoring.

Me: "OK. You like to work with your hands."

Sasha: "Yes."

Me: "If you were the owner of a shop would you rather hire someone who was a hard worker who did a good job, or would you want someone lazy who you had to yell at all the time to get the job done?"

Sasha: "A hard worker."

Me: "If you were looking for a job, do you think they would hire you if you acted like you did around here?"

Sasha: "No." At least he was honest about it.

Me: "Sasha, you have the choice to always do the easy thing and just get by in life or you can work hard and do an excellent job. It is your choice. Both here in our home and in your future job. Do you understand?"

Sasha: "Yes, I understand. I will do better."

We were hopeful he would.

January 2015 – The snowstorm aftermath. We had experienced a huge snowstorm and the teens were all enjoying a snow day. We live in a large neighborhood and the three Ukrainian boys decided to grab snow shovels and go earn money shoveling driveways. Two hours later Dima showed up alone with $125 in his hand. Tom and I looked at each other, quite impressed with the haul. In all the years our teens had been shoveling none of them had ever earned that much in just two hours. 15 minutes later, Viktor and Sasha came in the door. They had each made $40 working together as a team, clearing four driveways. Tom asked Viktor, "What happened with Dima?" Viktor replied, "He left to go shovel by himself. He didn't want to work with us." Then Tom asked Dima, "How many driveways did you shovel?"

"Five." Dima replied.

Tom and I looked at each other thinking this isn't adding up. How did two boys shovel four driveways and earn $80 and one boy by himself shovel five for $125? Tom said to Dima, "Get your coat on. We're going for a ride."

As they pulled out of the driveway Tom said, "Which way are the snow shoveling jobs you did? We are going to drive around and you're going to show me the five you did." Tom drove around the neighborhood with Dima pointing out five different driveways. Once Tom was clear on the five, he stopped the van at the last driveway, got out, told Dima to get out, and they walked up to the door.

Tom rang the doorbell, the owner opened the door, and Tom asked, "Did this boy shovel your snow?" The owner replied, "Yes." Tom thanked her and he and Dima walked back to the van and proceeded back to house number four. They repeated the walk to the door and rang the doorbell. The owner answered and Tom asked, "Did this boy shovel your snow?" He replied, "No." "Have you seen this boy before?" Tom asked the owner. "No." he answered. Tom thanked him and got into the van with Dima and proceeded to the third house. At the third house Tom already knew that Viktor and Sasha had done the job because Tom had driven by while they were shoveling.

Tom looked at Dima and called him out about that house. At the second and first homes it was obvious they were done by snow blowers. Tom pointed that fact out to Dima and how it was impossible that Dima had done them with a snow shovel. Then Tom asked, "Where did the $125 come from because it wasn't from snow shoveling?" Dima responded, "No, I shovel snow." The lies continued despite the truth. They returned home.

Once home, Tom informed me what they had done and I asked Dima, "Where did you get the $125?" He stubbornly repeated, "I shovel snow." We realized it was fruitless because he would never admit the truth. I was not happy when, the next day, I realized exactly $110 was missing that I had hidden way back in my desk drawer. He was paid $15 for the one shovel job he had done, and the rest came from me.

Journal entry – February 12, 2015. It's not just things they are doing that are making us crazy. It's the lying, the blaming and the justifying. Here are just three examples of recent events:

First, Tom and I came home to a broken kitchen window. We called everyone in and asked, "What happened." Of course, no one knew anything about it. Finally, after over 30 minutes of prodding we let them all go. We had no idea. Later, we cornered Sasha, who was the one, if any of them, who might tell the truth, if the others weren't around. Finally, he said, "Dima and I came home, but the house was locked. Dima got the ladder and was going to use it to get into a window upstairs. The ladder accidentally hit the kitchen window and it broke." Tom asked, "What were *you* doing?" Sasha replied, "Nothing. It was Dima's idea. I didn't touch it." Yeah, right. Telling Dima we knew the story, he shouted, "I no do it!"

One day I tried to open the garage door and it was broken. Tom thought it had caught on something, then after looking at it, he realized that someone had pulled down on the beam and broken it right in the middle. Of course, we asked everyone, and no one knew anything. The three Ukrainian boys seemed sheepish, so we dug a little deeper. Tom told Sasha the neighbor had seen him hanging on it. Sasha immediately yelled, "NO! It was Viktor. He was doing pull up's and it broke. Dima and Viktor laughed when it happened, but I didn't." Sure you didn't. When Tom confronted Viktor, he got angry and blamed Sasha. Deny, blame, deny, blame.

Tom noticed big muddy footprints on the carpeting. He called Dima over who was the only one wearing boots and they matched the print. Dima looked at him blankly and said, "No me. I no do mud." Tom looked at him and said, "Your shoe matches the marks. It was you. I am going to get the cleaner and show you how to clean the marks right now." "NO! I no clean." He walked out of the door.

I wish one time they would own up to what they did. I wish it wouldn't take hours-long conversations to finally get the truth out. Tom and I understand accidents happen. With these Ukrainians there is just zero accountability. It's incredibly frustrating.

March 8, 2015 – International Women's Day. While in Ukraine we learned that International Women's Day was a very big deal. Women and girls dressed up in traditional costumes, flowers were given to every female and there were celebrations in schools and workplaces. Tom wanted Arina to experience a taste of the celebration, so he went out and bought a beautiful bouquet of flowers for her. He wanted her to feel happy and as honored as if she were in Ukraine. I was standing in the kitchen and Arina was sitting at the table when Tom walked in with the flowers. He smiled, handed them to her, and said, "Happy International Women's Day!"

She took the flowers, smelled them, and gave him a half smile. She set the flowers down and went back to painting her nails. Five minutes later she got up without saying anything, grabbed her coat and left for the library, leaving the bouquet lying there.

I felt so bad for Tom. He had gone out of his way to make her feel special. I hugged him and said, "Thank you for trying." I could feel the disappointment emanating from him and wished for once that she would have been grateful, for his sake. He tried so hard to be a good dad to her.

I put the flowers in a nice vase and put them in her room. I glanced in her room the next day after she had left to go to the library and saw the flowers in the trash, the vase next to the bin on the floor. I never told Tom.

Tom and I were at a loss. It seemed as if we'd had a hundred conversations between the two of us trying to figure out a new way to get through to them. Try this, try that. We'd pretty much thrown out decades of parenting tips and methods, which didn't work with these teens the way they'd worked with our bio children. We'd tried several methods promoted by various "adoption and other professionals" which didn't work. We found "Connection Parenting" which is taught in the book "Connection Parenting: Parenting through Connection instead of Coercion, Through Love instead of Fear" by Pam Leo. There are several groups on social media which focus on this method of parenting adopted children/teens. Then there was the Karen Purvis method of TBRI, Trust-Based Relational

Intervention® for attachment from her website and book, The Connected Child.

Everything we tried was used as ammunition against us by our RAD teens. We had to admit we were out of our league. Our family was disintegrating. I felt like the little Dutch boy with his fingers in the dyke in the old Han's Brinker tale. Only I didn't have enough fingers and the water was flowing way too fast.

We made the decision to remove Arina from public school in favor of home schooling her. The issues of her refusing to do her homework, lying to teachers, and constantly begging money from teachers and classmates, and causing problems with other students were mounting, so we pulled her. She would only attend the high school for a gym class once a day. Two days after the flowers fiasco she was angry about going to school for gym. She didn't want to go. It was a two-week swim segment and she couldn't find her suit.

I had been reminding her for the last week to find her suit, and now twenty minutes before the class she didn't have it. I found an extra suit (when you have a pool there are always extra suits lying around) and sent her off. She came back two hours later with completely dry hair, so I asked what happened. She refused to talk about it. I heard from her teacher later via email that Arina simply refused to get into the water and sat, completely dressed, poolside the entire class, sulking. One class and she was failing because she refused to participate.

Dealing with these teens reminded me of that old arcade game, Whack-A-Mole. Tom and I had a game with six moles and every time we'd whack one problem down another one popped up. We would get one of the teens in a good place, then another we thought was in a good place was not anymore. Something would happen to set off a trigger in them and all hell would break loose. Oh! And they fed off of each other – constantly!

Family X...

- Adopted daughter, 14, constantly finds a way to get on the internet and interacts with strange men. These men keep showing up at the family home, looking for a 24-year-old they "met" online. When the parents tell him he is really talking with a 14-year-old, sometimes there is surprise and sometimes not. The parents are afraid of the ramifications on the rest of their family. What if one of these men show up and they aren't home?

(This was something we also feared. Viktor, Arina and Dima were constantly giving out our home address to strangers. Their "new friends.")

- One time adopted daughter, 17, rode up in a car driven by a strange man. Later police told us he was on their list of possible human traffickers in the area. Great! And we have a beautiful 11-year-old biological daughter. These kids seem to attract the worst of human's right to your own doorstep. That day is when real fear took hold of us. When we realized that she was attracting predators to our address. I think that was when things really went from bad to worse for us. And we went into protect mode for our biological daughter.
- Before we adopted we didn't think the little girl who was so happy we were adopting her could be so evil once we were home with her and that I would hate the idea of adoption now. We don't trust ourselves anymore. I thought that if we missed this behavior, what else are we missing? Now I know that she was just very good at hiding it. We are stuck.
- Before I adopted I loved seeing happy stories and great things happening in my friend's lives on social media. Now I've deleted them all because I can't stomach seeing all the happiness when I'm living in daily terror and hell.
- Before we adopted I had no idea that young teenagers could be so resourceful in stealing things. It's as if they have a sixth sense on where to look for things I thought I had hidden well. Nothing is sacred in this house. If they want it, they take it.

CHAPTER 12

YES! We Padlocked the Refrigerator

Viktor was doing better for a while and then, out of the blue, he told me he got a message over social media from his bio-father. About a year prior to this news, Viktor told me he had heard from his uncle. His uncle had told him both his bio parents had been killed by the Russians in the Donetsk region of Ukraine. He'd told Viktor his bio parents were riding on a bus to the orphanage to find and pick Viktor up from the orphanage when the bus was stopped at a checkpoint and everyone was killed. It was extremely traumatic when he learned about the tragedy. Now, a year later, this uncle reached out to tell him this about his father and to make arrangements for the father to contact Viktor. When I asked how it was possible the bio father was alive, Viktor was not sure. Viktor was understandably angry and upset, because this guy, this father, was not a decent guy at all. His father had allowed Viktor's mother to place Viktor into the orphanage in the first place and left him there for over eleven years.

I talked to Viktor about forgiveness. I explained just because we forgive, doesn't mean we have to have a relationship with someone. We forgive so we aren't carrying the burden of holding onto the anger. We let Yahweh handle the burden from then on. If we don't forgive others how can Yahweh forgive us? He took it all in, nodding his head in agreement.

We thought we had made progress spiritually, but later found the idea of forgiveness hadn't made an impression on him at all.

It took us awhile to understand that the Ukrainian teens would agree with me and nod their heads and say they understood, but they really didn't. What they were really saying was they heard me and they understood the words, but not necessarily the concepts. Or whether they agreed or not. This led to constant misunderstandings.

I gently reminded Viktor that we didn't really know the truth about his bio parents. Ukraine was far away and we had no way of knowing the truth since all the conversation took place over VK. It could be anyone saying anything. Viktor was freaked out for days. One minute he seemed to be listening to us and understanding, the next he had regressed. He would become angry saying, "This is me. This how I am. I no change." He decided he wanted to go back to Ukraine. He told us he owned a house there from his grandmother and had a little brother, an uncle and other relatives, and now maybe a living father.

Journal Entry. March 25, 2015. It's been months of up and down, up and down. Constant Whack-A-Mole. Viktor, Arina, Dima and Sasha are sullen, argumentative, aggressive, secretive and angry. They have formed a united front. Them against the rest of us. Ukraine vs. America. Garrett and Katherine have become too quiet, guarded, and are hiding in their rooms most of the time. We've lost our family. I'm so sad I don't know how to function anymore. I want to throw up I feel so sick at what has happened to us. Tom and I don't communicate much at all. The four of us; Tom, Garrett, Katherine and I just exist. I cry, all the time. Over what I've lost, what I've done to cause it and the futility of thinking anything is going to change for the better anytime soon. I feel completely helpless. My family is being decimated right before my eyes and I don't see a way to stop the demise. We are reminded constantly by Arina how she didn't want to come here; didn't want to be adopted. I'm afraid for my family. I try to pray but no words come out. I don't know what to say to Him. I ask Him to make it all go away. To make them all go away. To make us right again. My eyes hurt from crying so much. How did we get here? Help!

Last night Arina stomped down the stairs to where I was cooking dinner. She stood before me with her hands on her hips, glaring at me. I picked up my phone so we could translate.

Me: "Is there something you need, Arina?"

Arina: "I hungry."

Me: "OK, dinner is in 30 minutes and we are having chicken the way you really like it."

Arina: "No. I hungry now. You give me food now."

This was such a common conversation, so I just shook my head no and said into the translator app, "Arina, dinner will be ready in 30 minutes. Wash your hands and set the table."

Arina: "I hate you. I hate you very much. I hate you adopted me." Then she is gone. Yup. Again. That's all it took. I spent 2 hours making a dinner she liked and would eat and she never came home to eat it. Most likely she went to the library and told her sob story to someone on VK who came to her rescue again. She never came home last night.

No matter how logical it is to say she is the one who asked for it, not only from us, but from the Ukrainian court, from the orphanage director and from the U.S. embassy in Kiev, I am the enemy. It makes me angry because all she had to do was say no right there at either the orphanage or in the Ukrainian court and we wouldn't be going through all this right now. It was all her plan to come here and my family now lives with the consequences of her deceit. I think of the very long line outside of the American embassy in Kiev of people wanting to come to America who, in reality, have little to no chance of ever coming to this country. These four were handed American citizenship on a silver platter and they act as if they were given pig slop. I am seething with anger.

April 2015. Ex-orphans had been in our home for more than two years. Two years for Viktor and seven months for the other three. None of them wanted to be in our home. Oh, they wanted the food and the place to sleep and money, but none of the "family" stuff. No belonging to a family, no consequences for bad behavior, no accountability, not even encouragement to be a better person, or any sort of love or affection. They didn't even participate in the fun. I felt like I was running a hotel complete with full maid service and 24-hour restaurant. They would come and go as they pleased, they acted as if they owned the place, and we were their servants. The threat of calling the police became a daily occurrence. We could never, *not for one minute*, let down our guard. We could never be alone with any of them.

Things came up missing. Even stupid things like kitchen gadgets. One afternoon while cleaning, I found my vegetable grater in the children's bathroom, pushed way back in one of the bottom cabinets. Family heirlooms were broken or had disappeared. Favorite items were never seen again. Katherine had a small iPod her oldest brother had given her several years earlier for her birthday. It disappeared off the kitchen table, never to be seen again. We had gained the work of supporting four extra people in our home who did absolutely nothing to contribute. We had to provide well for them or face the consequences. I felt empty. I knew my bio children felt empty and abandoned. We four were living behind our own walls of misery.

Almost every door in our home now had a lock on it. Tom and I each carried around big sets of keys, a jangling reminder of the orphanage director. I recalled her large set of keys and could still see her lock up her bag of coffee. My home had turned into an orphanage. Even our refrigerator was locked up at night. We put a chain through the doors with a padlock. (Very common in adoption circles.) I had come home one night with four extra-large pizzas someone had donated to us. Dinner for the next night all set – what a blessing! The next morning, the pizzas were gone. I asked everyone. Nobody admitted to knowing anything about them. All six left for school, Arina to her gym class, and I went on the hunt for pizza boxes. I found them. Two were smashed under Arina's mattress, the other two under Dimas's. From that time on, we locked all food up. It wasn't like they didn't get enough food. All they did was eat the food I constantly prepared for them. That was my new job - short order cook – on duty from 6 am to 10 pm.

Viktor, Arina and Dima would frequently say they were going back to Ukraine when they turned 18. It would go something like this. Tom and I would be sitting in the front room talking and the three of them would walk in and stand in front of us. Viktor the leader, of course. They would stand in front of us with Viktor announcing in a demanding tone, "We have something to tell you and you have to listen."

Tom said, "What's up?"

Viktor: "Arina is 18 next year in July and when she is 18 we are all going to Ukraine."

Tom and I looked at each other and shrugged. I said, "OK. Anything else?"

They looked deflated as if they expected an argument from us. After they left the room I turned to Tom and said, "Do you know how much I wish she was 18 today and they were already back in Ukraine?" He agreed.

Okay then. Why in the world did we do all of this if they were just going to go back to what they left behind? How was that life going to be any better for them there? We felt so used. Arina reminded me once again she never wanted to be here in the first place and, she added, it was all my fault. This had now become a daily rant from her. Really? My heart felt broken. I felt used as I reflected over the past seven months. I could see what a toll the struggles had taken on my entire family. All based on lies. All of the sleepless nights, the stealing, the police, the running away, the threats, the moving of Katherine out of her beautiful room into the basement in order to protect her. I'd inadvertently taught my bio teens what it was like to live in an orphanage. All to be screamed at daily by four teens who knew they had complete control over us. And then tell us it was all our fault.

Which was the one truth they told.

We should never have adopted!

April 10, 2015. We realized when Arina went to the library, she went with the purpose of going on the internet to look for men in the area to whom she could attach herself and who would buy her the things she wanted. They were the source of her new clothing. She bounced from person to person, sponging from them as much as she could while providing sexual services to them. Prostitution. Exactly what we intended to save her from by adopting her. When the men started asking questions she dumped them and moved to the next "john". She was incredibly nasty to everyone in our home, especially Katherine and me. We endured the worst of her moods. Katherine was constantly on guard. Whenever she had the chance, Arina would steal something of Katherine's. Clothing, stuffed animals - any object Katherine cared about was a target. One day I was going through Arina's room looking for old food to throw out and picked up one of Katherine's stuffed animals. The back felt hard, so I pressed it. I realized Arina had sliced the back open. Hidden inside the animal was another phone!

We had taken at least five smartphones away from Dima and Arina. Where they were getting them, we had no idea. Either people were buying them, they were stealing them, or they were stealing the money to buy them. The one I found in the stuffed animal had a calling plan with monthly payments which were being paid by some anonymous man. I confiscated the phone. They were not allowed to have phones. When I confronted Arina, the only thing she would tell me was the guy was in his 30's and she met him "at" the library. (What she meant was she was on the internet at the library and "met" him online.) She refused to tell me his name.

By the middle of April 2015, I had lost track of the number of runaway juvenile police reports I'd filed. It didn't matter the weather, or what was going on. At the slightest imagined offense, they ran. According to state law, I had to file a police report every single time in order to protect Tom and myself. I had a file with everything the police would need for their report. When they would come, I just handed the file to them. A copy of the teens' state I.D. cards, copies of Tom and my driver's licenses, and a typed statement of the latest incident. I tried to make it as easy on the police as possible. The police would find whichever one of the teens had run and bring them home. Once home, the teen or teens would be offensive and belligerent to both us and the police officer. I was so embarrassed by their behavior.

I constantly cleaned trash from Arina's room. One time after she had taken off and had been gone for several days I opened the door to her room because I smelled something really putrid when I walked by. Opening the door, I was shocked. I had never seen a room so trashed in my life. It was as if she had been in there years, not a few months, and garbage was piled up everywhere. There were large holes in the wall where she had thrown objects. She had found a sticker book and covered Katherine's beautiful hand stained dresser with at least a hundred Minion stickers. All the antique knobs were missing. One drawer was broken apart. The top of the dresser was covered with some kind of sticky mess she had spilled and not bothered to clean up. It couldn't be salvaged. The floor was piled high with clothes, shoes and garbage. Used, bloody tampons littered the floor, along with empty and half-empty boxes of food, candy wrappers and empty "cup of soup" containers. I realized she'd used the garbage can for a pee bucket. I gagged, but that reeking odor, as disgusting as it was, was not the source of the stench.

I had to find the source of that awful smell. It was overpowering. I found bags of food. Food taken from our pantry and fridge, and food from God only knows where. There were full cheesecakes and shrimp platters. That's where the nasty stench was coming from. Shrimp platters in this girl's room, tucked under a mattress, another down in the closet under a huge pile of dirty clothes. Another inside of a box, inside another box, up high on the closet shelf.

I wanted to puke. Where did she get all this stuff? Either someone bought it for them or it was shoplifted. I knew both Arina and Dima were involved. If they are eating all this old food, why were they not puking sick? Two whole cases of instant soup hoarded away. Food I never bought.

I understand they grew up hungry. Since they had been in our home, I literally cooked breakfast, a huge lunch, and another full meal after school, dinner and then a huge snack about 9:00 p.m. - daily. Five giant meals every day. And they had been told, over and over again, if they are hungry at other times they just need to ask. Even after locking everything at night they were told, "Just tell us if you're hungry and we will give you as much food as you want." It was one thing our house did really good – food!

Tom and I would swing from disgust to amazement to incredulous to sad to just "this is so crazy that no one would believe it" modes daily.

CHAPTER 13

Introduction of "Horrid Man"

One Saturday in mid-April I was out of town for a few days for business. (Yeah, trying to keep a business going while all this is going on. Don't ask me how I did that. A miracle for sure.) Arina and Dima asked Tom if they could go to church because there was a special teen event. Surprised, he asked, "What church?" They replied, "It's the church around the corner across from the library." There was a Methodist church almost across from the library, which was a 5-minute walk from our home. "Yes, that's fine." Tom told them. 5:00 pm rolled around and they hadn't returned. Tom hopped into his van to drive to the church. There were no cars in the parking lot. There were two other churches close by, so he drove there, and same thing, no cars. He called me while I was at the convention and told me they were not home and not at any of these churches. I told him, "Wait until 9:00 p.m. then call the police and file a runaway report." He waited, then called the police who came and took the report.

At 10:45 p.m. Tom noticed a dark blue SUV had pulled up into our driveway. Seeing Tom on the front porch, the driver rolled down his window. Arina and Dima got out of the SUV, walked up to the porch, and went into the house without a word to Tom. Tom walked over to the SUV.

We dubbed this character "Horrid Man" as events unfolded.

HM said, "Hello, my name is "Horrid Man". I picked up Arina and Dima at Great Lakes Crossing Mall". (A mall an hour away from our home). Tom said "Horrid Man" did most of the talking. "They called me and asked if I would drive from where I live in Detroit to the mall to pick them up and take them home. They told me John the Chinese man drove them there, bought them lunch, and then left them."

Tom replied, "Why would they call you and not call me and how do they know you?"

HM said, "I'm a friend of theirs from church and they called me because they had my number. I have been a Good Samaritan who drove all that way out to the mall and brought them home to you."

Tom (thinking to himself why in the world they would call this guy instead of just calling dad to come get them? And who calls themselves a Good Samaritan? But didn't ask because at this point Tom already knew he would not get a straight answer.) This sounded quite unbelievable already.

Tom asked, "What are they doing at Great Lakes Crossing when they were supposed to be at this church five minutes away and now all of a sudden they are calling you, who we don't even know?"

HM replied, "I'm connected with the Ukrainian Church in Detroit. That's where they have been going to church." Now Tom wondered how they were getting back and forth to this church in Detroit, 45 minutes away. And how many times have they gone to this church? And why today of all days did they actually ask to go to church? And did they attend church that day or were they really at the mall? The tall tale was growing quickly.

"Horrid Man" came across as a friend/mentor to the two teens. Tom thought he seemed a little old (somewhere in his 30's) to be friends with Arina and Dima. All of it seemed quite fishy.

Once "Horrid Man" was gone Tom called the police and they came to our home to verify Arina and Dima were back in the home and then closed the report.

When I returned from the convention in Vegas I called the number "Horrid Man" had given to Tom. I wanted to meet this guy and get the straight story. I invited him over for a talk. He was very enthusiastic to come and meet with us.

We sat in the front room with Arina, Dima, Sasha and Viktor. Suspicious of this new "friend", I purposely told Garrett and Katherine to stay put in their rooms and not show themselves. He sat in the chair next to the couch I was sitting on. He was short and thin, wearing very pointy dress shoes, dress slacks and a light jacket. He reminded me a little of Viktor in his demeanor – very Russian. My antennae was on high alert. Something in my gut was very unsettled. I got right to the point with him. "So how is it that you met Arina and Dima?" I asked. There was no meaningless chit chat. This was going to be an interrogation. I was polite but didn't mince words.

He replied, "I met them through VK when they were looking for other people who spoke Russian in the area. I asked them if they were going to church and then invited them to go to church at the Ukrainian church in Detroit where I go with my family and friends. I told them to ask you, which they said they did. One day a few weeks ago I picked them up at the library and drove them to church, and then out to eat and to the zoo before bringing them back to your home."

"How many times have you driven them to church since then?" I asked.

"A few times, most every Sunday." He replied.

"And you never thought to meet us and talk to us about it? That in all these weeks you just picked them up and dropped them off at the library. That didn't seem suspicious to you that you weren't picking them up and dropping them off here at their home?" I inquired.

"No, they told me that is what you preferred."

"And you drive all the way to Novi from Detroit to pick them up, then go back there for church, then back here to drop them off, then back home again?" I asked.

HM replied, "I'm a Good Samaritan." (Again, with the Good Samaritan bit.)

At this point I was at a loss. I didn't like what I was feeling, but there was nothing substantial I could put my finger on. How could I keep them from going to a Ukrainian church to be with other Ukrainian/Russians? Wouldn't that be heartless? "OK, then this is how it's going to be from now on. They must ask before going to church with you. I must be told exactly what time you are picking them up and you will pick them up from our home. I will be told what time they will be brought back and they will be brought directly to our home. There is no more of them coming and going whenever they want. If they walk out of this house without our permission, they are not going to be allowed to go with you. Is that understood by all of you?"

He talked to them in Russian and they all nodded their heads, "Yes."

I looked at Viktor and he confirmed what was said in Russian was exactly as I said. (That boy, sometimes he was just ridiculous how bad he was and other times, like then, he was so good and helpful.)

"Horrid Man" left and something told me to ask Arina about the latest phone I had found. "Arina, did "Horrid Man" buy you that phone?"

"Yes, so we could talk to him when we want." She answered. So that mystery was solved. I wished I had thought to ask about the phone while "Horrid Man" was still here. I wondered what he thought when he found out I had taken the phone from Arina. Arina and Dima ran upstairs and I told Viktor and Sasha to stay so I could talk with them. I asked them, "How did all this seem to you?" They both replied, "He is a bad man. He is not good for Arina and Dima." "That's my feeling, too." I told them.

The next day I called the detective we were working with and told him "Horrid Man's" name. I told the detective it was "Horrid Man" who had given Arina and Dima their latest phone. The next day I received a call from a Homeland Security officer telling us to be very careful. "Horrid Man" was a person of high interest to them, thought to be very dangerous; part of the Russian Mafia. He was suspected of involvement in human trafficking! And I let this man into my home!

The following day there was a knock on the door. The police. After learning about "Horrid Man" they decided they wanted the phones I'd been collecting. They wanted to check the photos and text messages. They were also going to the library to check the surveillance tapes. They wanted to see who had been talking with Arina and Dima. They didn't know if it was only online or if there were men who showed up in person to talk with them. Since the truth came out about "Horrid Man", they were very concerned about trafficking and thought there may be a possibility Arina and Dima were jeopardizing our entire family. The library cooperated with the police and provided the security tapes. The police kept all the phones for evidence.

Good. I hated having them in the house, especially the last one from "Horrid Man".

Advocating for orphans. I made the decision I'd never advocate for adoption again. I was so angry my family has been turned upside down by these four teens. Garrett had withdrawn and refused to be in the same room as any of the Ukrainians. He stayed in his room most of the time. We tried to get him to come and hang out with us, but he said, "I feel safe in my room, mom. I'm sorry. Can I just stay in my room?"

Katherine was showing signs of severe trauma. She had become withdrawn and was constantly angry; snapping at everyone. I found out she was so distraught one night that she rode her bike to the house of a friend at midnight, over four miles, crying the entire way, alone. She was there until 4:00 a.m. and then rode home again so she would be home before I woke up at 6:00 a.m. I found out when she was still so upset that morning when everything spilled out. My mind raced with everything that could have happened to her, in the dark, on those rides to and from our home. "I hate my life now. I hate them. They've ruined everything. I'm so scared." She sobbed into my shoulder. I didn't know what was causing the terror I knew she was feeling. She opened up to me later – much later – and told me an account that made my blood boil.

Biological Children Molested.

One night Katherine was in the kitchen cleaning up. Garrett was up in his room, Arina was gone and Viktor and Sasha were at work. Dima walked up to Katherine and put his arms around her, touching her breasts, in an attempt to molest her. Thank Yahweh my daughter is a fighter and was stronger than he was. She broke away from him, kicked him in the groin, and told him if he ever touched her again he wouldn't be able to walk again for a long time. She went downstairs and locked herself in the basement for the night. Any time she was in a room alone with Dima he attempted to rape her. After Dima was gone from our home permanently, Katherine told me all of it saying, "Mom, I just did my best to always be with someone else or locked in the basement where he couldn't get to me, but sometimes I came home and he was the only one here and I couldn't get to the basement fast enough. But I kicked him as hard as I could, then ran to the door and locked it behind me. I wouldn't come out until someone else came home."

Had we known he would've been arrested and out of our home for good. I asked why she never told us she said, "Mom, you had so much you were trying to handle and I didn't want to make it worse for you." She was scared and traumatized that someone attacked her in her own home but didn't feel able to tell us. I was sickened.

I stopped sleeping in pajamas. I began sleeping fully clothed, with my socks and hoodie laid out on the floor next to my bed. It was a time saver. You see, when the police come to your home in the middle of the night they don't just softly knock once or twice. They pound the door loudly while at the same time ring the doorbell fast seven or eight times. They wait about 15 seconds and do it again. I was conditioned to respond quickly. At the first pounding my feet hit the floor and after putting on my socks, I would grab my hoodie and pull it on over my shirt all while running down the stairs to open the door. My goal was to get downstairs and turn on the porch and inside lights before the second round of knocking and ringing began. I wanted to let everyone else in the house continue to sleep. I couldn't remember the last time I slept through an entire night. Probably in Ukraine prior to picking Arina and Dima up from the orphanage.

F.B.I., Homeland Security and More!

On this occurrence, I opened the door at 2:45 a.m. to see nine people on my front porch and sidewalk. Cars were parked everywhere. I momentarily wondered what our neighbors thought of us. I invited the crowd in. Apparently, we were having a police party in my foyer! All around me stood two local police officers, two sheriff's deputies, one State Police trooper two F.B.I. agents and two officers from Homeland Security. And me, in my sweats and hoodie, wiping the sleep out of my eyes. "Where are Arina and Dima?" I was asked in a very gruff voice by one of the Homeland Security officers. "One minute and I'll check." I replied. I ran upstairs to check and they were gone! They must have snuck out after I fell asleep. The police suspected they were back with "Horrid Man". I never found out how they knew the teens were gone. The questioning lasted about 40 minutes and then they all drove away after scribbling in their notebooks and collecting information. I lost count how many times we had a middle of the night police party in my foyer.

Arina and Dima showed up in school the next day and came home afterwards. They refused to say where they'd been. I called the police to let them know they were back home. The police came to interview them, but they were tight lipped and refused to speak. They just sat in kitchen chairs with arms folded. We all knew something was going on, but what?

The next morning Arina was still in bed when she should have been in her gym class. I couldn't force her out of bed, so I picked up her backpack. She sprang out of bed in one hot second, grabbed the bag and ran out the door with no shoes on her feet. A few months prior I would have been so upset, but I had become desensitized to the drama. I wondered what was in the bag she didn't want me to see. Most likely another phone, a replacement for the phone from "Horrid Man"

I knew she had run to the library because I received a Facebook® private message from her saying, "I hate you. You are bad mom. I wish you dead. I want new family. I hate your family. I find new family. I find orphanage to live. You dead to me." Tom and I were certain there was some plan in place. She was burning bridges.

I responded that she has a nice home here with people who care about her and it was her choice to run away this morning. She continued to rage and threaten. I stopped responding and ignored her. I let the police know she was threatening me and that she was at the library on the computer. There was nothing they could do, but they made note of it.

Upside Down World

We live in a weird time in our society. Recently there was a school shooting. Social media overflowed with people asking, "Why didn't someone say something?" My answer is: people like me say things all the time, but nothing gets done about it. Why? Because in our society until someone proves they are deranged by killing a bunch of people, or at least making a credible attempt, threats aren't taken seriously by law enforcement. Adoptive parents make police reports yet nothing is ever done to protect them. We are told nothing can be done unless the child/teen actually does something. It takes a shooting, or a murder, to wake people up. This is really messed up. A mom on our adoption group is in fear for her life because her adopted son swore he was going to kill her. Police say they can't do anything unless he makes the attempt.

A few hours later Dima came home from school, ate two huge plates of food and went to sleep in his bed. He woke up and went outside just after 8:00 p.m. I looked out a few minutes later and there he was talking with Arina. Just before 9:00 p.m. I went out to call them inside, so we could lock up and go to bed. They were both gone. At 10:00 p.m. I filed another police report. It was a new officer this time, one we didn't know. I thought we knew all of them by this time. He was chatty and wanted to know the back story, so I told him some of the events of last eight months. He also talked with Viktor who told him we were great parents, good to Dima and Arina and they were stupid kids who were always in trouble. (This from the teen who just the day before had spouted hatred at us. I closed my eyes and thanked Yahweh for changing Viktor's heart just when it was needed. There were many times we would have been in harm's way. All it would have taken was for Viktor or Sasha to corroborate Dima and Arina's stories. But they never did. I am grateful.)

The police called at 12:30 a.m. They had them. They found them in the vestibule of the library again. It was funny how they kept going back to the same places. They were caught watching a movie on a cell phone, using the library Wi-Fi. Another cell phone as I had suspected. She didn't want me to find it in her backpack, so she grabbed it and ran. The police spent 45 minutes writing out the report and talking to me. We talked how Arina and Dima had been going on VK and that's where they were meeting these men who were giving them phones, food, money and other stuff. I told the police it was also where they were learning how to work around the law. The police were shocked.

I told the officers we had told them many times how dangerous it was to go off with strangers they'd met off the internet. I had them watch human trafficking videos. I told police how the Arina and Dima were driven to the mall across town and left stranded, then brought home by "Horrid Man". Arina and Dima sat there as I talked with the officers, smirking and laughing. Then Arina rudely said, "Nothing happen to us. We smart. "Horrid Man" is nice man. We go with him many times to Detroit from library." I turned to the police and said, "After Homeland Security warned us about "Horrid Man", I instructed them to never, ever go with him anywhere again. Obviously, that instruction has made no impression on them." The police then tried to talk some sense to them. They told Arina and Dima what they knew about "Horrid Man". They laughed out loud at the police. Nasty laughter. They said the officers, "We leave again when you leave. No make us stay." They had absolutely no fear of authority.

None of us, the police included, had any power and Arina and Dima knew it. The police attempted to take the cell phone but said unless Dima turned it over they couldn't physically take it and neither could we. I told Arina to go to bed and she laughed at me in front of them and sat there, not moving. The police were dumbfounded at their behavior. She and Dima sat there and laughed and talked in loud Russian the entire 45 minutes the officers were in my kitchen. Arina and Dima had complete control and we all knew it. We had become prisoners in our own home and servants to these teens. How in the world did this happen to us?

I want scream this!

If you are someone considering adoption. Please hear me. This is **NOT** an isolated case. This is more common than anyone in this adoption business would like you to know. Imagine your home as it is now. Now imagine a person, or persons, coming into your home and you are forced to have them live with you. While they live with you they can come and go as they please at all hours of the day and night. You cannot make them leave. You cannot make them stay. You are forced to provide them with a room to sleep in, food to eat at least three times a day, amenities like showers and toiletries. You cannot force them to go to school, and yet if they don't go to school you can be in trouble with authorities. They can make all kinds of threats against you and your family, but unless they actually are violent there is nothing police can do. Even if they do something violent you will still be forced to allow them back into your home because you are responsible for them and their safety. They can scream at you. They can destroy your things. They can threaten to kill you and your family. They can make your life a living hell **and there is...**

...NOT ONE THING YOU CAN DO ABOUT IT.

Think about that before you adopt and bring a new family member home. This is not a dog that you can take back to the pound if he becomes aggressive and bites your child. Once on American soil, you are stuck. No way out. None. Zero. Zilch. Until the day they turn 18 they are your responsibility. Be warned. I'm not kidding here. I'm dead serious.

The police left and within five minutes the two were gone again. They were laughing at me as they walked out the door. Arina turned and waved to me with a fake grin on her face. I gave it fifteen minutes and called the police again. I hated bothering them but they kept telling me I had no choice. I had to file, at least on Arina. Dima would be 18 in June and we were counting down the days.

The police called in the morning and reported both teens showed up at school, and that they had reported us for abuse. The school called CPS and the police. Both the police and the school knew the teens were lying but they were bound by law to contact CPS. We were told to stay at home and wait for the CPS officer to interview all six of the teens who were at school.

This is where the trauma escalated to an entirely new level for Garrett and Katherine. Forced to sit with this CPS officer at the high school and answer questions about Tom and me, from the standpoint that we were already guilty, broke them both. The officer assumed we abused them all, drank excessively, took drugs, and more. He didn't care about the history of the past year. Garrett and Katherine came home from school that day sobbing.

When CPS interviewed Tom and me at home, it was an intense interrogation. I wondered if it was going to end in either Tom or me going to jail. There was no doubt we were guilty to them and they were out to prove it. There was no "innocent until proven guilty" with CPS.

I told the CPS officer, "During the time the teens said we were abusing them they were both absent from the home and I have a police report to back it up. When the teens were brought back home last night by the police neither teen mentioned the abuse to the police even though the police were in our home for more than 45 minutes. During those 45 minutes both teens were sitting at my kitchen table in front of the police laughing and talking loudly in Russian while the police were trying to get them to behave for us. Within two minutes of the police leaving, both teens left out the front door yelling obscenities at me. I immediately called the police and filed another report. There was zero time for any of their claimed abuse to have happened."

CPS officer: "After speaking with your other teenagers they have corroborated your story, but we have to continue the investigation and we will let you know what we decide."

Me: "WHAT? Are you kidding me? How much more are you going to put our family through?"

CPS officer: "We will let you know." And he left.

WHAT??? You can't be serious!! But, oh yes you can when it comes to CPS. Like our Ukrainian teens, CPS had all of the power and they knew it. There was not a dang thing we could do about it. Can you say stressful? On all of us. Except for the two who had instigated the mess. Another nice VK education for them. Turn the parents into the authorities for abuse. Four days later we were told we were cleared.

I asked if anything was going to happen to Arina and Dima for filing a false report. Nope. They are free to do it again. And they did, over and over again. For months their behavior was reinforced by the lack of legal consequences. And even though Arina and Dima had a record with CPS, each time CPS treated the accusations as if the past had never happened. We were all rubbed raw time and time again. Who needed proof when accusations would suffice?

I wouldn't be alone with either of them again and neither would Tom. If we were home alone, or even the two of us together and one of them came home, we sent them to the library until another teen came home who could be a witness. This practice would save us on several future occasions when we could prove them liars with paper trails and witnesses.

I prayed my heart out to Yahweh to protect my family from this evil that had invaded our home. I saw evil in the eyes of these two that night when the police brought them home. Dima would act so meek and mild until he was caught red-handed, involved in some infraction. Then the mask would come off and he was unnervingly scary to be around. I tried to figure out who was the leader of the two. Sometimes I thought it was Arina, the other times, Dima. I wasn't sure who the dominant one was. All I knew was my peaceful home had become a battleground and my beautiful family was losing the battle.

The "should-have's" kept running through my mind. We should have done more research on them. We should not have made such a quick decision. We should have taken a moment to think instead of relying strictly on emotion or driven by fear. However, my hope was in Yahweh to bring us through this trial. I prayed for protection and wisdom.

Viktor and Sasha were so angry at Arina and Dima for putting the family through those grilling interviews, so they told them the news we had been cleared as soon as they found out. When Arina and Dima found out we had been cleared and everyone, including their teacher, knew they lied about us, they ran again.

We filed another report. We were to the point where we were hopeful they would not be found too quickly. It was much more peaceful without them around and we all relaxed a bit. A week passed, then another. Every time the doorbell rang or someone knocked a little too loudly, I jumped out of my skin. I tried to care about Arina and Dima, but I was too worn out and the intimidating CPS investigation was still fresh in my mind. I lived in a war zone, in my own home.

Family X. If only we had known...

- I never imagined I'd be counting down the days to them turning 18 years old so I'd never have to see them again.

- When we adopted I never thought I would need a safe for money and credit cards so my adopted child wouldn't steal them and rack up thousands of charges.
- When we adopted, I never thought we would put up security cameras in our home. More to the point, I never thought we would put up security cameras in our home to record US to protect us from lies our daughter might tell about us.
- When we adopted I always thought PTSD was for soldiers. I guess in a way I am a soldier, too, just in a different kind of war.
- I wish I had known **our 6-year-old adopted son was going to burn down our home** with our two dogs and our beloved 15-year-old cat inside. Afterwards he actually told police we were lucky because he meant to do it when we were all home and asleep. He is now in an RTF (residential treatment facility).
- I didn't realize all of the promises of after adoption support were lies and that suddenly I would be the suspect in a CPS investigation because our adoptive social worker, who was supposed to be support for us, called them on us.
- I didn't know that by trying to reunite siblings and adopting the 11-year-old brother of our adopted four and five year olds, that he would rape them for over a year before we found out.
- I used to be known for my contagious smile and uplifting personality. Now I struggle to make it through a day without crying or screaming at some point and my bio kids look at me all the time and ask, "Mom, are you ok?".
- I used to read newspaper stories of situations like ours and judge so harshly. I wondered how a mom could not know her children were being abused right under her nose. Now I know.
- I never knew people who didn't know me before RAD child came into our home would think this is how I really am. And I don't care anymore about what anyone thinks of me. They don't live my hell.

Chapter 14

Human Trafficking Too Close for Comfort

First week of May 2015. This is when some really crazy stuff started happening. The bizarre ramped up to a whole new level of insanity. The behaviors became worse. Much worse. The day after Dima and Arina ran away I got a call from "Horrid Man". I was terrified because of what the Homeland Security officers had told me about him.

"Horrid Man" asked how Arina and Dima were doing. Between the police and Tom and I we thought it very likely Arina and Dima were with him again but there was no proof. I told him they had run away again. He was overly friendly saying, "I'm so sorry. Is there anything I can do? Do you have any idea where they went? I've told those two how nice you are to them and they should be grateful to you for adopting them."

Okay, then. My head was spinning. I thought, "Why in the world are you still having conversations with Arina and Dima when you know they were told to have no contact with you?" I was dumbfounded he thought he had the right to talk to me about them. I told him I had to go and hung up. The next day he called again to ask if I had any idea where they went. No. The next day he called again and told me Dima had reached out to him on VK and he was doing fine. Dima was at a friend's house somewhere in our town and was looking for a job. "Horrid man" said Dima asked him if he knew of any work. Dima, he said, didn't want to go back to school. He wanted help finding a job. These conversations continued daily for two weeks. Unbeknownst to him, every time "Horrid Man" called, I gave the information to the police detective who was working our case. Everyone was suspicious and the detective told us to be on our guard. "Horrid Man" kept calling - every day. After several more days, the detective advised me to stop answering and let the calls go to voice mail.

Three weeks later.

Dima had a new social media account. He sent some of the people on my Facebook® friend list friend requests. His profile said he was now living in Florida with a very nice family. He had found them at church, and he liked them very much. He said in his bio he would be 18 in a few months and his new mom would help him get an American passport and he was going to fly to Ukraine for a visit. He had a new job and he earned $60 a day. It was dusty work, but good. He stated he was going to school but needed money to buy food. Clicking on the map on the account showed him just east of Tampa. I found it interesting he was living with a very nice family but needed money to buy food. It all sounded a bit confusing.

My first reaction, if we assumed the information was true, was anger. So, he got a nice family like he wanted. REALLY???? At our expense! After months of lying and stealing and running away and being completely horrible to us all. After we spent thousands and thousands of dollars, eleven weeks in Ukraine, away from our family, to do what they both said they wanted and now this!!!!!

Then, we quickly settled down and thought things through. First, how did this happen so quickly and how in the world did he get a job or get enrolled into school without any legal documents? I had all of those. Social Security card, birth certificate, citizenship. He had nothing. The only thing he had was his school ID. I called our Homeland Security liaison. He called me back to say most likely it was "Horrid Man" posing as Dima to lure our friends to "friend" Dima so he could find more people to solicit and/or keep an eye on what we posted, or both. He told us to reach out to everyone on this new page friends list and privately tell them to unfriend the account ASAP. Tom spent the next three hours contacting our friends who had accepted Dima's friend request. We were to keep an eye out for new pages for either Arina or Dima and do the same thing. That became Tom's new job.

Soon after, a private message from Arina popped up saying she was in another state but wouldn't say where. She said, "I am very happy to be away from you. You are terrible mother. I hate you very much. I never love you. I wish your family dead. You are all dead to me. I never want you for my mother. I never want your family. I hate you. You are bad mama".

That was one of the worst experiences through all of this. The hateful words constantly spewed at us. Seriously, it broke our hearts every time. I constantly thought of the sacrifice my family made for them, because they asked, and this was the treatment we got in return. It was hard to live with. I sat down to pay bills and saw the almost $80K we still owed (after already paying close to $40K) and wanted to throw up. Honestly, I'd gotten to the point where I just couldn't care anymore. I told another adoptive mom we continually throw pearls before swine and we need to stop.

> *Matthew 7:6 "Do not give dogs what is holy, and do not throw your pearls before swine, lest they trample them underfoot and turn to attack you."*

We kept trying, time and time again, to convince Viktor, Arina and Dima that they could have a wonderful future if they would just let themselves. We beat our heads against a brick wall over and over and came away bloody, then did it all over again.

I wanted this to mean something. I needed this to have happened for a good reason. I begged Yahweh to show me why He allowed us to adopt, because we truly thought it was all from Him.

The next night was beautiful with mild temperatures, so Tom and I sat on the front porch enjoying some well-deserved peace. Tom had messaged all our social media friends who had friended Dima and Arina. He told them to block the two because someone was using Dima and Arina's account to stalk us and glean information. I received a call from a friend who also had an adopted teen. They lived near us. My friend called because as she was blocking the accounts she hit the wrong button and called the number which was listed for Arina. I didn't know you could do such a thing!

She hung up quickly when Arina answered, but Arina called right back. Fortunately, my friend was sitting at her computer with her adopted son and the boy was smart on his feet, answered the call, and told Arina he had taken his mom's phone, run away, and was in Detroit. He told Arina he was scared and didn't know what to do. Arina told him she would call him back, which she did a few minutes later. She asked for a picture to show where he was in Detroit. (It was obvious someone was coaching her, and they didn't know whether to believe this boy or not.) The amazing thing was the family had just been to Tiger Stadium the day prior and they had taken a picture of the boy standing in front of the stadium. They sent the picture, and Arina gave him the address where they were staying and told him to come to them and he would be taken care of by the same man who was taking care of her and Dima.

I called the police to let them know and a few hours later the police in "Horrid Man's" city rounded up Arina and Dima. Interestingly, while we were on the porch waiting to hear back from the police, I got a text from "Horrid Man" again, fishing for information. He was all chatty in the text asking how we were holding up and if we had heard anything new. I told him via text, "We are doing just fine. We are at the movies. Thanks for asking." He asked me to text him when we got out of the movies.

Here is where it gets even stranger. When they were found, both teens gave different names to the police. They told the police they had just flown in from Ukraine and were only staying there for a short time. They were found in some type of boarding house. The man at the boarding house told the officers a man (the one we suspected – "Horrid Man") had told him that the teens had just come from Ukraine and needed a place to stay for a couple of weeks. "Horrid Man" had paid for their rooms in advance. The police now knew who he was for sure and we were told by that police department that "Horrid Man" had a very bad reputation in their city. They had been after him for a long time and had a long list of complaints against him. The police were looking for "Horrid Man" now, but so far, no luck. He had gone into hiding.

Arina was taken to a juvenile detention center to be held overnight so she couldn't run again. Dima was turned over to our local police and then brought back home since he was 17, almost 18. I had an appointment in court the next day at 11:00 a.m., where Arina would be arraigned on the charge of incorrigibility. What a horrible time this was. I wanted off this ride! Then I thought maybe we would be able to take a really bad guy off the street through all of this. Maybe that was all part of the good that would come of this. I was hopeful this was part of making a difference.

The next day – well…middle of that night.

"I'm going to get through this day. I will." I told myself at 2:30 a.m. when the police brought Dima home in handcuffs. He was wearing brand new clothes and dress shoes. He was utterly defiant. He would not speak to the officers or me except to say he would leave again as soon as they left. The officers said to call them if/when he left. They couldn't do much because of his age, but at least it would be on record that he was not in the home in case he decided to report us for abuse again. The police definitely had Dima's number and were looking to protect us as much as they could.

Dima sat on the hard tile floor in the foyer and refused to move. I told him to go to bed and we would talk in the morning. Nothing. At 3:00 a.m., exhausted, I finally went to bed. At 3:30 a.m. there was pounding and ringing the doorbell. Officers back with Dima. They had been watching for him to leave. Up for another 30 minutes and back to bed again. I was emotionally and physically drained. I was woken up early the next morning to a text message from "Horrid Man" asking me if Tom and I were still at the movies. Really? After dragging myself out of bed I found that Dima was gone again. We filed another report.

How can a person function on so little sleep? I felt like I was in a constant fog. I couldn't see clearly. I couldn't think clearly. Once while driving, I nearly ran a red light with a semi coming from the left at 45 MPH. I don't know what caused me to brake. I'm pretty sure it was an angel. I would have died, no doubt. Heaven sounded pretty good right then. Peaceful. Who was I that I thought those thoughts? I shook my head trying to clear my brain.

Adoptive Family PTSD/Trauma

I had no idea this was something people could have outside of being in war. I had no idea my family and I would develop PTSD. I was sitting on a chair reading and someone pounded just a little too hard on the front door and rang the doorbell at the same time. I almost fell off the chair. I was instantly transported back to the time we went through with these adopted teens when the police, or the FBI, or Homeland Security, or the local sheriff's department or the State Police pounded on my door night after night, day after day. Now, it's January 2018 and I haven't had the police pound on my door in over a year, but you couldn't tell my brain and body that. They still react as if it were yesterday. My heart was pounding and my stress level instantly went through the roof. I was shaking. I started to cry. My mind said, it's not the police, but every cell in my body was ready for trouble. I was shaking when I opened the door to a window salesman. I could barely say "no thank you" to him. I closed the door and closed my eyes, talking to Yahweh, asking for His help once again. Will I ever be healed of this trauma? Will my family?

As our story continued our bio teens and I all suffered from PTSD. We all developed adrenal fatigue. This is very common for adoptive families and more needs to be done to help. Actually, darn it, more needs to be done to prevent this from happening in the first place.

STOP this madness from happening to families

Family X...

- I wish part of the adoption process included U.S. Department of State being required to inform adopting families they could go bankrupt or be forced to spend a fortune on post adoption 'unforeseen' expenses. Adoptive families should have to sign and notarize a document prior to adoption, agreeing it is understood

adoption could cost us our homes, retirements, savings and even tables, couches and heirlooms.
- We never, ever anticipated the post adoption costs (destroyed personal property, attorney fees, missed work, court costs, etc.). We expected to pay for food, clothes, and some therapy, but who knew we would pay $25,000 for just one attorney after he was arrested or $7,500 to just one mental health doctor in an attempt to get him help or, on and on and on. I have a friend who adopted who had to sell furniture just to buy groceries. They now live in a small rental house because they had to sell their home to pay for unknown mental health costs. When adopting they were told their son was perfectly healthy.
- Living the brokenness right now! And "well-meaning" people just make our situation exponentially harder.
- Before we adopted I didn't know that one day I would be enjoying a nice, hot shower after a long day and suddenly feel eyes on me and hear rustling outside the window. Staring back at me through a crack in the blinds was my 15-year-old adopted son. My bathroom is on the second floor with a steep metal roof. He later told us he wanted to go outside and look at the stars.

I drove the hour to the court appointment concerning Arina. We were hoping they would keep her at the facility so, at the very least, she would be kept away from "Horrid Man", off any electronics, and possibly get some counseling to work through her anger and attachment disorders. I still believed if she would get help she would be the Arina we saw in Ukraine. I know, I know.

In the meantime, Homeland Security and the State Police were hot on the trail of "Horrid Man". They believed he was part of a widespread trafficking ring. Since he had been caught red-handed harboring a run-away minor, they now had probable cause to investigate deeper.

They suspected Dima had called "Horrid Man" earlier that morning and Dima was likely back with him. Hence the text this morning. "Horrid Man" wanted me to communicate with him for information. Nope.

On Monday we would have to file a petition with the court so when they found Dima again they could arrest him and keep him detained. They said it was more for our protection since he was still under 18 and if anything should happen, we could be responsible. As long as we kept filing reports with law enforcement, we were protected from liability. Everything was documented.

This was a day filled with police, court and a lot of drama. Too much drama for me who hates drama. I felt like I was in the middle of a tornado and crazy things were flying around my head and all I could do was duck and hope nothing hit me. I was now working directly with two detectives who had gone through an intense human trafficking training. They told me Michigan was ranked 2 in the nation. They had contacted both the State Police and Homeland Security with updates about our situation. The police told me "Horrid Man" had been under scrutiny for quite some time. This guy was very bad news according to them.

I showed up at Arina's hearing just before 11:00 a.m. The judge and juvenile officer seemed to be very concerned with keeping her safe, so that was good. They believed she was being taken advantage of by a really bad situation and person. I thought so, too, at the time. (As time passed, however, I realized that this was exactly what she wanted.) At the hearing, the referee granted our request to keep her safely in custody while the police did what they could about "Horrid Man". Arina actually gave me a hug and said she didn't want me to leave. I wanted to believe her so badly. She asked if Dad could come back with me the next day so she could see him. It was a scam, but we longed so much to believe her. Soon we realized it was just like the orphanage. She wanted out of the facility at all costs and was willing to put on whatever show she had to in order for that to happen.

The police recommended we file a PPO (personal protection order) against "Horrid Man". (I did the next day.) I finally got home just before 5:00 p.m. and laid down for a nap. I had no more fallen asleep then the doorbell rang and there was pounding on the door. Now what?

It was Dima, standing there with a police officer.

(Can I just say again how much I love our Novi police department? Really. I know police in many of these cases get a really bad rap, but our local police were amazing.) Officer W. stood in our foyer and talked to Dima for a long time. He tried to convince Dima that we were his best option. To realize we are a great family, and how much we'd done for all of them. All because we want them to have a good future. This particular officer had known us for a few years and he is a real class act.

After the officer left I talked with Dima about "Horrid Man".

Me: "Dima, why did you go with the man?"

Dima: "He buys me things. Whatever I want."

Me: "What about us? We brought you here to America and we have bought you a lot of things. We bought you many new clothes and even a new bike."

Dima: "That was before. You no buy me things now and you no let me have a phone." That was the crux of it – the phone. It's always about the stupid phone!

THIS is what these people do to prey on these teens and children. In a way I get it. They didn't have the upbringing like our bio teens. Don't go with someone who offers you candy or shows you a little puppy. No stranger danger training. But this teen is almost eighteen, not four.

I offered to make him food and he refused. He walked upstairs to his room and laid down on his bed fully clothed. I went to bed to lay down for a few minutes. I was exhausted. I woke up at 12:30 a.m. with a start that I had slept so long and checked on him. He was still there. That was something. He didn't run this time.

The next day I told the detective "Horrid Man" was still texting me, asking what was going on. I hadn't responded to him. The detective told me to text "Horrid Man" and to tell him to stop texting me and to stop contacting my teens. I was to tell him he was not allowed near me, my family or my home. And if either Arina or Dima contacted him, he was not to respond. Zero contact. Well, wouldn't you know it? All the playing nice from him was gone in an instant. The pure hatred that spewed from him was actually a little funny to me. He had the audacity to tell me he understood why I was mad. It was because my kids didn't want to live with me and I couldn't cope with that truth.

He knew nothing. I wasn't angry. I was just done with all the deceit and triangulation. There could not be any healing done for Arina and Dima as long as he, and others like him, kept injecting themselves into our lives. We all knew "Horrid Man" had ulterior motives for Arina and Dima to be with him and I was through with his lies. And I was done with my family being put through hell for two teens who were bent on destroying my family in whatever ways they could.

This was the same person who had been texting me for the past three weeks, all supportive, telling us he was looking for them for us. And he had them all along. I passed along all the texts to the police and Homeland Security.

Family X...

- When we adopted I didn't know my bio kids who had given up so much to get our adopted daughter home would constantly be ignored by relatives while the same relatives fawned over our adopted daughter. And the more problems our adopted daughter caused, the more the relatives stepped in and "tried" to help her, which made it all so much worse on my bio kids. And what's even worse is the ones who sacrificed so much and are still sacrificing every damn day are invisible.
- I never realized how many people lie to get what they want. The lies told to us in Ukraine, by adults who should have known better, have ruined our beautiful family.
- **That a cute 6-year-old could be a psychopath fixated on blood, fire, porn and killing.** I actually tried to tell a "friend" the other day and she shut me right down and told me that she couldn't believe I would lie about him like that. She even hinted that maybe she should call the authorities on me if that's what I really thought about him. Seriously? Woman you've known me for more than 30 years!!!!
- Before adoption I didn't know being hated could hurt so badly. My heart is broken.

CHAPTER 15

Triangulation Insanity

One of our detectives went to the library to alert the faculty about Dima and Arina and to tell them they were not allowed in the library anymore. They were not allowed to have internet access there. I thought to myself it would be difficult to enforce with all the employees and volunteers there. They couldn't possibly keep a constant watch out for these two.

Arina had been released from the center to come home. It was costing us $175 a day to keep her there and she wasn't getting the help she needed. We had Arina and Dima watch another movie on human trafficking and it was so clear this was what they had experienced. They both agreed they would not run away again and they would not reach out to strangers from the internet like they had done. They both stayed close to home, playing board games mostly. I thought maybe we'd gotten through the worst of it and they had learned their lesson. I thanked Yahweh nothing terrible happened to them. They both acted as if nothing had happened at all. We had all met up at the courthouse the day after the court hearing and filed the PPO's against "Horrid Man" and had him served. I was still hopeful we could turn this around.

Stupid People Triangulating.

I have a HUGE pet peeve and that is people who have no clue what we've been through, and who know nothing about attachment trauma

(RAD) in children/teens, who inserted themselves into our situation as an expert. They ALWAYS made a bad situation much worse, then disappear to their own lives thinking they've done a good thing, but not realizing they've left us to deal with the dreadful after effects of their meddling.

On the day we went to court to sort all of this out and decide what was going to happen to Dima and Arina the court appointed them a translator. (Which I had to pay *way too much money* for). Let me just say this. A translator is someone who translates. Period. They don't insert their own opinion. They take a word in Russian and translate that word to English and visa-versa. That's it. End of story.

We experienced a perfect example of triangulation with this translator.

This woman. ACK! I still want to scream just writing about this. She was originally from Moscow but had lived in America for over 20 years. This woman could not stop herself from continually interjecting her own opinion. And let me say she had ZERO experience with teen adoptees or RAD. She had the audacity to lecture me, *in front of them*, for deciding to home school them moving forward from that day. For not allowing them to have phones. For keeping them from the library. For not allowing them on the internet so they could talk to people in Russian. ARE YOU KIDDING ME?? I had FOUR Russian linguists in my home. THAT'S **ALL** THEY DID! It is why, after eight months in America, they had such poor English skills. They refused to speak English. Even Viktor had lost a good portion of his English skills and reverted back to Russian.

This is just a tiny portion of our more than three-and-a-half-hour conversation.

Stupid Woman: "You need to let them drink cow's milk."

Me: "No, I don't."

SW: "Yes, you do. And you should not tell them what they can and cannot eat. It's not right. You don't know how they lived in Ukraine. I am Russian. I know. Candy is good for them. You need to talk to a doctor so he can tell you that you are being a bad mother for how you feed them."

Me: (Keeping my cool). "No, I don't."

Remember she was also talking in Russian with Arina and Dima and they were feeding her information on what I did and didn't do with them at home. And she was telling them how wrong I was.

SW: "What is wrong with you? I am Russian. I know what they should be eating. And there is nothing wrong with them having sugar. It is good for them. And why don't you let them have a phone. All teenagers should have phones."

Me: "No, they shouldn't have a phone."

SW: "Yes, they should and you are being a bad mother to them for how you treat them. And why are you home schooling them? They should be going to school to make friends."

Me: "No, they shouldn't. They only get into trouble in school."

SW: "That's because you are being such a bad mother. It is making them bad in school."

Me: "No, it's because they are choosing to do the wrong things there."

SW: "You need to be a better mother. You need counseling."

The only reason I didn't slap this woman was I was surrounded by court employees. I was livid! She blathered on and on about how I was *just* a mom and I didn't know anything about food or nutrition and if I wanted to learn I should take them to a doctor and let him educate me. For those of you who know me you will be completely impressed with how well I controlled myself. (For those who don't know me I've studied nutrition for more than 20 years.)

She continued there was nothing wrong with pop and candy and I was being a horrible mother for not allowing them to eat sugary treats. Can you imagine my brain wanting to explode? The fact is sugar is a drug to these adopted teens. It literally made their bad behavior much, much worse. I'd watch it happen right in front of me. I could tell when they had eaten candy. Sugar only escalated their outbursts.

She went on and on about giving them freedom to do whatever they wanted and how I was being a bad mother for keeping them from those things. My head was pounding from the stress of it all.

Later, I wrote a letter to the court about this woman and told them what she did was inappropriate, and she should never be hired as a translator again. That ridiculous conversation with her went on for an excruciating three and a half hours, and I had to foot the bill for the "translation services". She kept talking to my teens in Russian, so I had no idea what was really said. I was sure it was more ammunition for Arina and Dima to misbehave. Her actions set them up to be even more defiant with us. Later, driving home, I was quite amazed with my level of patience and thanked Yahweh for His help. If it had been just me, there was no way I would have shown that level of restraint. I appreciated His work in me very much. Thanks for the "Fruit of the Spirit" that day!

This woman did more harm than she will ever know or would acknowledge if she did know. Her contribution set Arina and Dima up for more dangerous behavior and our family for more suffering.

Two weeks later. The local police had now given everything they had on our case to the Michigan task force on human trafficking. (Crazy there needs to be an organization to fight against that. Horrible.) The Novi police were working with the police in "Horrid Man's" city to arrest him for harboring and whatever other crimes he committed. The PPO's were served. I had all those text messages and "Horrid Man" lied to the detective as well. All four Ukrainian teens had been quite docile for a few days since Arina was released from the facility. We had all four of the Ukrainians watch three different movies on human trafficking. Arina and Dima were reminded they were banned from both the library and high school.

Dima started work at a local restaurant as a dishwasher making $9 an hour. They told him as he learns the job and more English they would train him as a prep cook, then a line cook. The manager who hired him started as a dishwasher and was then the kitchen manager earning over $60K a year. He told Dima he could do the same. They started him working 30 hours a week, which came to about $270 a week.

The average MONTHLY income where Dima lived in Ukraine was $188 as of 2016. Yup! Dima was an American citizen, with no high school diploma, working as a part-time dishwasher, and was making more in one week than the average Ukrainian from his region made in a month. Within two days of starting the job he was complaining about how hard it was.

Arina started at a local store as a bagger/utility worker and was told as she learned more English they would promote her and start teaching her different positions around the store. She was told there were managers that started as baggers who now ran the store and she could do the same if she worked hard and learned English. She was introduced to a woman who ran one of the departments. She was originally from Russia and she had worked there 20 years. She spoke fluent Russian, achieving what Arina might someday. Arina also started at $9 an hour and they expected her to work 35 to 40 hours a week. This was a very positive thing for both of them. We were relieved and saw these as signs that life would be better going forward.

Things had settled down a bit at home. Arina and Dima had decent jobs with advancement opportunities. I didn't care about school for the two of them anymore. School was a constant battle and I was out of energy to fight. What they really needed was to learn English and they would get more exposure working their jobs than they would at home or school. School had become a place for them to scam things and money from people. Dima was now 18 years old and Arina would be 18 in about a year. They both needed to learn actual life skills so they could someday live productive lives on their own.

We thought, whew, we made it through. Everything would be just fine from this point forward.

CHAPTER 16

Return of "Horrid Man"

I received an unexpected call from a man who claimed to be a member of the Ukrainian church where "Horrid Man" attended. This man told me he hated "Horrid Man" for things he had done in their community and church. He also told me he was an attorney and wanted to represent me for free at a hearing scheduled for June 23rd. Hmmm....what hearing??? He said, ""Horrid Man" is contesting the PPO's you served on him." I replied, "I've gotten nothing from the court about appearing and until I do, I won't be going to court."

Right after his call I received a call from a different Homeland Security officer. The officer was very nice and told me the PPO's with "Horrid Man's" name had come across his desk and flagged an alert. "Horrid Man" was a person of high interest to their division. Down deep I had hoped this man really was nothing to be concerned with, but as more of these calls came confirming it, I was convinced "Horrid Man" was involved in trafficking, which meant we were involved.

Two weeks earlier, I had come home from a walk to find an old woman standing in my driveway. Picture in your mind an 80-year old Russian grandmother, bent over from years working in her garden, wearing traditional dress. Yup, standing in my driveway on a Sunday afternoon. No car to be seen. I walked up to her and she started telling me, in very broken English, how bad "Horrid Man" was and how he had stolen money and property from many people in their city and how she knew he had taken our teens and wanted to do bad things to them. She gave me her phone number and told me what kind of cars "Horrid Man" drove and the different phone numbers he used. She was very animated and genuinely seemed afraid for all of us. She kept telling me he was a very bad man and we needed to be careful. I related all of this at the time to our police department and now again to this Homeland Security officer. He was concerned and told us to always go places together and never be home alone. Great! I also related to him the call from the attorney and he agreed with me that there would be no hearing without some type of notification to me from the court.

The next day, the Homeland Security officer came to our home to visually see the text messages. He talked to us at great length about the things that had happened. Everything the "attorney" on the phone and Russian grandma told me was true. "Horrid man" sounded worse and worse. Homeland Security officer said the words, "textbook human trafficking scenario". They were after this guy. Good. I didn't want my family to be in the middle of it all but here we were. How did this happen? All we did was want to make a difference for some orphans. Crazy! All I could think was how could we protect Garrett and Katherine through all this?

At 1:30 p.m. I received a call on my mobile phone. It was the judge from Oakland County. She was on a speaker phone. (I briefly wondered how she got my number.)

Judge: "Mrs. Ray?"

Me: "Yes."

Judge: "This is "Judge M" from Oakland County and we are here in the courtroom waiting for you. I have Mr. "Horrid Man" and your attorney here on speaker."

Me: "Judge, I was not informed about this and I don't have an attorney."

Judge: "You were attempted to be served on June 16th at 4:30 p.m. by "so and so" who stated you refused to accept the summons or give your I.D. to her."

Here started a 30-minute conversation, on speaker phone, with the judge, "Horrid Man", supposed attorney from the church who judge said was there to represent me. "Judge M" wanted to know where I was and why I wasn't in court.

I said to the judge, with "Horrid Man" listening on speaker, "Really Judge? So, I spent hours of my time filling out and filing papers in Oakland County, then drove downtown Detroit to the Sheriff's office and paid $85 plus parking to get those papers served and then I'm going to refuse to show up in court after this guy took my teens for three weeks, lied to both me and the police about having them, texted me throughout the three weeks acting all concerned for me and the teens and continually said he had no knowledge of where they were? And that in the past two weeks I have spent several hours with Homeland Security, the State Police and our local detectives talking about this incident and "Horrid Man". Judge, had I known I would have been there. Something very weird is going on here. And by the way, Judge, at the time "Horrid Man" claims I was served, I was actually in Chicago the entire day and didn't return home until very late that night. I was nowhere near my home."

"Judge M" was HOT! Someone was obviously lying and I could hear it in her voice she believed me. She asked if I could get to the court immediately. I told her I could be there in 90 minutes or less. She decided to re-schedule instead so "Horrid Man" could produce his process server. Court was adjourned until July 1st at 2 p.m.

"Judge M" asked "Horrid Man" three times to just drop his motion against the PPO's. She stated, "She is these kids' mom, she said to stay away from them, and you should honor her request." "Horrid Man" didn't answer her. Instead, he demanded the judge order me to bring Arina and Dima to court on the 1st. I interjected and said, "No way. That man is never going to see my kids ever again if I can help it."

"Horrid man" then stated "Those kids didn't actually sign the PPO. She signed their names. They would never have done this against me." I said, "Judge, you know the teens had to sign in front of a clerk to file the papers. I could not sign for them. In fact, an officer of the court had brought Arina from the facility where they were keeping her, to the courthouse, with a translator, so she could understand and sign, which they both did in front of the clerk."

Then "Horrid Man" declared, "Judge, if she drops the PPO's I will not sue her."

I answered, "Really!! You are threatening me in front of the Judge?"

He claimed he would sue me for defamation of character unless I dropped the PPO's. The PPO's were hurting his reputation! (And what a stellar reputation that was!) Horrid, horrid man. I could tell the judge was extremely irritated with "Horrid Man". She told him, "Going to jail is not pretty for someone like you, Mr. "Horrid Man".

After the conversation ended, I called our Homeland Security officer and he agreed something very shady was taking place. He said he would call the Novi police detectives to update them. They needed to be aware and to keep us safe. He said to be sure none of our teens and most especially Garrett and Katherine didn't go anywhere alone: that they stayed with an adult at all times. He told me this guy was very dangerous and now we were his target. He would try to hurt us where he could the most. I asked the Homeland Security officer why "Horrid Man" was still on the street and wasn't yet in custody for what he had done." "We are working on it." He replied.

I prayed Psalm 91. I trust! This snake will be stopped. My family is protected. This "Horrid Man" picked the wrong mama. This mama and her family was protected by the Creator of the Universe. HA!

Family X...

- When we adopted we didn't anticipate not being taken seriously by the medical community and not having the support we needed to manage his medical issues. We were blatantly lied to about him in the orphanage and he is so much worse than we were ever told. We were not even approved on our home study for the issues he has, and we were not prepared.

CHAPTER 17

More Missing Money

Tom and I had gone out for the evening to a business meeting. Garrett and Katherine were sitting in the front room doing homework when Dima walked in and started yelling at Katherine for something he thought she said to us about him. The point was unclear because he was mostly yelling in Russian. (I realized much later Dima thought Katherine told me about his attempt to rape her.) Garrett told us Dima approached Katherine and threatened to beat her until Garrett stepped in between them and told him in no uncertain terms that Dima would not lay one finger on his sister. Dima viciously kicked at Garrett, and Garrett grabbed Dima's leg, throwing him off balance, and Dima fell to the floor. Dima leapt up, screamed at them in Russian, and then screamed Arina's name. Arina came dashing down the stairs and together, they flew out the door. We returned home to find both of them gone. They showed up in time to go to work the next day, with no explanation where they had been all night.

Arina was working and I was clearing dirty dishes and trash from her room again when I found another phone. I felt like a detective, always on the search for contraband. I had no idea how long she'd had it or where it came from. I was angry. I had hoped we were past this stuff. Confiscating the device, I said nothing to her when she arrived home after work. She couldn't ask me about it, because according to the court order, she was not allowed to have a personal phone. I had confiscated more than a half dozen phones. I looked at the history on this one and just that morning she was on

VK. And on a porn site. Ugh. I could have gone my whole life without seeing that junk. I wasn't going to look in the closet this time. It was stuffed with piles of dirty clothes. Then something told me to look beneath the clothing. And there it was, rolled up in a sweatshirt. Well, actually I do know what made me look. Or should I say, who? Yahweh. I am so grateful for His guidance. It's priceless!

$200 was missing from my office. I had hidden it in two books on my bookshelf. How did they know where to look? We were up to over $1,000 missing. Tom was looking into buying security cameras. I hated having a thief, or thieves, in my home.

Then a call from the Novi police. Sasha had been caught by Walmart security, stealing. Another Whack-A-Mole moment. He stole $2 in fireworks, of all things. He kept repeating, "It was only $2". Walmart security had Sasha sitting in a back room waiting for the police when he took off when they turned their backs on him. He was in serious trouble for running. The police tracked him down and held him in the jail until Tom arrived. After Tom finished talking with the police, Sasha was released into our custody pending his court appointment for shoplifting. He walked into the house spitting mad, as if he was the injured party. He didn't think he did anything wrong and yelled, "It's not fair I have to go to court and pay a lot of money. It was only $2." We talked with him for over an hour to help him understand that the amount didn't matter. Stealing was stealing. I asked, "How would it make you feel if I took $2 out of your wallet just because I wanted it?" Sasha replied, "No, I wouldn't like that." Of course not but he was still mad about it. We told him he was grounded so he ran off. He was gone until 9:00 p.m. that night.

What was it with these Ukrainian teens when they did something wrong, then when they got caught, they got mad and ran off? We were always the bad people, the police are always the bad people. They were always the injured party. No remorse. No, "I'm sorry."

They were never wrong.

More money disappeared, this time from my purse. It could have been any one of the four Ukrainians, but this time I suspected Viktor because he was wearing new clothes. We had a deal where he turned over his paycheck to me so I could save it for him. If he kept his check, the entire thing would be spent within 24 hours. He had no sense of responsibility. If he wanted something, he bought it. I allotted him $30 out of his check for the two weeks, so he didn't have a lot of extra for all the new clothing he was wearing. We knew at some point we would catch whoever was stealing. We just needed to give it time. We were sure the proof would come.

I couldn't wait for the cameras to go up.

June 27, 2015 – One Year! It was the one-year anniversary of arriving at the orphanage to meet Arina and Dima. I felt at least ten years older. I saw a memory picture pop up on Facebook. It was Arina snuggling close to me in the garden outside of the orphanage. She had a contented smile on her face. I looked happy. I started bawling seeing the picture. Images from the past year raced through my mind. My world and that of my family had been turned upside down. I didn't recognize it, or me, anymore. How could so much have changed in just one year?

As July 1st, 2015 and the court date approached, I prayed Psalm 91 every day. I was ready to face this "Horrid Man". I visualized an army of Yahweh's angels around our home, our family and me as I got ready to go to court. I also found out grandbaby #7 was coming on the 1st in Nashville so the plan was to go to court and then head to Nashville immediately afterwards. I wasn't happy about the timing at all. On Monday the 29th I received a voicemail from "Judge M's" assistant to call her ASAP. I did and found out "Horrid Man" had dropped his motion to have the PPO's dismissed. Praise Yahweh. I laughed with her because we both knew he dropped it because he couldn't produce the process server. There was no process server. She agreed with me and said "Judge M" had said the same thing. So no court and I left to be there with my son and daughter-in-law when my new grand girl arrived! Yay! The bonus was Katherine accompanied me, giving me some private time with my girl, something we both needed very badly.

I was so thankful for the peace in my heart leading up to the court day. Instead of worry and anxiety, I was completely at peace and rested in Yahweh.

Katherine and I arrived home from Nashville five days later and BAM! No Arina. She supposedly rode her bike to work around 11:30 a.m. to check her schedule for the week. Tom assumed she stayed to work. It happened a lot, so he didn't think much of it. Two of the boys got called into work the day before when others didn't show up for shifts. By 8:30 p.m. we were concerned she'd not come home so we drove to her work. Her brand-new bike we had just bought for her was in the rack but unlocked. We found out she never worked that day, so we called the police to report her missing. On the way to us they picked her up at the gas station where she was hanging out with a 20-year-old man she had met in the parking lot a few days before while she was retrieving shopping carts.

The police learned this guy lived in the apartments across the street. Arina had agreed to hang out with him, in his apartment, and they had decided to walk to the gas station to buy snacks. He had a warrant out for his arrest from another city and had a criminal record. The police arrested him and took him away to be transported to the other city. That freaked Arina out and she started thrashing around in the police car. She refused to get out of the police car and into our van for over an hour. There were seven police cars from two different cities all trying to get a 16-year-old into our van so we could take her home. CRAZY!! Nothing we said moved her. All she kept saying was, "NO!" They got a translator on the phone but that made no any difference.

Tom started chuckling and one of the officers looked at him like he was crazy. Tom said, "You don't understand. We deal with this crazy stuff every single day. Sometimes you just have to laugh at how bizarre it is." The officer nodded his head and said, "Yeah, I get it. We deal with crazy stuff every day, too." I finally reached Sasha on my phone and he talked to her. We don't know what he said to her, but she hopped out of the police car and into the van. We thanked the police and headed home. Arina ate two bowls of borscht that I warmed up for her, with some bread. Then she went to bed without saying a word to us.

Later we found out she was irate because she had "given" this man favors, and he had gotten picked up by the police before he could give her the money he had promised to her. And of course, we were the bad guys, once again, because we had called the police.

Family X. I received an email from a mom. It started out asking, "What have I done to my family and how can I take it all back". They were a happy family of three. Happily married with a little girl, four years old. Friends of theirs had hosted a teen girl and boy, sister and brother, over the holidays. That family was not interested in adopting but after spending some time with them, Family X decided to pursue adoption of the two. They were told by the hosting agency that the girl was going to be kicked out of the orphanage onto the streets the next summer when she turned 16. And the brother the next summer after that. They were told the teens had no family and were true orphans. They were also told the girl was sure to be taken into prostitution and most likely she would be dead by age 20. The boy would not survive much past that age either, they were informed.

The parents were horrified and decided they were not going to let that happen to these precious teens. So, they adopted. The email I received was nine months after returning home with them. The dad was no longer in the home. He was living in an apartment with the adopted girl. The baby girl was in foster care after being abused physically by the girl (she was jealous of the baby) and sexually abused by the boy who, when the truth came out, had a history of abusing younger children while in the orphanage. The criminal behavior of these two teens were well known by orphanage staff, yet no one questioned allowing them to be adopted into a home with a toddler. It was also disclosed that the teens had family in Ukraine, waiting for them to age out, so they could come home. The adoptive mom is alone, the adopted boy in jail waiting for sentencing. The mom is devastated and can't see any hope for the future. She has lost her world. Her only hope is getting up every day to fight to get her baby girl back. This scenario is much, much too common for this current adoption business to continue. Changes must be made. Families protected.

Family X...

- When I adopted I didn't know my daughter would be a prostitute and meth addict by 13.
- When I adopted I didn't know breaking a worthless dish would bring me to my knees in tears. I didn't know that doing normal day to day chores would be completely overwhelming, and that crawling out of bed in the morning would bring instant anxiety.
- When I adopted I didn't know it is impossible to overcome trauma with love. I didn't know he would always stay an orphan in his mind.
- We didn't know that a four-year-old could constantly sabotage us becoming a family.
- When we adopted I didn't know she would <u>want</u> to be a prostitute.
- I didn't know the child we love so much would threaten my life and seek to destroy our family.
- That a little boy adopted at just 14 months could turn into a monster at 11 years and whose only goal would be to kill us all. The only thing that gives him pleasure is destroying something that belongs to one of us. Then he laughs it's a horrible laugh that I can't get out of my head. To others, he shows himself to be the sweetest, kindest boy.
- **When I adopted I didn't know I would hate myself for bringing this disaster into my family.**
- When we adopted we didn't realize the addition would take away so much from our family, and then break it into a million pieces.
- When I adopted I didn't know how devastating it could be living with someone who doesn't have the capacity to love.

CHAPTER 18

Another Gestapo (I mean CPS) Witch Hunt

July 2015 was just plain crazy in our home. Every day was a new drama. One day Viktor and Sasha decided to pick a fight in a park near us with some other boys over a stupid lanyard which belonged to me. They came home angry and told Tom what happened, and Tom told them to just let it go, it didn't matter, and we had plenty of lanyards around the house they could have. No, no! That wasn't going to cut it with them! Ugh! I wondered when or if these boys would ever listen to wisdom.

Somehow Viktor found a black BB gun and removed the orange cap, so it looked like a real gun and Sasha grabbed a baseball bat. Russian tempers are something to behold I'll tell you. There was no talking them off the ledge. They continually went full force and always ended up in heaps of trouble. Of course, the police were then involved. They showed up at our house looking for the Viktor and Sasha, who by now had disappeared. The officer asked if I owned a gun. Yes. I checked, and all were locked up tight and none were missing. I finally tracked down Viktor and Sasha, told them to get to the police station immediately, and to take the BB gun with them. After ten minutes of furious arguing from Viktor, I told him either they do what I said, or the police will find you and you'll go to jail. They finally conceded. After two days discussion with the city prosecutor, and the families of the other boys, all charges were dropped. They were banned from the park for thirty days. And of course, Tom and I were the bad guys with the boys – again. They were mad at us because we made them turn themselves into the police. They could not comprehend how much worse the outcome if they hadn't gone.

The next day Tom and I were in an all-day business meeting and hadn't been gone an hour before we got a call from Dima's work. They told me Dima had been at work, then asked to go home for a few minutes to get his MP3 so he could listen to music while he ran the dishwasher. They were fine with that, but he never returned, and they were concerned something happened to him. I told Tom about the conversation then said, "Dima doesn't own an MP3. He is not allowed electronics. What is going on now?" We were mystified.

We called Emma, our grown daughter, who drove over to our house to check on things. She called us, "All four Ukrainians are here, but no one will talk to me. I don't know what happened, but everything seems fine now. She had told Dima to go back to work right away and he had left."

We got home later in the evening. None of them would talk to us. The next day Tom was working in the front yard and our neighbor walked over. He informed Tom a police car had pulled up and an officer picked Arina up out of the police car (he called her "the girl, not Katherine") and dumped her on the grass. Then the officer took Arina's bike from his trunk and set it next to her. The officer yelled at "the girl", got into his car, and drove away. Tom came to where I was in the back yard to tell me and I called "our" detective to get the rest of the story.

The police had gotten a call from a concerned citizen who saw two teens sitting in the middle of a road arguing. When police arrived at the location, they found Arina sitting in the middle of the road, with Dima standing over her. They were screaming at each other. The police found out another phone had surfaced, and Arina and Dima were fighting over it. We concluded later she had taken it out of his backpack and then when he arrived at work he realized it was gone. (They even steal from each other!) He was furious and left work to confront her. When he got home, she saw him and took off on her bike with the phone and he followed her on his. Somehow, they ended up in the road about four miles from our home. They refused to stop arguing so the police bodily picked her up and put her in the police car. Dima told officers he would ride his bike home and took off on it, and that is where Emma found them.

When I asked Arina about having another phone she told me she was mad at Dima and threw it in the nearby lake. I didn't buy it. These two were so addicted to phones there was no way she would intentionally destroy one and she had no opportunity. More likely she had hidden it somewhere and was waiting for things to calm down before going back for it. I reminded her the judge said no more phones or she would go back to the teen center. She screamed at me to leave her alone, ran upstairs and into her room, then slammed her bedroom door so hard it put a crack in the wood. She came down ten minutes later and said, "I go to work now." I was hopeful she would actually show up for work and then home afterwards. My gut told me something wasn't right. She had a phone and that always led to trouble. My gut was confirmed when she didn't come home. Tom and I drove to her work and talked to a supervisor. She told us that Arina had left hours earlier, saying she was sick and needed to go home. Her bike was there, in the rack but not locked, but no Arina. We filed another police report.

Viktor was causing problems again. Since he turned 18 in April 2015 he acted as if our house rules no longer applied to him. "I'm a man", he would angrily tell us. We told him since he considered himself a man, and since he decided to drop out of school against our wishes, he would now have to pay rent, help out with extra daily chores, and be in by curfew at 10:00 unless he was working. The night before he showed up an hour past curfew with a smirk on his face. Tom told him it was his final chance. From then on the house would be locked at 10:00 and he would be sleeping on the porch or a friend's couch if he wasn't in the house by that time. We knew he was drinking and getting alcohol from someone. We hadn't kept any in the house for a long time, but we could smell it on him and his eyes told the real story.

The day prior he had ranted at me for 30 minutes about how I should care more about Arina. He told me we should be out looking for her and that she was my responsibility. I asked him, "Where am I supposed to look?

I filed a police report and have asked at her work." He didn't even like Arina. He was just mad at me for forcing him to grow up so throwing barbs was a way to take the focus off himself. That night he was in before curfew but became more and more argumentative every day. I realized he was deliberately doing things he knew I disliked, watching my reactions. I learned, very quickly, to stay peaceful, then calmly turn to him and call him out, saying "Viktor, I know you are a good person and you can be better than this." He would mutter something under his breath in Russian and walk away. He learned his tactic didn't work and stopped. One day I looked at him and knew something was different. Then I realized he had no braces. I asked, "Viktor, what happened to your braces?" He rudely replied, "I take off. I no want braces. I done." He had removed them with pliers. I walked away furious. Another $6,000 wasted.

A full week had passed since Arina disappeared and the police had no leads. As far as I could tell she was still going to her job. Money was being deposited into her work account, which I had access to, but she didn't. She continued to work for no money. I drove to her job several times to inquire about her and each time she had gone "home" sick. Her supervisor finally told me she would have no choice but to let her go if things didn't improve soon. I told the supervisor Arina had run away with someone she either met there at work or online and there was a police report filed. They were shocked. I wasn't shocked anymore. Really. The shock had worn off a long time before. I was just numb, and tired. I asked the supervisor to call the police the next time Arina came to work. Arina never showed up again. She dumped her job. The job that took me two weeks to secure for her. One with a real future.

So much work and potential down the drain – again.

By the end of July 2015, Arina was still MIA. One minute I was angry, the next I wanted to cry. I felt so stupid. My mind wandered through the past year since we picked them up from their orphanage. It was hard to believe it had only been one year. My family was broken. We had already dealt with so much trauma and deceit. Arina and Dima expertly lied about

Tom and me to other people, telling those people how badly we were treating them. How many times had they thrown away perfectly good food I prepared and then lied about us not feeding them? We had been so manipulated. Their teachers, and counselors had been manipulated. Their employers, too. How many times had we driven for hours in the middle of the night looking for them, worried for their safety?

Just days before she took off, I took both Arina and Dima to the movies to see Minions because she was obsessed with them. The very next day she trashed her room badly – again - and it would take time and money we didn't have to repair. How many times had she stormed out the door screaming not to bother calling the police because she was never coming home again because we asked for a phone that, according to the judge, she was not allowed to possess? A phone that came from who-knows-whom. And now the next thing.

BAM!

CPS called me saying they had opened another investigation on us. YUP! What was the charge this time? Tom was always drunk, and I was physically abusive to Arina and Dima. We realized it had been instigated by Arina, who we found out, had accused us of kicking her out of the house and leaving her no place to go. (There are no words to tell you how hurtful this all was. And we still had no idea where she was.)

It was the day of our CPS interview and we were all home waiting. Officer J. came to the door and he was gunning for bear. We could tell from the tone in his voice and body language he had already decided Tom and I were guilty and he was there to prove it. It was incredibly intimidating. I was shaking. He didn't shake our hands or even introduce himself properly. Tom told him, "You can ask anyone here anything you want. It doesn't matter. They are going to tell the truth." J. told us he would talk to the teens first, then me, then Tom. Each person was interviewed privately. After he was gone we all sat down and compared interviews. The teens were all asked questions like the following:

How many times a week does your dad drink?
How many times a week is your dad drunk?

How many times has your dad hit you?
How many times has your mom hit you?
How many times has your dad touched you inappropriately?

Notice these questions were not "does your dad drink", or "does your mom hit you", but "how many times". It was assumed Tom and I did those things. J. was only looking for how often we did it. There was no room in J's mind to consider it had never happened at all. All our teens were extremely angry and upset. They felt backed into a corner where someone was falsely accusing their parents of horrible acts. This was a witch hunt. How dare he do this to our children?

Because, J. is with CPS and he could do whatever he wanted.

My turn. In my mind I told myself to stand strong. Easier said than done. I knew this man was looking for any little thing he could find to lay guilt on me. He went through a litany of accusatory questions, which I answered, then I said, "This is the deal. We brought Arina here because she said she wanted to come. We did not force her. Once here she realized we were not the TV family she wanted. We actually had rules (gasp) and gave her responsibilities (the horror), which, by the way, we talked to them about at great length while in the orphanage and they agreed to, and we didn't allow 24/7 access to the internet and porn and strange men and boys (how terrible we are). So, she rebelled. She throws temper tantrums like a five-year-old, says terrible things to and about us to others and then runs away because she doesn't want to be responsible for her words or actions. Once she cools down she realizes she is in trouble, so she has to make up stories to blame someone else in order to take the heat off herself. We have been here so many times in the past year. It's always someone else's fault. WE made her angry. WE gave her sandwiches instead of lunch money. WE made her get up early and go to school. WE made her practice her English. WE didn't allow her to go on porn sites on the internet. WE didn't allow her to stay up all night talking with older, strange men about having sex with them. Because WE made her do these things WE are the evil ones and because she couldn't tell the truth she had to make up stories. Stories to her teacher, school counselors, police and now to you, CPS. And what do you know about RAD – Reactive Attachment Disorders?" ACK!!

J. looked at me and said, "I don't know what you are talking about."

I told him, "Spend some time learning about attachment disorders, RAD in adopted children. Arina and Dima both have severe reactive attachment trauma which is causing all of these behaviors."

J. said nothing. Just made notes in his book. I felt deflated. As if, nothing I said would matter anyhow. I was frustrated and angry she was putting us through this again and no one was listening to us. He looked at me and told me he was ready for Tom.

Tom was the last person interviewed. They sat down at the table facing each other. It was tense; it was very evident they were opponents. Before the conversation began, Tom asked to see J's identification. J. was startled by the question but complied. Tom said, "We don't know who you are, and we've dealt with some pretty unsavory people in the past year. I want to be sure you are who you say you are." After reviewing the identification, the interview began.

J. leads the questioning with, "How much alcohol do you drink per week?"

Tom answered, "I have a few beers through the weekend. I don't normally drink during the week. The drinking on the weekend is with a meal such as pizza and beer. I have a system where I put two beers in the refrigerator and that's my limit for the night."

It went back and forth on hitting, mom hitting, and other abuse such as kicking the teens and then Tom stated, "This girl Arina doesn't bend on anything. No matter what we have as a meal she refuses to eat, whatever plans we make as a family she does everything to sabotage it, she comes, she goes, she does whatever she wants, and the police have told us there is nothing we can do about it except to file a police report when she leaves. We have filed every single time."

J. barked, "You are responsible for her until she is 18. You need to do more to be sure she is safe and doesn't go wandering around."

Tom replied, "Absolutely, I know I'm responsible. I have never told her to leave. My wife has never told her to leave. In fact, on many occasions when Arina had left my wife stood on the porch calling her back. Yelling to her as Arina walked away, "Arina, this is your home and your family. Please come back." Arina walked away without looking back and then told everyone we kicked her out so she can mooch from them. She walked out this door all by herself. In search of the "better family". It's not that we're a bad family. We are simply not the family who gives her everything she wants and lets her do everything she wants. I also know I can't force her to stay here in this nice home and not go off to who knows where. I can't force her to stay here where she is well fed, well clothed, and people care for her. I can't stop her from going off with strange men she finds on the internet. She is 17 and she knows she has all the power."

J. countered, "If anything happens to her while she is not in your home you are responsible and will be held accountable."

Tom (thinking is this guy crazy?) said, "We are doing our best to keep her here."

J. stated, "You come across like you are the authority of this home."

Tom replied, "I am. I'm the dad."

J. then said, "That is an awful way to run a household."

(Tom is thinking at this point what in the world is up with this guy? Is he crazy? On one hand he is telling me I have to be more forceful to keep her from running away, but then telling me it's awful for me to do just that. Who is supposed to be the authority? Her?)

J. was a bully. He had the power and he knew it.

Tom then said, "What happens when she turns 18?"

J. replied, "That is out of my jurisdiction. Now I need to look at a few things in your house."

Tom said, "Go for it."

The first thing J. did was to open the refrigerator. It was stuffed to the brim with food, including six-quart jars of freshly made borsht.

I said to him, "Just so you know. This borscht, it's authentic. It takes me over 6 hours to make it. It's her favorite food and one of the few things I can get her to eat so I always keep it on hand for her. I make a huge pot once a week." Then he looked in the pantry, which was also full. Then we all walked upstairs to her room. We opened the door to the destruction she had left. He looked at us as if to say you let her live like this? Tom said, "Nice, huh? This is how she chooses to live. You may not realize, but I made this room perfect for her before she came home with us."

I said, "She did this. In fact, she has done this several times. Every time we make it nice she destroys it. The police have recommended we file a destruction of personal property report against her, but we keep hoping she will calm down and we don't want her to have a record." He said nothing in return and walked back down stairs. Really? No comment huh?

Then he said, "I need to check the water in all of the sinks and showers." Huh? Seems she claimed we had no hot water and she always had to take cold showers. Where did she come up with this stuff?

I said to J., "CPS has a huge problem, but none of you care. We have been falsely accused by Arina and Dima several times now. All false claims because one or both did something wrong and rather be held accountable, and because they have RAD, they called CPS to turn the heat on us instead. After our entire family is put through a brutal investigation, we are exonerated. Each time, going into the investigation, we tell the assigned CPS officer about the previous times and they tell us it doesn't matter. They have to investigate without prejudice. Really? Without prejudice. Prejudice to whom? You certainly are prejudiced *against* us. And *for* them. No matter what they say they are believed and no matter what we say our words hold no weight. I'd say that is pretty darn prejudiced." J. said nothing. I wanted to scream in frustration. Our bio teens were put through the ringer – again. Katherine cried every day. Her grades were slipping. Her running suffered, the thing she loved most. I prayed this didn't have long term consequences for her and Garrett.

Before J. left I asked, "How is it that we have all these other teens, including two other Ukrainians, who tell you we are wonderful parents. They are doing well at home and in school. Then there is Arina and Dima who constantly cause problems, but they are automatically believed and the rest of us are run over the coals? And those two are never held accountable for their lies. I hope you realize that CPS is giving them more power over us in the future and they will keep calling and making false claims. Do you realize that?"

He replied, "I'm just doing my job." Then he walked out the door.

After the door closed Tom turned to me and said, "There are two evils in this world. 'I'm just doing my job' and 'that's the way we've always done it.' You know he already believed we were guilty as soon as he walked into our house and he was out to prove that because that was his job. He was a total jerk. This was our house, we live here, we pay the house payment, and he was completely disrespectful. That was a witch hunt."

J. did tell us what Arina had been up to the past several weeks. We found out she had met a man online while on break at work and told him her "poor little orphan girl" story. He told his parents. They believed her story and took her in. On one level I was so angry with them. Who does that? Without even talking to us? We had no idea where she was, if she was hurt, with another trafficker, etc. Of course, I understood what she told them about us abusing her. She was such a good actress. They believed her. HA - so did we a long time ago. I understood believing her story. But they waited three weeks before they called anyone about it and that was not okay. They should have reported it immediately.

It was left that J. from CPS was going to contact this couple to tell them to call us to "work things out". I wondered how long they would keep her once I told them the truth. I thought to myself, I should allow them access to my private blog, so they can read her history and see if they still felt the same.

A few days later we were notified we had been cleared of any wrongdoing by CPS. I asked – again - if there would be accountability for her lying. NOPE! Seriously. This girl would keep doing this over and over, every time she needed an out. What a nightmare! What a violation against our family. It seems these teens could say anything and turn our lives upside down with no consequences. Our character and integrity would be continually questioned as long as Arina and Dima felt they had something to gain by telling lies about us. The other four teens were upset once again after being asked such intrusive questions like, "How much does your dad really drink every day" and "How many times has your mother hit you?" REALLY???

HOWEVER. This particular CPS investigation would end up being a blessing in disguise. We just didn't know it at the time. Thank Yahweh for good that comes out of trouble.

Arina was still with the couple. She was being treated like a princess. They bought her new clothes and, of course, another phone. They took her out to eat, took her shopping and treated her like the little girl they never had. She had no responsibilities and I found out later they had suggested she quit her job. They told her she was too young to be made to work. I waited for the phone call from them.

Family X. I didn't know I would lose all belief in our American justice system. CPS, the police, the courts. I used to be so proud to be an American. No more. There is such a travesty of justice going on against adoptive families and no one cares. The only thing they care about are their paychecks. Our family meant nothing to them except money.

CHAPTER 19

Triangulation Part II

July 31, 2015. I WANTED TO EXPLODE! I received a voicemail from the man who was harboring Arina. I said aloud to myself, "How is it okay for some couple who did not spend eleven weeks in Ukraine, tens of thousands of dollars to help give her a future, then practically killing ourselves to find something which would work to heal her so she could live out that future, plus all of the trauma of the past twelve months on our family, to tell me that WE have your daughter now and she WILL be staying with us? Without even talking to me? Leaving a message ON A VOICEMAIL!!!"

I told myself to breathe, then I called J. at CPS to tell him about the voicemail. I was told J. would tell the couple to allow me to talk with Arina. I told him it would do no good for me to speak with Arina. The couple needed to turn her over to me immediately.

We found out via a call from another police detective that more than a week before I had talked to Arina's supervisor, Arina's store manager had called them about Arina. She was concerned because Arina was seen talking with an older couple. Arina told her they were parents of a friend. This "friend" was named Al and he was 31 years old!!! You've got to be kidding me! AND the police detective told us he had relayed that information to the CPS officer. So, CPS officer J. knew this information before he interrogated all of us yet didn't say anything to us. When I told the detective about the investigation we had gone through and that Arina was still with these people, he was very concerned. He sounded angry and told me he would immediately call the State Police.

We hung up and I called J. at CPS. I said, "It was such an emergency to investigate us and now we've been cleared it is no longer a priority to get our daughter back to us. I just spoke with detective M. and I now know what he told you the week before you investigated us. I know Arina contacted that couple's son, A., through an internet site, and he was someone she had never met before. I know he is 31 years old and there are naked pictures of him all over the internet. You knew all of this, yet you wasted time putting my family through an invasive, destructive investigation, all while Arina is with some couple who may very well be traffickers and with a son who is depraved.

Detective M. is calling the State Police task force at this moment to apprise them of this situation and you can expect a call from them." Silence. J. told me he would call the couple immediately to tell them to turn Arina over to us. We hung up. Right. Of course you will – now that you are backed into a corner.

Within ten minutes I received a call from another county's CPS office. (Honestly, if one more person tells me that "SOMEONE ELSE" is a respected member of their community I'm going to throw something at them. When I was ten I was molested by a "respected member of the community, a deacon in the church," who told me to keep my mouth shut because no one would believe me over him.) This CPS woman said, "I'm a close friend of "so and so couple" who have been taking care of your daughter and they thought they were simply rescuing her."

I replied, "Really? Rescuing her from what? From whom? If they are such upstanding people, why didn't they contact the police immediately upon hearing her story about being in such danger? Why did they wait almost three weeks to contact the police, or even CPS? If you are their friend and they know you work for CPS, why didn't they call you? Why did they go into her work to change her contact information from ours to theirs? Why did they tell her to quit her job? You know, I really question if they are as respectable as you say. My husband and I are respected members of our community, too. We already did the hard stuff to rescue this girl from life on the streets in Ukraine. She doesn't want a real life. She only wants a handout. And a cushy life. And no accountability or responsibility. I don't care who your friends are, they have been harboring a minor child for weeks, without reporting it to law enforcement. How is that respectable?"

I was livid and continued. "My family has been put through incredible trauma, and your friends, those upstanding people, contributed to that trauma. And NONE of you has a clue what Reactive Attachment Disorder is or what it does to a family. The enabling by your respectable friends did not help Arina one bit. In fact, it only added to the destruction of my family by her and it told Arina, my RAD daughter, that she simply needs to move on to greener pastures and reinforced her disorder. She now knows she can say what she wants about us and it will take the heat off her. I guarantee you it has escalated Arina's anger toward the person she deems responsible for losing out on this new cushy life – me. You wait and see, Miss CPS lady. I am in big trouble from Arina now because she sees me as the one removing her from this new great new life she found. I expect her back to me TODAY. Do you understand? I have already alerted my contact at the State Police and they are ready to get involved and file kidnapping charges if Arina is not back with me today."

She replied, "I will have them call you right away to make arrangements."

As for CPS, their failure to enforce consequences for Arina for her poor choices simply empowered her even further. All she had to do was tell someone in authority a fairy tale and she was off the hook. It made no difference what the truth really was.

THIS!!
Something MUST be done to protect good families from invasive and traumatic witch hunts.

My phone rang less than 30 minutes later. I spent an hour and a half on the phone arguing with the man. His wife was on a second line, but rarely spoke. (Can you say drained?) It seemed no matter what I said he replied with, "Maybe over time Arina will want to go home." NO! Are you crazy? Arina was living the high life! Easy access to a phone and computer, someone buying her whatever she wants, a Visa card with money on it…are you kidding me? This is the life she had dreamed about. He kept repeating his diatribe even after I told him the whole sordid story from last summer until now. They were CLUELESS!! STUPID!! He actually said to me, "Perhaps you don't know how to parent her the way she needs to be parented."

At this point I'd had enough and said, "Really? And you're such stellar parents that your 31-year-old pervert son has his naked self all over the internet and picks up young girls he meets online." Yeah! He ignored what I said and repeated, "Arina does not want to go to your house and she does not want to go on vacation with you." You think??? Stupid people. I said, "Of course she doesn't. And give it enough time she won't want to do anything with you either. She has Reactive Attachment Disorder!" My blood was boiling. What right did they have to talk to me like that? Who were these people?

I finally had enough and stated, "When, not if, Arina starts destroying your home and/or attacks either of you verbally or physically, I am telling you right now we are not responsible in any way. As soon as we hang up, I'm calling my contact officer at the State Police, our local police detective who has been working with us, our Homeland Security liaison officer and your lady friend at CPS to tell them the same thing. You are welcome to Arina and all of her problems from here on out. I will no longer be responsible financially or in any other way for what she does IF you decide to keep her past 6 pm today. Do you understand?" There was silence. For a really long time. I thought they had hung up. Finally, the woman spoke, "Well, we could meet with you this afternoon. Perhaps we can meet where she used to work, and you can pick her up there at 4:00."

You think!!!!

This is the thing. People want to interfere as long as it doesn't hurt them. And hurt was guaranteed if Arina stayed with them.

The plan was we would meet in the Meijer parking lot at 4:00 p.m. They would tell Arina the plan once they arrived there and tell her she needed to go home and work everything out with us, her parents. I alerted the police and they were ready to come if needed. I told Tom I was leaving.

Tom asked, "Where are you going?"

I replied, "To Meijer to meet with the stupid couple."

Tom: "Why?"

Me: "To pick Arina up from them. They are meeting me at 4:00. I'm taking Sasha with me for a witness and to help translate if needed."

Tom: "Does that mean she is going to Florida with us tomorrow?"

Me: (sighing deeply) "Yup."

Tom: "Oh...crap."

Me: "I know."

To both of us this meant Arina would be in the car with us for the 20 hour drive the next day and our entire trip would now revolve around facilitating her moods, which fluctuated by the moment. We also had to be concerned about her getting out of the car and running away at any of the various stops along the way, or even in Florida.

Chapter 20

Domestic Violence

July 31, 2015 - continued. Arina was in jail. Domestic violence. Against me. She was to be arraigned the following Monday or Tuesday. Charged as an adult.

I showed up in the parking lot to meet the couple as we had arranged. The man told me his wife had taken Arina into the store so we could straighten things out between us first then he immediately leaned in and got close to my face and asked, "Is there anything punitive going to be done to Arina over this?" I was so over this guy by now and just wanted to get Arina and go. His words made me want to scream, but thankfully Yahweh helped me hold my temper. I was thinking, "Who the heck do you think you are, guy? You've had MY daughter for the past three weeks, not telling me or anyone else where she was and calling your big buddy, who works for CPS, who got us involved in ANOTHER false investigation. You've completely undermined us with OUR daughter, taking her to a doctor and a psychiatrist without our permission, and you have the nerve to ask me this?"

Instead I simply asked him, "Why do you want to know?" He replied, "Well, you talked about God in our phone call and I know you Bible people and how you are." REALLY? I wanted to explode, but instead exhibited amazing self-control, thanks to Yahweh. I had prayed the entire drive there because I knew I was terribly on edge. Yahweh definitely heard my prayers and was right there with me in that parking lot. Me, alone? I would have taken the guy's head right off for being so condescending and disrespectful.

I said, "I don't know what Bible you think you know, but it sure doesn't sound like the one I live by." He said, "I know a lot of 'Bible people' and they all believe in very harsh punishment. I think that's why Arina ran away from you and perhaps why she is upset and doesn't want to go with you." WOW! (Seriously, when I told Tom about this conversation he asked me how he wasn't picking me up from jail for attacking this ridiculously stupid man. I told Tom, "Yahweh was right in my head the whole time.")

To this know-it-all I said, "Yahweh is my God and He is amazing. He is the author of kindness and gentleness as well as justice. I don't know what kind of Bible people you hang around, but I would get new friends if I were you. We have never lifted a finger against this girl and we've done everything in our power to give her a good life. Don't you recall anything I told you over the phone earlier about Reactive Attachment Disorder?"

Instead of answering my question he continued to push buttons by saying, "Also, I don't like it that you refer to her like she is a five-year-old." Clearly, this man knew NOTHING about RAD or attachment, trauma, or emotional underdevelopment in adoptive children/teens. It was as if he remembered nothing of our 90-minute phone conversation earlier that day, except to take bits and pieces out of context. I told myself to take a deep breath, then said to him, "I understand what you think. I suggest you do some research on RAD and the other disorders I spoke to you about. You, your wife, and your son have done more harm than you will ever know to Arina and our entire family. I won't discuss this with you any further. Get Arina out here, then you and your wife leave immediately." I think to myself, "Will you please just shut up and go, idiot!"

He looked at me as if he wanted to say something more. Seeing the look on my face he decided against it and walked to his car and opened the trunk. He removed two large black garbage bags and handed them to Sasha, who was standing next to me. "What is all this?" I asked. "Just some stuff we bought for her, clothing and some other things we thought she needed. We spent quite a lot of money on her. (It came across as if I should reimburse him for his expenses. I ignored the hint.) We bought her a new bike, too, but couldn't fit it in our car." GREAT! They bought her a bike after she left her brand new bike we had just purchased, unlocked, at her work. (Yeah, we were so abusive to her that we had purchased two new bikes since she came to live with us because she "lost" one of them.) All of this "stuff" was more "proof" to her that she had it good with them and I ruined it all for her. This couple had NO CLUE that everything they had done the past few weeks would contribute to our future hell with her.

You see, in her eyes, I was now a REALLY BAD PERSON. She was all nice and comfy in this home with these nice people she had bamboozled, who treated her like a little orphan princess and now, I had RUINED IT! And she was steaming mad. When she came out of the store with the woman and saw me standing there with the man her eyes projected pure, unadulterated hatred. Unconsciously, I took a step backwards in fear.

She walked directly to their car intending to get in it when Sasha told her what was happening. She started screaming in Russian and tried to open the car door, but it was locked. She ran back into the store. I told Sasha to follow her. The couple started to follow her, too, but I stepped in front of the man and stood face to face with him, blocking his path. I told him forcefully, "You have both done quite enough damage. Get into your car and drive away – NOW! If I hear that you, or your son, has communicated with Arina at all, ever again, I will report you to Homeland Security and the State Police." They turned and walked toward their car. I jogged to the store entrance to find her and Sasha.

Arina was sitting in a chair in the café section of the store, leaning back against the front window. Sasha was silently standing about five feet away from her, waiting for me. I approached and stopped near him. I assured her in a soft voice, as if I was talking to a frightened puppy, "Arina, everything is going to be all right. You are not in trouble. Let's go home and have some dinner. I have borscht ready for you." Sasha translated, and she screamed at the top of her voice, "NO, NO, NO", as if she was being attacked. She leapt up, grabbed the heavy metal chair and launched it at me. It smashed into my lower leg. I stumbled back, bent over in pain, and she lunged at me. I had my phone in my right hand with the number to the police ready to push send. She was digging into my arm and grabbing at my phone, so I couldn't hit the button. I was bent over trying to protect myself when she tackled me to the ground. She screamed again, "No police. No police." She grabbed my left arm to pull me around towards her still trying to grab the phone. I yelled, "Please, someone call the police!" There were several people in the café area, but no one did anything! Part of me was mortified this was happening in public, in front of people. Now on the floor, crouched away from her, trying to protect myself from further abuse, I finally hit the send button and was connected to the police dispatcher. I told her what was happening. She said to stay on the line and a car was being dispatched immediately. Arina's nails were digging into my arm and twisting it backwards. She grabbed my hair and pulled hard. Arina's only focus was to get my phone from me. She jumped on top of me, pulling my right arm to her, then once she realized the police were alerted she released me and started running for the door. I motioned to Sasha to follow Arina, then painfully grabbed ahold of the chair and pulled myself up. Limping after Sasha, I stayed on the phone with the dispatcher, giving her the blow by blow. I thanked Yahweh there were witnesses to the assault, and security cameras everywhere recording the incident.

Sasha and I tracked her out of the store. He was close behind her and I was doing my best to follow him. I was limping and talking with the police while trying to keep them both in sight. My leg was on fire. My arm hurt horribly and was bleeding where she had raked her nails. My head was pounding from the pulling of my hair. Arina raced out of the parking lot, then across the road and into the woods. Sasha kept up with her better than I did, but I could still see both. The police found Sasha and me near the woods. I pointed her out about 100 yards into the woods. They went in after her and brought her back to their car in handcuffs. She was raging and screaming at the top of her lungs in Russian. The police wrote the report and asked me to sign it.

I was sobbing. My leg was throbbing, and the police took pictures of it, which had already begun to show bruising, as well as the cuts, scratches and black and blue welts on my arm. I hurt so badly, inside and out. Arina was booked on aggravated assault and domestic violence. Since she was over 17 she was charged as an adult and sent to adult lock up. The police said maybe the outcome of being charged as an adult would make an impression on her. Maybe she would finally take things seriously and stop acting out. I told the officers we had to leave the next day for Florida on a family vacation. One of the officers said, "Go and enjoy." He said, "She will be in jail and she will be arraigned either Monday or Tuesday. Then it would depend on what the judge sets as a trial date. You don't need to attend the arraignment so go and enjoy your vacation."

After limping slowly back to the store parking lot to get my car, Sasha and I left for home. My plan was to drop him off, then drive to the urgent care to get checked out. The phone rang. It was the couple who had just dropped her off to me. He said, "We just wanted to check and be sure that Arina is doing okay." "Yes, she is doing fine." I replied. "She is currently being transported to the jail after she attacked me in the store. I am driving myself to the urgent care to get checked out because I am badly hurt." Silence, then he asked, "What did you do to her that caused her to attack you?" I hung up on him. I looked at Sasha and said, "That couple caused all of this, you know. She is raging because I took her away from them." He nodded in agreement and said, "I know." The man called right back and said, "Did you hang up on me? All we want to know is if there is anything we can do to help Arina." No, Idiots! I think you have done quite enough. I said, "This is RAD. This is caused by the attachment disorder I told you about and that you decided to ignore. I was nicely asking her to come home, telling her everything would be fine, when she brutally attacked me in front of several witnesses. Would you like to have her in your home now?" "Well...we are not sure we are equipped to handle it now that she is physical." He replied.

YOU THINK!!!!!!!!!!!!!!!!!!!!!!!!! Such idiots!! Thank you – NOT – for your contribution to this disaster Hopefully they would be out of the picture for good now.

The phone rang again. It was one of the police officers. He said, "Because Arina is being charged as an adult with domestic violence, under no circumstances is she, by law, to be allowed to be in your home or within 1000 feet of you." I was a huge melting pot of emotion: Sick, upset, defeated and so sad thinking back to the sweet girl we had met in Ukraine. Realizing it was all an act then and that she was destroying the future we wanted so badly for her. The future she told us she wanted, too. It was all going down the toilet – fast. I couldn't stand to watch the destruction.

After a visit to urgent care, I arrived home. I told Tom, "My leg is fractured, and they said my arms are going to hurt pretty bad for the next few days." I had bandages on the deeper scrapes on my left arm from her nails, and a walking cast. I looked like I had been in a car accident. When he saw the bruises on my arm he pulled me to him for a long hug and all the tears I had kept in until then came pouring out.

In the shower the next morning I started bawling again. I couldn't explain the heaviness on my heart. It was incredibly hard watching someone throw their future away in such a vicious, violent manner. My dreams for her crashed and burned. I hurt so badly, both heart and body. I had enormous bruises on both arms and my leg. Huge black and purple marks. You could see images of her fingers. Tom took pictures. I lifted my arms to wash my hair. The pain was awful, and the tears just started down my face, mixing with the spray of the water. Before long, I was sobbing uncontrollably, deep, soul wrenching sobs. We were leaving for what was supposed to be a great family vacation that day.

How would I ride to Florida hurting like this?

CHAPTER 21

Vacation! What Vacation?

While in the car driving to Florida, I received a call from the city prosecutor in charge of Arina's case. He told me they didn't have a date for Arina's arraignment yet. They had to hire a Russian translator and the date would depend on finding one. I informed him we were on our way to Florida; that the police had said we could go and he agreed. He said, "We don't need you at the arraignment. We will let you know when we have a trial date. You will be needed for that as a material witness since you are the victim. Arina will be kept in lockup until the arraignment. Once she is arraigned, the judge will decide whether to keep her in jail or let her out on some type of bond. If Arina is let out on bond, she is not allowed in your home. Domestic Violence is a serious crime and we don't want you in further danger." I said, "I'm pretty sure she wouldn't come home anyway. She will reach out to one or more of the five hundred men on her one of her social media pages to rescue her." He replied, "I am hopeful the judge will keep her in jail until her trial, but it is not up to me. Arina will be represented by a court appointed attorney and you, as the victim, are not allowed to finance her attorney, or any of the court costs. Do you understand?" "Yes." I answered.

August 3, 2015. We made it to Florida. The prosecutor called to tell us the arraignment would not be taking place that day and he didn't know when it would. He told me, "I'm going to ask for a severe sentence for this one. You are her mother, and this was done in a public place." After his call, one of the police detectives called to ask me how I was holding up. She was very concerned about me and wanted me to know they were not taking this lightly. Their support made me feel a little better. I hung up and went to find Tom to bring him up to speed. I told him, "I could breathe a sigh of relief if she is put in jail for a while. If she is in jail, she won't be able to hurt us, and she won't be able to hurt herself, either. I hated thinking this way, but I didn't know how much more of this hell I could take. We all needed a break." Tom nodded in understanding. Only he really knew our hell.

Tuesday August 4, 2015. Another update from the prosecutor. Arina still had not been arraigned, but the judge had ordered a $2,500 bond, plus, to be released on bond, she needed a verifiable address, which couldn't be ours. He reminded me I was not allowed to post bond for her. The hope was they would arraign her the next day. They knew if she got out on bond, she would disappear, so he was working hard to keep her in custody. He also told me during the bond hearing, the judge had reiterated to Arina she was not allowed within 1000 feet of me or our home.

It was a hot August in Florida, and I was walking around looking like I'd been a victim of abuse, which I had been. Poor Tom walked next to me in the grocery store and endured evil looks from other shoppers. I felt bad for him. I looked like a battered wife. I couldn't sit in the sun either, one of my favorite things to do, or the bruises wouldn't heal properly. The pain in my leg and arms made it tough to sleep. I tossed and turned each night, trying to get comfortable. I cried a lot.

Friday August 7, 2015. I felt like I was in a nightmare and couldn't wake up. I got a call from a court probation officer. Contrary to what we had all assumed, Arina pled guilty of the charges, so there would be no trial. Sentencing took place immediately at the hearing. At sentencing, she was convicted of domestic violence and sentenced to 90 days in juvenile detention.

Thirty minutes later the prosecutor called. He was HOT!!! He said, "Apparently, the judge felt sorry for her."

I thought, "How about someone feeling sorry for me?"

He said, "Domestic Violence is NEVER let off this easily. I can't explain it." The prosecutor continued, "The court received a call from juvenile detention that Arina wasn't allowed to be incarcerated there because of the adult conviction of domestic violence. And I hate to tell you this next part. The judge let her go with time already served!" YUP! Just let her walk out and go. No punishment at all. Unless you considered the few days she spent waiting for her arraignment. Arina walked out of the courtroom free. 45 minutes away from our home. In a strange city. With us in Florida. Before she left the courtroom, the judge reminded her she was not allowed near me or our home or he would put her back in jail.

Thank you so much judge, I thought sarcastically. One more person who could have done something to help her, and us, and didn't.

Arina knew we were in Florida and there was no one at our home. I called the local police and let them know. They were happy to keep an eye on the house. I also reported her as a missing person again. A few minutes later, I received a call from the officer who had arrested Arina. She was outraged the judge let Arina off with only a few days served for domestic violence. And that they had let her out without any clue to where she was headed. In her words, "It was completely irresponsible." The officer said she didn't understand it, because in abuse cases judges are normally harsh. That was a repeat of what the prosecutor told me.

Five minutes later I got a call from an officer from CPS. This was turning out to be the "best" vacation of my life!

CPS: "Mrs. Ray?"

Me: "Yes."

CPS: "This is Mr. S. from Child Protective Services. We are charging you and Mr. Ray with neglect and abandonment of a minor."

Me: "What?"

CPS: It has come to our attention that Arina was released from jail today and you were not there to pick her up. It was your duty to do so."

Me: "You're joking, right? We were told by both the police and the city prosecutor to go on our family vacation and to stick with our plans. I have been in contact with both every day the entire time we've been gone. We found out a few minutes ago from the city prosecutor the judge released her with no jail time after we were told by the court probation officer earlier today Arina was given 90 days. The judge specifically told Arina, and we were told by the police and prosecutor, that she was not allowed in our home or near me due to the conviction of domestic violence. How in the world are you charging us with neglect?"

CPS: "She is a minor child and you are responsible for her. I don't care what the judge said. You are required to have her in your home. I am filing neglect charges against you and your husband, and I am also looking into the possibility of removal of your other children. You are unfit parents."

Me (completely furious now): "Well, Mr. S., as soon I hung up with the prosecutor, I immediately called our local police department and filed a missing person's report on Arina. They have it on file and are already searching for her."

CPS: "Oh. (Sounding deflated.) Well, I guess you are fine then." He hung up without another word.

I stood there staring at my phone, feeling like I dreamt the whole bizarre past hour. Was this world completely mad? When this conversation took place, I had been a great mom for more than 32 years and raised four amazing children to adulthood!! I was a grandma! OH MY WORD!! I didn't know how much more of this I could handle!

This system sucks!!!!

NEGLECT CHARGES by CPS

When parents are charged with neglect it causes a ripple effect on the entire family. Here is a roadmap how this can evolve:

- Adopted child/teen runs away, or refuses to go home, or like in our case was told by a judge not to go home, or something similar.

Or charges are made by the adopted child/teen or another person about the parents in regard to the child/teen. Maybe a teacher, or other school administrator. Maybe a neighbor. Or even someone from your church. Or it's the only way for the adopted child/teen to get the medical or mental help they need.
- CPS steps in and charges the family with neglect. We were threatened with neglect on four different occasions. And oh boy, it comes across like a threat, too. They know they have all the power and they use it however they want. This is a family living with severe trauma and CPS does not help, but actually adds to the already stressful situation.
- Once parents have a neglect charge in their file it NEVER GOES AWAY. It can, and often does, affect employment, and other aspects of the parents' life.
- Once parents have a neglect charge in their file CPS now controls their life, in every way. There is an open door to investigate anything at any time, with no notice.
- Once parents have a neglect charge in their file any other children in the home can be removed by CPS at ANY time. We were threatened four times that they would remove Garrett, Katherine and any of the other Ukrainian teens who were under 18. They would put them into foster care if we refused to comply with CPS demands.

Honestly, we now know what the Gestapo was like. That may sound like an exaggeration to anyone who has not had interactions with CPS, but after living on this side of several investigations, I say it without hesitation. CPS (or whatever it is called by various states) is a federally funded, multi-billion dollar per year business. That means it is 100% funded by taxpayers. But, as its name implies, CPS only has the best interest of the complaining child.

In an article by Health Impact News the author states, "Those who work in this "business" have a vested interest in removing children from homes and rehoming them into the foster care system. It is all about the almighty dollar."

(http://medicalkidnap.com/2016/02/25/child-kidnapping-and-trafficking-a-lucrative-u-s-business-funded-by-taxpayers/)

In my opinion it's just another way to make money by trafficking children. CPS is an organization with no oversight and full autonomy to make decisions in their own best interest. They are judge and jury, and parents are automatically guilty and very seldom proven innocent.

How is that American?

Family X. More CPS horror stories...

- I am a licensed marriage and family therapist, specializing in attachment parenting. We are now embroiled in a CPS investigation due to allegations by my now 15-year-old adopted son. CPS has made findings for both physical and emotional abuse against myself and my husband, based entirely on the testimony of our son, who has an established vendetta against us. The "investigation" was a process where they found the allegations they wanted to find, and completely ignored our pleas to interview anyone else who had knowledge of the events (neighbors, family, school administration, etc.). While several of the CPS complaints on the court petition can be easily refuted with documented evidence (hospital/police/school/therapist records), others are based solely on the inferences of CPS, not backed up by any actual facts, and were not even the complaints of our son! We are battling these findings in court, to the tune of $3,000 spent to date, with an additional $15,000 necessary if we are forced to go to trial. CPS refused to make a decision at mediation and forced us to trial. I feel like we live in a military state, where the government convicts you of something you didn't do, without any real judicial process, just because they have the power. Our family is completely broken. And as if our family was not already in enough crisis just trying to get through each day with a violent child, with major mental disorders, and very risky sexual acting out toward my 7 and 8-year-old daughters. Added to that we are under this undeserved CPS supervision. And to add insult to injury, CPS asks the perpetrator of all this horror if we are treating HIM well during the weekly visits they continue to make to our home. They ask him if HE feels safe with us!!! After talking with him, they come to me to tell me we need to adjust our diets because he doesn't like eggs, or tomatoes, or some other crazy thing. Unbelievable!

- My adopted son had run out of the house barefoot after threatening to kill me. After he'd been gone 15 minutes, I locked up the house and left. I didn't realize he was standing on the front porch. He lunged at me and attacked me by pulling out a handful of my hair and smashing my head through the front window. Two of my neighbors saw what was happening and ran over to pull him off of me. They held him while one of their wives called the police. My son asked me if he could go into the house to get his sneakers. I said no because I knew he only wanted to go in to cause more damage. The police took him to the mental health hospital. The hospital called CPS and had me charged with neglect for not letting him put on shoes. It was August, by the way. I was put through an investigation by three different CPS agents. It was brutal. I believe the only reason I wasn't dead was thanks to my neighbors and then I had to endure a ruthless CPS investigation where it was clear that in their eyes I was the guilty party. I was the abused, but I was treated as if I was the one causing the abuse. I felt as if I were living a nightmare and couldn't wake up. Not even the testimony of my neighbors made a difference. Finally, it was the fingerprint bruises around my neck that finally got the case dismissed.

- My adopted daughter 16 pulled a knife on me. I was instructed by the police to call CPS and they would get her the help she needed. The CPS worker came, and I explained the situation. The worker told me that for them to get involved they would charge me with neglect and I would pay child support to her foster parents. She told me a neglect charge would mean they would most likely take my bio children. So we are stuck.

- When our oldest adopted daughter turned 18 she called CPS on us, with the help of someone at our church who believed her story. This was after an entire year of her running away, us dealing with the police on her behalf and brief psych ward visits where she was released due to her refusing medication. The accusation was that we adopted children in order to abuse them. Human trafficking. There were other charges that CPS refused to tell us. (Where in America is it okay to charge someone and not even tell them what they are charged with?) It was an invasive investigation, interviewing all our children and looking through every inch of our house. They took pictures of everything. I felt terribly violated. We had to fight it with everything we had. My husband was in the military and had the neglect or abuse charges stuck he would have been dishonorably discharged. CPS is out of control.

- It was an afternoon when our adopted son had his mandatory in home counseling. He refused to come into the house to get ready for it. Our case worker showed up while he was outside and spoke with him. The case worker came inside and told us that our son had accused my husband of beating his head into a wall the night before during an argument and our son had a knot on his head. There was no argument and no knot on his head could be found. The case worker insisted on reporting us even though his counselors advised against it based on his violent history. When CPS arrived, it escalated quickly, and we are now being told that we are in danger of losing our other children. They are basing all of this on the story of a destructive, vindictive child with an abusive history toward others and no evidence. Nothing we say is being taken into account. I'm terrified.

- My son's first year of kindergarten ended in February, after fighting tooth and nail for the bare minimum of needed services and still not having an IEP. They were intentionally harming him and going against his 504 (which I had to demand in an effort to protect him) and five letters from five different doctors. The day we withdrew him, they called CPS on us in retaliation for taking their cash cow. (Military kid + Sped = $$$). The CPS officer who came to talk to me, after talking to all my kids in school without my knowledge or permission, said she was going to administratively close the case without further investigation due to the fact that I had tons of evidence. I shudder to think what would have happened if I had not documented everything. This was unbearable.

- We are currently going through our second allegation from CPS over our adopted daughter's lies. She is 12. The first time she gave them an entire list of abuses by us that were never proven, but we were left with the knowledge they "knew" we had done it, they just couldn't prove it. It is the same with this second investigation. The probing questions that make you realize they already believe you are guilty and they are out to prove it make you want to scream. I feel like I'm losing my mind.

- My adopted daughter turned me into CPS telling them that I had gone after her with a razor blade and cut her legs badly. You could see they were very old scars. Luckily, I had evidence that in 5th grade, without my permission, she had tried to shave her legs several times and cut up her legs. She had a bad "picking" habit and the cuts weren't allowed to heal. During that time frame she was seeing a therapist regularly and I had her talk to my daughter about the cuts on her legs. I told the therapist how they happened, and my daughter corroborated it. CPS was not friendly to us, didn't want to believe us and even questioned the validity of the therapist documentation. That documentation saved us. I shudder to think what would have happened without it.

- My adopted daughter accused one of my biological sons of raping her. Even though there were witnesses and the case was dropped because she recanted and said she lied, all of our names are now in a permanent sexual assault database, including my son. I have worked tirelessly to get our names off that list, but we are told by CPS there is nothing they can do to remove it once it is on there. Funny (not), there is plenty they did to put it on there, but nothing they can do remove it. It will follow my son around all his life. There are jobs he will not be able to get. The damage that has been done to him (and us) is immeasurable. This incident almost destroyed him and our family. What she did was unconscionable. What CPS did was even worse. It was clear their goal was to find us guilty. Once it came to light they were wrong, they walked away without an apology. The stain will live with us forever, unless they take our names off that list.

- I called CPS about our adopted son who we adopted from foster care. They showed up at my house to take my biological daughter instead. "We need to remove her for her safety", I was told. It took me ten months and over $30,000 to get her back. CPS is out of control. They have ruined our lives. All for money.

- CPS showed up at school to talk to my children. Seems adopted son, 9, had told his teacher that my husband had beat him up the night before for not taking out the trash. They pulled my two bio children out of class and asked them questions like, "how many times has your dad beat you". OH MY GOD! They are six and seven years old. They came home in tears. CPS called me two days later to tell me they were coming out later that day to interview my husband and me. I told them that my husband had been in Germany for two weeks for work and would not be home until the end of the week. I asked them what this was all about and they wouldn't tell me. They came out that afternoon and were angry that my husband was not there. I again told them that he had been out of the country for two weeks and they refused to believe me. I had to show them his travel itinerary and give them his employers' information for verification. They finally told me what the charge was, I told them that my husband has never hit any child and that he was in another country when the alleged beating took place. There were no bruises or cuts on the boy. I then showed them reams of documents about my son and his behavioral issues. They left after a three-hour interrogation and said they would get back to me with their findings. Three weeks later I got a letter saying they had closed the investigation.

- Our adopted daughter, 12, talked to a neighbor and told them we kept her locked in her room and wouldn't let her use the toilet. He reported us to CPS. They came out and from minute one acted as though we had actually done this horrible thing. They never once asked us about her. We showed him her room, which was very nice, and showed there was no lock on the door or window. He talked to our other children and asked invasive questions like how many times has your dad hit you and how many times does your mom lock you in your room when you do something she doesn't like. I was appalled that CPS gets away with this kind of Gestapo tactics on families. It was only after two weeks of interviews, accusations and talking to others about us that the file on us went away. It has left me not trusting anyone anymore. We've been good neighbors on this street for over 20 years. No one believed us. Everyone automatically believed her. I'm crushed.

- The day that CPS showed up without calling and removed my three bio children and took them to foster care is the absolute worst day of my life. All it took was my adopted daughter, 11, telling her teacher that I was sexually abusing all of them on a regular basis. There was zero proof. NONE! It came out months later she lied because she was mad at me for taking away her phone. After the truth came out it took over two weeks to get my children back home. They are not the same anymore. What they went through in foster care is going to take years of therapy. I don't think I will ever recover. My family has been destroyed.

- We've been victimized by the very entity we adopted from in the first place - CPS. We adopted out of the American foster care system. I can't tell everything in a few words, but eight visits in ten years. The first four in eight years were pretty simple open shut cases where we felt minimally victimized, and we still believed that good people who've done nothing wrong have nothing to worry about. That thinking changed when our 13-year-old was taken to the mental hospital for making threats to harm us. While there she got picked on by the other kids for having nothing really wrong. To make her case seem worse she then claimed I hit her and gave her a bloody nose to make her case seem worse. In the meantime, her doctor told us she shouldn't return home because our family was in danger from her. When CPS came things seemed to be going our way until I mentioned what the doctor said about us being in danger from her. Things got ugly quick with them threatening to take our bio one-year-old baby. The harder we fought, the more they tried to crucify us. It was clear to us they were on a mission to take our baby. I finally called the supervisor and we ended up using most of savings to protect ourselves and our baby. Now every time a CPS officer shows up at our house we look to see if there is a car seat because it means they are here to take our baby. We now have a plan in place to move to another state. Both our therapist and attorney told us we should do that because CPS was out for blood in our case. It's a terrifying way to live.

- We have been battling CPS allegations of emotional abuse for a year and a half now, to the tune of about $10,000 in attorney fees. Before things got really ugly, we asked CPS for help - respite, anything - but they said we didn't need help. Less than 2 months later, our RAD adopted daughter who is now 14 (then 12) ran away and was taken by police into county custody. We refused to allow her back into our home; it was our one chance at avoiding additional physical and emotional abuse FROM HER! In the past year and a half, she has been kicked out of 3 placements (foster home, treatment foster home, and even an RTF – residential treatment facility), and has been in 5 different mental health hospitals. There was only one RTF in the state that agreed to take placement of her because of her aggressive nature and her severe behavioral and mental health issues. Somehow, after all of this,

CPS continued to believe we are emotionally abusing our daughters - we also adopted daughter's younger bio sister (also RAD, but not quite as severe) - because we won't let our youngest daughter spend time with her older abusive sister. Really? Would they want to put their own children in harm's way like that? Of course not, so why should we be forced to? The girls have a very intense TRAUMA bond, not a healthy relationship, and when they see each other they both spiral out of control for months. We have been villainized by CPS. They have called me HITLER in their case notes. They have opened 10 different cases on us based on our daughter's lies. They attempted to take our youngest daughter away, but the judge shut them down, because they had no grounds to do this. We were luckier than most. They appeal every decision that goes our way, which means more attorney fees for us. Six months ago we sold our home and moved out of the county to get away from their evil intent. Even with no jurisdiction, they have continued to harass us. CPS sent a file on us to our new county and the new county said, "this is the opposite of emotional abuse, by its definition." CPS didn't like that answer, so they are appealing it in order to rack up more attorney's fees for us. I am disgusted by the absolute power CPS is given. I am in constant fear that my job will end because of all of this (I am a special education teacher). My husband and I are exhausted from fighting.

- Our adopted daughter with RAD, who had an extensive psych history, was mad at us because we wouldn't let her spend the weekend at her boyfriend's house, so she accused my husband (of 20 years) of sexually abusing her. She had accused multiple people of this same thing in the past. We had her sent to the hospital to have a rape test done, which we were told would take about 2 months. Fast forward 10 months and still no results! In the meantime, my husband took, and passed, a polygraph test, but it's been hell waiting for the report to come back. She was always trying to get people in trouble. She has absolutely no friends and she couldn't stay in public school due to the problems she caused there. She is now in a group home and we pay child support. We have no contact with her and at the court hearings CPS goes out of their way to make both my husband and me out to be horrible people, saying we should be doing more for her. We have done more for that child in the three years we had her than anyone did her entire life! Our lives have been hell, thanks to her and to CPS, and how I wish we never adopted her!

- Our children were adopted through our state CPS system. We were told we could contact them if we needed any post placement supports. When we contacted them for those supports for our oldest child, we were notified the next day that they were proceeding with opening a case against us. We have since had our family's case/file/name flagged in the CPS system so it can only be accessed by employees at a certain level and we have been banned from fostering or adopting ever again. CPS is not to be trusted – ever!

- Our adopted daughter, 14, accused my husband of 'touching her boob' after being home with us for three months from Colombia. DCF Florida took both of our children immediately, without any investigation. They never investigated, never spoke to us or any of our family, friends etc. Within 16 days they filed for a Termination of our Parental Rights. The case manager assigned to us never met with us. We did a background check on her. She possessed two social security numbers. One of a dead woman from Maine. She had several judgements and evictions on her record and numerous citations/tickets. This is the caliber of their employees making decisions about my children. We fought (and continue to fight) and won the TPR (termination of parental rights), but what does winning look like? We still don't have our children, they do. DCF has no understanding of trauma in children and they destroyed our family. They fed into the narrative my daughter continued to develop. DCF never once asked for any history on our daughter. The last words my son heard my husband say to him that morning was, "You're doing such a good job in school. I'm so proud of you. After school let's go fishing." I can't imagine what has gone through his mind since then.

There are thousands and thousands of heartbreaking cases like these, and worse. **There are far too many families being ripped apart by this "business" called Child Protective Services. Something MUST be done!**

Family X. I'm a dad. Post CPS destruction of my family. I live in nothingness. What is my 'feeling'? PAIN. Pain that cannot be measured. I don't even know how to convey my feelings about the pain I live with now that a group of government contract agents has destroyed my family. CPS. The pain left me lying in a fetal position on the floor in my son's room after they were taken from us. My hands were clenched, and I was crying like a seven-year-old. Something happened in my brain, and I began a downward spiral into a depression that haunts me still. It was, and still is, a physical as well as emotional pain. I am stabbed with pain every time I see a commercial of a happy family or get a reminder of "what should have been." I don't know if I will ever be right again. A friend told us, when you go through something like this, you will always walk with a limp.

I am a veteran of the U.S. Marine Corps. I have been through war and experienced things most people never think of, but I have never experienced anything as traumatic as having our children removed from our home without our permission, never to see them again, for nothing we did to cause it. It is unimaginable, and I am trying to find a way to live through it.

Family X. Our adopted daughter went to school, which was also my workplace, and told a teacher that I was abusing her - hitting, slapping, etc. I got to my classroom one day and was greeted by my principal and the high school principal telling me that they were filing a report. I immediately fell to the ground. I couldn't believe it. I have to say that both principals knew all the issues we had been having and were extremely sympathetic but if she reported it to them, it's the law to call CYS. We spent months with CYS visits at home and to our four bios at school. Our bios were horrified. I cried every time CYS called or came to the door. Adopted daughter flat out told them she did not want to live with us. I started to be hopeful that they would actually help us get out of the hell we were living in. In fact, at one point I begged the caseworker to help us. My husband got so upset with a CYS worker on the phone when he asked for help and she said, "We can't help you, there is no violence. There are no drugs. There is nothing we can do." He replied (not seriously), "Then I guess I will pick up some drugs on my way home and go beat my wife, so we can get help!" In the end although they dismissed our case we still had no supporting services or help. Some of my coworkers, who adopted daughter had manipulated enough for them to believe her, avoid me. We lost friends and family over the accusations. We just had to wait it all out until her 18th birthday and she could leave our home. I think it was the final straw for our bios. They just couldn't believe even with all the other things she had done to us that she would do that. It took me a very long time to recover emotionally. And I learned quickly who my true friends were and who was just around for the drama.

CHAPTER 22

Tattoo Man

August 10th. We drove home from Florida and from social media we learned Arina had hooked up with a 35-year-old motorcycle guy with tattoos all over his face and head. "Tattoo man". Who knew how they found each other. She posted on social media pictures of them together and said they were in love and were going to live happily ever after. He became her "go-to: guy every time she would run away in the future. They began a love – hate relationship.

Dima asked if I knew anything about Arina. I told him what I had read in the social media post.

August 11, 2015. 1:00 a.m. My phone rang. It was the Novi police asking me to come to the station right away. (I was dead tired from driving through the night to get home from Florida the night before.) All three Ukrainian boys were at the police station to report Arina missing. Dima thought I was lying when I told him about Arina the day before. (Their belief system was all skewed because of their own proclivity towards lying so they believed everyone lies.)

I told them again there was already a missing person's report on file and the police had been alerted that she was with "Tattoo Man". I tried to convince them that Arina is 17 and we couldn't make her come home. There was nothing the police or we could do.

Me: "Boys, we need to all just go home and get some sleep. There is nothing anyone can do to make Arina come home."

They just stared back at me. I looked at the officer and shook my head.

Me: "Officer, is there anything any of us can do to make her come home?"

Officer: "No, she is 17 and can make her own decision."

Me: "Boys, let's go."

Finally, they walked to the car.

We returned home from the police station and I logged onto social media to show them Arina's posts hoping they would believe me and we could all go to bed. It was now after 3:00 a.m. I pulled up the page and there was Arina, almost completely naked, in bed with tattoo man who was also mostly naked. The boys looked at each other, shook their heads and began talking fast in Russian. I asked Viktor what they were saying, and he said, "She is a dog. She disgusting. That man disgusting."

They all climbed the stairs and went to bed - finally.

Tom took a screenshot of the pair just in case we might later need proof of what she was doing. Later, we showed that screenshot to numerous police officers and during future CPS investigations. Within two days the photos disappeared from her page. Gotta love screenshots.

DOCUMENT. DOCUMENT. DOCUMENT.

Keep detailed records of **everything**. Papers, recordings, video. Police reports. Medical reports. Keep a journal. Take pictures. Documentation saved us on many occasions. When CPS came after us the fourth time, having pictures of Arina's destroyed room, the broken door and images caught on social media went a long way in our defense. If you don't have documentation, it's your word against theirs and they are "poor defenseless orphans" (sic). You **WILL** lose.

Family X. Imagine sitting in your easy chair after a long day taking care of your four children, all adopted. Three of the four are in bed and the older teen girl is sitting at the table doing her nails. You get up to treat yourself to a soda and the girl, completely out of character, sweetly asks if she can get you anything. You're surprised because historically this girl has been verbally abusive and argumentative about everything. You are hopeful this means you're in for a nice evening instead of the normal arguments and say, "Yes, please, and thank you."

A few minutes later you are sipping on a nice cold soda thinking happy thoughts. Then something isn't right. You feel strange, as if you aren't actually in the room. The next thing you know you wake up in a hospital bed. You find out that you started hallucinating and no one knew what was going on with you. Your husband drove you to the hospital where it was found that you had taken a hallucinogenic drug. The police are on their way to question you.

You find out a few days later that your teen girl had purchased drugs at school and put it in your soda with the hope you would die. Lucky for you it wasn't a high enough dose.

Since it couldn't be proven you didn't take the drug yourself or that she was the one who gave it to you there is nothing done to her. The girl ends up moving in with another family in town who is happy to treat her like a princess. They start bad-mouthing your family all over town for not taking good care of her, telling them you are druggies and that you've been abusing her. That is, until princess starts treating them badly, too. The cycle continues.

RAD
Destroying good families everywhere.

CHAPTER 23

Catching the Thieves

More money was missing. We did our best to keep very little cash around, but life is life. I began keeping my purse in a locked drawer in my office, which was also locked. Tom's security camera finally caught Viktor, Dima and Sasha breaking into my office, then breaking into the locked drawer and rifling through my purse, pulling out money.

Keep in mind, we spent more than $100,000 to give these four teens a future, different from what they undoubtedly would face in Ukraine. We are still so deep in debt I don't know how long it's going to take to pay it all off. Long after they are all gone I'm sure. Then we caught them stealing from us.

We confronted all three boys about the missing money with the video tape of them stealing. Tom and I decided I would talk to each of them privately in my office to see what they would say. While I was talking with one, Tom would stay with the other two so they couldn't collaborate. It was the same conversation, three times. Almost exactly, which was weirdly funny.

First denial.

Me: "Dad and I know you have been breaking into my office and locked drawer to take money from my purse."

Boy: "No, I not. I not steal from you." Faces looked affronted I would even accuse them of something so terrible.

I show the video. Faces changed. From arrogant to upset they'd been caught, then immediately defiant. It was so interesting watching their faces. They all demonstrated the exact same reaction sequence.

Then the justifications began.

Boy: "It was just one time."

Me: "I don't think so."

Boy: "It only a small number of money."

Me: "It doesn't matter how much money it was, you still broke into my office and into my drawer, went through my purse and took my money."

Then, realizing we had them taking money on several occasions and we knew exactly how much was taken, the next tactic was to roll over on each other.

Boy: "I only did it a few times when they make me. It was "their" idea and they make me steal with them. (They each blamed the other two). I not want to steal from you. They make me."

Me: "Really? You didn't want to steal from me?"

Boy: "No. I love you."

Only when you want something or are in trouble and want me to go easy on you. I didn't actually say that aloud. Later to Tom, though.

One after the other said the same things.

Me: "How did this all begin?"

Boy: "We up in Viktor's room. He tell us how he steal from you a long time. He say you leave money on desk or in purse and it easy to take. You lock door. He show us how to break door with knife. We change to watch for you come and other take money. Sometime Viktor watch, sometime Dima, sometime me. We go Viktor's room with money."

Me: "Did Arina do it when she was here?"

Boy: "Yes."

Viktor was slightly more evasive when it was his turn. Once we watched the video he jumped straight to defiant mode.

Viktor: "I steal from you, you steal from me."

Me: "Oh really. When did I steal from you?"

Viktor: "You take my pay and only give me $30. You steal rest."

Me: "Viktor. Every week when you get your paycheck we sit down at my computer to go through your account. I show you how much money you have and what you have spent your money on. Isn't that true?"

Viktor: "Yes."

Me: "Didn't I just show you last week you have almost $700 saved up?"

Viktor: "Yes."

Me: "Can you tell me where I stole money from you?"

Viktor: "You no let me have my money so you are stealing it."

Me: "Viktor, didn't you agree for me to save your money so you can buy a car when you have enough?"

Viktor: "Yes."

Me: "It was wrong for you to steal from me. I have not stolen from you. And Sasha and Dima told me you've been stealing for a long time, even before they came home. And you showed them how to steal from me. What do you have to say about that?" Shrugged shoulders.

Me: "How much money have you stolen from me?"

Viktor: "$100."

Me: "Really? I think it's more like $1,000 from you alone."

Viktor: "Maybe." He shrugged his shoulders again.

Me: "Well, you are all going to pay me back for all of the money you stole from me." He got up and yelled at me in Russian, ran out of my office and slammed the door, then ran out the front door.

Tom and I felt completely betrayed at this point.

(Arina was just as much a part of it when she was with us and the boys admitted she instigated not only stealing from my office but rifling through Tom's stuff and in Garrett and Katherine's rooms, too, with no remorse.)

None of them grasped the concept that stealing was wrong. They completely justified they were owed money and we were in the wrong for keeping it from them. They told us we should be giving them money every month to spend on what they want. Back to the American T.V. shows. I thought the only thing that would stop them in the future is thinking we had cameras and would catch them. I showed them tiny cameras on Amazon and they realized they wouldn't get away with it anymore.

They all had jobs. They all made good money. They all had savings accounts. They had no need to steal from us. They even took my good Ukrainian chocolate a friend brought back for me. They blamed each other. They said they were sorry. They said they wouldn't do it again. We didn't believe them. They were pathological liars and thieves. We weren't their family. We never would be. We were simply people for them to take from, I resigned myself. I felt violated. I just wanted to move on with my life and be done with the nightmare.

August 14, 2015. I realized I was in a place I'd never been in my life. In 57 years I'd had my share of tough times like everyone else, but nothing compared to this. I was fighting for my sanity. I cried all of the time. And I'm not a crier by nature. Now tears were ready to fall at a moment's notice. I cried when I woke up, when I was in the shower, driving to an appointment, when I hit my leg against a chair and the pain of the break shot through my body. I cried for the pain, but more for the wreck my family had become. I hated wearing the walking cast. I hated the guilt of what had happened to my family more. My heart was broken. Anger, sadness, frustration. Dreams dashed. Futures ruined. A totally messed up family. More than a year of no sleep and being completely on edge waiting for the next assault on our family. Never being able to relax. It was two weeks since the attack and my leg was healing too slowly. The pain was a constant reminder of failure.

Honestly, I don't know what I would have done if I hadn't been able to talk to Yahweh at all hours of the day and night. He was (and is) my rock. And then in dawned on me. To be grateful. For all of it. WHAT? That's insane. I guess it would be to anyone not in relationship with Yahweh. For anyone who is though, it makes perfect sense.

Let me say it this way: I say I have a relationship with my husband. I love him dearly, but I never spend time with him. Or I only spend time with him when I need something or want something. That wouldn't feel very good from his end of things. It becomes very one sided and selfish.

That's how I treated Yahweh before all of this. Not anymore. Through this I learned to talk to Him all the time about all kinds of things. I praised Him through the storm. I actually formed a relationship. Dang. I guess it took a lot for Him to get through this hard head and as hard as it was and still is, if it brought me to where I am with Him then I will count it as good. Very good. And I'm grateful. I trusted Him to bring my family through this trial and at the same time, into a better relationship with Him. Then it would all be counted worthy.

Side note. If you have a selfish relationship with the Creator of the Universe and the only time you talk with Him is when you're in trouble, well, guess what? He just might allow trouble so you'll talk to Him more. I know if the only time I talked with my husband was when I needed his help with something he would most likely go out of his way to make sure I needed his help more often. It's no different than our Heavenly Father. Sad it took me 57 years to realize that one. Maybe you'll get it faster than I did. Hopefully. Learn from my mistakes. Don't do what I did.

Or do it differently.

We found out from friends that Arina was all over social media begging for money and as usual telling everyone how horrible I'd been to her, in a bid for sympathy. Thankfully, most of my friends knew the back story and were not buying her sales pitch.

I think I understand RAD now and as painful as this is at least I understand it's not really about us. With RAD children/teens it doesn't matter who the person is, it could be anyone. Sadly, Arina, Dima and Viktor will most likely continue their cyclical behaviors their entire lives unless they decide to seek help.

And then I wonder about this RAD. How much do we blame on RAD and how much on them? Arina was 17 then. She knew she was lying to us in the orphanage. She knew what she did was wrong. She knew exactly what she was doing when raging out of control and destroying her bedroom. She knew exactly what she was doing when she got online and started flirting with men, then sleeping with them so they would buy her what she wanted. The same with the two boys. They knew what they were doing was wrong. Where is the line between justification for RAD and taking responsibility for their own actions? They were not stupid. They were actually quite intelligent. I write this because if I'm thinking it, most likely someone else is thinking it, too. Maybe the right person will see this who does know more than I do and start making changes where it will count.

AND please...please...please...for anyone thinking about adopting please research background on the orphan and look for possible attachment issues/RAD. Pay for an outside therapist. If there are possible issues, think long and hard, then decide if you are willing to take on a potential bomb. And you are going to have to get counseling. Serious counseling, for years, from a RAD trained therapist. And the RAD needs to agree to the counseling. AND...if they are over 8 years of age with RAD, beware it will take even more effort on your part, and theirs, to modify their behavior. They are so conditioned it will take a miracle to make a difference. And it **will** have an impact on your family.

We had no idea about RAD. None. Zilch. It's like an incendiary bomb went off in the middle of our family. There is shrapnel everywhere and every single person in our family has been hurt by it.

We received a notice in the mail of court costs for Arina's trial. Not my problem, thankfully. I was not allowed to pay the bill even if I wanted to. I couldn't afford to. Then, out of nowhere, I got a call from a blocked number. Many times the police came up like this so I answered it, then wished I hadn't.

It was "Tattoo Man" of all people. (Seriously the audacity of some people. This 35-year old man, who was shacking up with my 17-year-old daughter, called me, her mother, to ask for Arina's papers so she could get a job. His tone of voice as if he was a trusted family friend. In what universe was this okay?)

I asked him, "Are you aware Arina is just 17?"

He replied, "Yes." Yuck. Pervert.

He talked to me like we were working together in her best interest saying, "Yes, I am trying to get her a job and she is helping around the house while I'm at work. I have a good job and I make over $100,000 a year so she will have a good life with me."

I stated, "I need to talk to Detective B. first before I do anything. Please do not call me again."

Tattoo Man answered, "She needs her documents."

Me: "Well, that's nice for her, but from here on out I am doing what is best for my family and not for Arina, who has done her level best to destroy my family. I am no longer putting her and her needs first." I hung up.

Did I sound mean? I was out of patience with her and her dreams.

Can I just insert here how sad I was at that moment? Sad we adopted Viktor, Arina and Dima and not some of the other teens I see posted on social media? It's like there was a big beautiful bowl of apples and we got rotten ones. I know that's not true, now that more time has passed. Out of that giant bowl of apples there are most likely only one or two that are good. That's one of the problems here. Social media lies. Well, people on social media lie. They create stories resembling something out of a magazine. I found that out when I started writing my blog and some folks messaged me telling me they were living my life. Really? That's not what I read on social media. From all accounts you have a dream adoption and life. It's part of what is wrong with this industry of adoption.

Hosting agencies lie.
Adoption agencies lie.
Facilitators lie.
Orphanage caretakers and directors lie.
Orphans lie.

Then, when all is said and done, and you are back home with a nightmare, **you lie.** Because it's easier to lie than to tell the world that you made a big, fat mistake which just ruined your life and your family. So, you lie.

And the fantasy about adoption is perpetuated. The truth stays hidden under a basket of broken dreams. Then someone else comes along, reads the fairy tale that is being written on social media and thinks, hmmmmmm…we should do that, too! A year goes by and there goes another broken family.

Try and tell me Satan doesn't have a huge hand in this. He has taken "help the widows and the orphans", a directive to Christians, and twisted it in his nasty hands until families are breaking right and left. There is NO WAY this is Yahweh directed. Yes, He will use these situations for His good and glory because He can. Just like bringing me to a closer relationship with Him. But the lies are definitely not of Yahweh.

The lying needs to **STOP!** No more hiding the truth. My hope is if you are one of those who is living desperately that you will get this book into the hands of every person you know so they know what you're dealing with and hopefully will support you. AND stop lying about your situation. You are perpetuating the problem.

August 25, 2015. Viktor left. BAM! Just like that. He was supposed to be saving his money, so he could move out and into an apartment. I had access to his savings account and it wasn't supposed to be touched. He kept $30 out of his paycheck to spend and the rest went into savings. One day I noticed he had no money in his savings. And his checking was overdrawn by $50. **All** $700 of his savings gone!!! I asked him, "What happened to all of your money?"

He said, "It none of your business. It my money. You steal from me and my friend is helping me now."

Me: "What friend?"

Viktor: "Not your business. My friend."

Me: How long have you known this friend?"

Viktor: "I met last week."

Me: "How old is he?"

Viktor: "Old. Not your business. Stop with questions."

So, the $700 he worked to save was gone, given to "some friend" with "no name".

I asked him, "Do you trust this friend more than you trust me?"

Viktor: "Yes."

There was no winning this.

Me: "Well, now you have no money and you owe the bank $50." He shrugged. I sarcastically said, "Viktor, if you don't trust me after all I've done for you the past two years and you trust this guy you just met maybe you should be living with him instead of with me."

He walked out of my office and I went back to work, shaking my head. How could anyone help a person like this? I was stumped.

About 15 minutes later Tom walked into my office.

Tom: "Did you know Viktor left?"

Me: "No, where did he go?"

Tom: "He was just talking to me upstairs and told me thank you dad for all you've done for me and then said you kicked him out and he was going to live with a friend."

Me: "I sarcastically told Viktor if he trusted his new friend who he handed his $700 to more than us then he should go live with his friend. I guess he took me seriously."

Viktor left and never said a word to me. The "thank you" to Tom was meant as a dig to me. I'm tired. I'm tired of being the bad guy in every single scenario. I was the mom who helped with everything at a moment's notice and then was treated like dirt. Every paycheck we sat and talked about his goals, his savings and his spending. I showed him on a spreadsheet I kept how much money he had spent in the past year and what he had spent it on. Instead of being angry with himself for constantly overspending, he was angry with me for "taking his money" - again. We had the same conversation every other week for more than two years. I would tell him I didn't take any money from him and show him the account. It was there in black and white. All his decisions.

I had never met such entitled, ungrateful people. To go from nothing, to having all we'd given them, to this.

So now it's two gone, two to go. I began wondering who I would be once they were all gone. Would I even exist anymore?

September 1, 2015. After Viktor had been gone about a week, he came home, rang the doorbell and I answered. He stood there while anger radiated from him. Why? I could not say.

Me: "Hi Viktor. How are you?" Using my most cheerful voice.

Viktor: "I want my documents?"

Me: "What documents and why do you need them?"

Viktor: "My birth certificate and citizenship and security card."

Me: "Why?"

Viktor: "I get passport and move to Russia."

Me: "Why are you moving to Russia?"

Viktor: "I have friend there. I go live with him and maybe join Russian army."

Me: "Oh! That sounds dangerous. Why do you want to do that?"

Viktor: "I like Russia. Maybe I shoot Americans."

Me: "Really! Wow. That's interesting to hear. I have your Ukrainian passport which is good until February of 2016. You will find it much easier to travel to Russia with a Ukrainian passport than an American one and you already have it so it won't cost you any money. Do you want that?"

Viktor: "Yes."

I retrieved his passport and other documents. He was 18 so was legally entitled to them.

Me: "Here you go. Viktor. If you lose these I can't help you get new ones. Please take care of them."

He grabbed them from my hand and walked away, saying nothing. I found out a few days later from Sasha that Viktor was telling everyone, including Sasha and Dima, that I had stolen all his money and kicked him out of our house. I sat down with Sasha and Dima and showed them the accounting. I didn't include all the stealing Viktor did. At the end of the column it showed he still owed me $13. Once the boys saw all the money Viktor had spent and what he had spent it on, they knew I had told them the truth. However, they said they were still both worried I would steal their money and kick them out. UGH! What would I have to do before they would believe I had their best interests at heart?

Viktor continued to make stupid decisions. He quit his job at the restaurant and wouldn't tell us where he was living or working. I didn't get it. He let strangers in, but not us. Crazy stuff we dealt with in adoption land. Crazy stuff this RAD. We didn't know if he actually left for Russia or was still in the area. He talked at one time of moving to California to work as a stunt double. No one had heard from him.

And the roller coaster continued.

September 19, 2015. Arina was no longer with "Tattoo Man". That didn't last long. Dima told us she called him and she was back with "Horrid Man" who was still under investigation by law enforcement. "Tattoo Man" called to let me know she was gone and who she went to; as if I cared. (Do I sound heartless? Probably. I wasn't sure I had a heart anymore. It had been stomped on by these teens so much I felt it was just a blob somewhere in my chest. Our home without Arina was more peaceful and I didn't have to worry about being around her and her hurting me again or her going to CPS.)

Then "Tattoo Man" called me again to complain about Arina.

TM: "I want to talk to you about Arina."

Me: "I don't care to know what the two of you are doing. I've asked you to stop calling me."

TM: You don't understand. I know I should have listened to you. (HA!) I make a lot of money and I told her she didn't have to get a job as long as she cleaned up the house while I'm at work, cooked dinner and that's all. She refuses to do anything but sit on her phone all day looking at porn. I told her to stop but she won't. What do I do?" I shook my head and said, "Isn't that what I told you would happen? You didn't listen to me and there is nothing I can do so please stop calling me."

TM: "I told her she would get into real trouble one day if she doesn't stop this."

Me: "Again, I told you all of this. You didn't listen. There is nothing I can do. Please stop calling me."

TM: "I know I should have listened to you, but now I don't know what to do. She left me and went to some other guy in Detroit."

Me: "Well, that's what she does when she doesn't get her way. Now please stop calling me." I hung up.

Later that evening Dima walked up to me and said, "I just talk to Arina on message. "Tattoo Man" kick her out and she with "Horrid Man" at his house." Same story, different person. Never accountable for her actions. Always the other person's fault and she is the one kicked out. Broken record from all of the Ukrainians.

Arina must have a death wish, was all I could think. After everything we had told her about "Horrid Man", she went back to him. "Tattoo Man" told me twice he should have listened to me. You think???? He also told me one of the guys sending nude pictures to her was her "brother – A." Remember the guy, the son of the couple who took her in just before she broke my leg and went to jail back in July? The ones who were afraid I was too much into God? The parents who, even after I told them I knew what their son had done, only wanted to focus on how I would punish Arina?

The next day, irate Viktor showed up at our door again. He was spitting mad – at me - again. He was talking to me and when I say "talk" it's not your normal conversational talking. It was mean, angry, loud and accusatory. He was yelling fast with a very broken Russian accent. I had to really concentrate to understand him. I remained calm.

Viktor: "Why you call and cancel our apartment?"

Me: "What? I didn't call anyone. What apartment?"

Viktor: "Me and Dima apartment. Yes, you cancel. They say you call and cancel our apartment."

Me: "Viktor, I don't know what you are talking about. If you had an application for an apartment I was not on it so there is no way I could call and cancel it. It's not legal for them to cancel by me calling."

This back and forth went on for at least 15 minutes with me trying to convince Viktor that I could not and did not cancel his apartment.

I finally asked, "Viktor, have I ever lied to you?"

Viktor: "No."

Me: "Well, I'm not going to start now. By the way, why is Dima getting an apartment with you when he just asked to be enrolled back into the high school?

Viktor: "He can go school in apartment."

Me: "No, he can't. It's in a different school district. He would have to transfer to the other district."

Viktor: (Looking at Dima) "She wrong. You can go school Novi. You can live where you want and go school where you want. I drive you." (He had no car.)

Dima: "If they no let me go school in Novi I quit."

Me: "So Dima, I just spent all of last week getting you re-enrolled and you told Miss Shannon you were going to work hard in school this time and now you are just going to quit?"

Dima: "Yes."

I knew what was going on in Dima's head. "If I move in with Viktor I can do whatever I want, sit around all day and play on my phone and then go to work to make money to spend on whatever I want." I looked at Viktor and said, "I know the only reason you want Dima to move in with you is you can't get the apartment on your own and you need Dima's paycheck."

Viktor: "Yes, and I no care. I selfish, so what?"

Dima just looked at me and shrugged his shoulders. NOTHING we had tried to teach them had sunk in. Dima nodded it was okay by him. All I could do was shake my head.

I looked at Dima and asked, "So what about Miss Shannon? You just made an agreement with her that you won't sleep in class anymore. You won't be on your phone or play music and you'll do good work for her."

He just shrugged and didn't say anything. No big deal. What is it with these teens that they will listen to anyone but us? That Dima was listening to Viktor about being able to continue at school is absurd.

Me: "How would you get to school now that winter is coming, and the apartment is five miles from school and you only have your bike?"

Dima: "Viktor get a car and he drive me."

Viktor: "Yes, I drive Dima. You not my mom so you no tell us what to do."

In my mind I think, "Viktor, I hate to break it to you bud, but I figured out a long time ago I have *never* been your mom. I have simply been a caretaker in the long line of caretakers to you." I was sad, but there was nothing I could do to change his way of thinking.

Then Viktor dropped a bombshell. He said, "Yesterday I talk to "Horrid Man" on phone. He tell me you lie about him. He tell me you ruin his business. He tell me you lie to Arina and Dima about money for court. He tell me when Arina run away court was no money so you steal money from Arina and Dima. You lie to them. He tell me you a bad person."

I am defending myself to these boys and against this "Horrid Man" - again.

Me: "First of all, the day Arina, Dima and I went to court, "Horrid Man" was not there to see anything so he doesn't know what he is talking about. And, because Dima and Arina ran away to "Horrid Man's" house and all the trouble they caused, Dad and I had to pay for two attorneys and the translator and court costs and Arina's costs for housing for six days. The judge instructed me to make Arina and Dima pay for the costs so they would understand running away was bad so they would not run away again. Do you understand?" If there were never any consequences, nothing would stop them from continuing this behavior. (Great idea, but even that didn't deter them.)

Viktor: "That not what "Horrid Man" said. You lying."

Me: (Writing out a phone number from my phone on a piece of paper.) "Here is the name and phone number of detective B. at the police station. Please call him and ask him about it. I'm not going to argue with you about this anymore."

He stormed out of the house and slammed the door. We had no idea where he was staying but at least we knew he was still in the area. Apartment move in day was supposedly October 20th. We would see. A lot could happen in that time.

I told myself, "I am determined to have joy in spite of circumstances. I am determined to have joy in spite of circumstances." Repeat. Repeat.

Family X...

- I never experienced insomnia until we adopted.
- I never imagined that adoption could be so lonely.
- Who knew that adoption meant negative judgement by your peers?
- How could the happiest time of my life turn into my worst nightmare?
- I didn't know I could love and loathe someone so much, at the very same time.
- When I adopted I didn't realize I would be so exhausted and depressed from the adoption that I had only enough strength some days to shave just part of one leg. Sometimes it took me an entire week to get through both legs. And then I would cry because I had to start all over again.

CHAPTER 24

CPS Confrontations Continued

October 15, 2015. Bad turned to worse. I received a call from another CPS worker. "Do you know where Arina is?" "No." I replied. "Do you have a police report?" "Yes, we filed a missing person's report in August when the judge let her out of jail after she was convicted of domestic violence against me. I'm sure you've read the report stating they couldn't put her into juvenile detention because she was convicted as an adult. Then the judge felt sorry for her, so he let her go with no punishment whatsoever." I was angry and it all spilled out. I had to keep telling the same story over and over. Why was it they didn't have all these police reports? And did they ever check their own records about this girl? CPS worker stated, "Arina was dropped off at a shelter in Macomb County by an unknown male who, she told the intake worker, had picked her up at a gas station nearby. Arina was in the shelter a short time, then they noticed she left with a pregnant woman in a dark SUV. The shelter contacted us. Do you know who that might be driving the SUV?" "Not a clue." I answered.

Then, three more calls; Bam, Bam, Bam. CPS guy, Novi police and Warren police. All within ten minutes of each other. All said the same thing. Warren police had picked her up wandering around Walmart about 30 minutes from our home.

WP: "We have Arina Ray at the station. What do you want to do?"

Me: "I don't know what to do. The judge who ruled for her domestic violence conviction ordered she can't come near me or my home. I have no clue what to do."

WP: "Okay, we will keep her here until morning then and see what can be done."

A few hours later I got a call from a CPS woman from Wayne County. "Mrs. Ray?" "Yes." I replied. "We have your daughter Arina and we need you to come immediately to pick her up." I responded saying, "I don't know that I should do that. Arina was restricted from our home by the judge who presided over her domestic violence trial. She pled guilty to domestic violence against me and the judge told her she is not allowed near me or our home. I don't know what to do here." She said, "I'll check and get back to you."

At 10:00 p.m. I received a second call from her. "Mrs. Ray, you need to be in Mt. Clemens (an hour away) at the courthouse by 8:30 tomorrow morning. CPS will be charging you and your husband with neglect of Arina." She hung up before I could catch my breath. There would be no sleep for us that night. Would this nightmare ever end?

Tom was not able to get off work on such short notice, so I drove to court by myself the next morning. I walked into the mediation room and found that the court, without my knowledge, had assigned an attorney for me, one for Tom (even though he wasn't there), and one for Arina. They were all in the room along with the county prosecutor and two CPS workers; one for Oakland County and one for Wayne County. It became clear this was a battle between CPS and me. I wondered to myself how much this fiasco was going to cost. I wondered where Arina was and if she was going to be there. I hadn't seen her since the attack.

What a huge mess. This is hard to even write.

After two hours of bickering back and forth, no one in the room had a clue how to handle the situation. On one hand there was a 17-year-old, who didn't want to be in our home and constantly ran, for whom we were responsible. If we didn't allow her back home, we would be charged with neglect, which is a RED FLAG to CPS. At that point, CPS could *and most likely would,* go into our home and remove all our other teens and place them into foster care. A scenario both CPS officials made exceedingly clear to me was their goal. (I wonder if they take a class on how to look menacing to parents?) In the back of my mind I wondered how fast I could get out of town with Garrett, Katherine and Sasha and stay in hiding with them until they were 18. I'm not kidding. As I sat there listening to them threaten me I weighed various scenarios. I would NOT lose my children to these tyrants.

CPS told me we had three options: Option one I could go pick up Arina, my attacker, from where she was being housed and take her home. Option two we would relinquish parental rights for Arina and we would immediately be labeled with neglect and it was made clear that we would likely lose custody of our other teens. Or option three we could go to court, fight it out, and hope for a better outcome from the judge. Getting a better outcome was unlikely and would cost upwards of $10,000 on top of the money already being spent that day. I was terrified to have the neglectful parent label attached to us and have CPS remove Garrett, Katherine and Sasha from our care and custody - or that I would disappear with them and have kidnapping charges filed against me.

They discussed the order from the judge who presided over her conviction and the fact that Arina was not supposed to be near me. They had no clue what to do with that information. CPS kept talking about neglect charges. Time was ticking away, and the more time passed the more I felt boxed into a corner. Tears were burning behind my eyes, but I refused to let them fall in front of those horrible people. I closed my eyes for a moment and prayed for guidance. Then I stood up and firmly said, "Okay, this is how it's going to be. I will pick her up from the shelter. I will take someone with me as a witness and protection. If she gets into the car, fine. If not, the police, who will be on hand, can arrest her. If she comes home, I know she won't stay long. She'll be gone again in a hot minute. Then I will file another missing person's report. I will do that over and over and over again for the next eight months until she is 18 when I am no longer responsible for her." Everyone stared at me. "Where do I pick her up?" I silently thanked Yahweh for giving me the strength to be this person in front of all of them and in reality, do their job for them. I felt I was one against the ten of them. David against Goliath. But I had Yahweh on my side.

Leaving the court I got into my car and started sobbing. I was so angry and so frustrated we had no options except to bring this girl back into our home. What a nightmare!

I called my good friend Rebecca and asked her to go with me to go pick up Arina. I was sobbing so hard I could hardly speak to tell her what had gone on in court.

Family X...

- I thought because I had majored in Early Childhood Education and ran a day care for almost twenty years that I knew everything there was to know about little kids! Then I thought by fostering and adopting young children (all three girls arrived before age two and baby brother at twelve days!) that they wouldn't have had as many problems as older kids! I was dead wrong!
- Before I adopted I was considered a great mom by my friends and family and I'd been parenting for 21 years. After adoption I was told I needed parenting classes, needed to learn to love more selflessly and needed to learn to treat my poor orphaned children like my bio kids.
- I thought we'd be one big happy family. I never thought I'd lose my family and be fighting to build relationships with my bio kids again. My least favorite phrase - "you've changed" well, no kidding.
- I didn't know my adopted son would sexually assault two of my daughters and then me. I didn't know a therapist would suggest we keep him in our home after this and how much that would destroy us. I don't know if we will ever recover.
- Before I adopted I never thought I would be so bold as to tell a "friend" when they were giving me unwanted advice, "well, maybe you could take them for a few weeks and give me a break". They haven't talked to me since.
- I never knew how jealous I would become of people who have good adoptions. I hate, hate, hate, reading those stories on social media. I thought that would be me and that's so far from what we live every day that I can't stand the thought of adoption anymore.

Chapter 25

Tom Moved Out

October 16, 2015. The world was so messed up. I was alone in my home with Arina, my abuser. Who five minutes ago announced, "I want you dead. You make my life bad." I felt like I was living in a world where everything was upside down, but I was the only one who could see it.

Only in this messed up world would the victim in an abuse incident be required to bring her abuser back into her home AND to care for her. I wanted to SCREAM! Instead, I locked myself in my office and cried into a towel so she wouldn't hear me. Because it would make her exceedingly happy to know she upset me."

The day before, I was at home waiting for Rebecca to arrive so we could drive together to pick up Arina. I was already so upset, not wanting to get in the car to go pick up Arina once again, when a huge bomb dropped with another call from CPS.

CPS: "Tom needs to leave your home."

Me: "Why?"

CPS: "Because he is being investigated for sexually assaulting Arina. He needs to be gone immediately or we will have the police pick him up and have him taken to lockup."

Me: "There is no way this is true. She hasn't even been in our home for almost four months?"

CPS: "An allegation has been made and we have no choice but to investigate and he must not be in the home. When is he leaving?"

Me: "He will leave within 30 minutes. Before I leave to go pick up Arina from the shelter."

CPS: "I will be at your home tomorrow morning to interview you. I will interview your children at school."

I was stunned. I walked up to Tom who was in the kitchen. I would have given anything to spare my husband the pain of my next words.

Me: "Honey, can you go to Joe's house for a few days?"

Tom: "Why?"

My heart was breaking for him. I knew what this was going to do to him and I couldn't bear to utter the next sentence.

Me: "CPS just informed me that they are investigating you for sexually assaulting Arina and you have to move out of the house immediately or be arrested."

Tom: "What?"

Me: "I know. It's insane. They are going to talk to you tomorrow. The teens and me, too. Hopefully we'll get this all straightened out and you can come back home soon."

He packed a few things and drove away while I sobbed my eyes out. I didn't know what to tell Garrett and Katherine when they got home from school. I was afraid for my teens. First, I had to tell them Arina was coming back that night and now this!!!! "Yahweh, please help us through this nightmare!" I tried to think of words to soften those two huge blows.

Why had this happened? Because Arina found out I was driving to pick her up and she told someone she was afraid to go home because Tom had sexually assaulted her. We decided for precautions sake, that Garrett should go to a friend's home because at 17, and at 6'4" he would easily be targeted by her. I wouldn't take any more chances. It was time to start being proactive about protecting my family.

Remember how I said RAD's would go after anyone and anything they could to hurt the person they want to hurt? I got my son out of harm's way. I knew she would do anything not to come back to our home. She made up this horrible lie thinking CPS would give her to another family instead.

The next day we found out that both CPS and the police knew she was lying. Again, she thought she would be in big trouble with us. (With no history of punishing her, we were mystified why she kept thinking this way.) She thought putting someone else in the spotlight would take the focus off her. It was her pattern.

How did we all know she was lying? The timeline. Remember, I hadn't seen her since she was arrested in July. Tom hadn't seen her since early July when she originally ran off with that couple and their pervert of a son.

During July she was with the other couple. There was the extensive CPS investigation at the end of July, including Arina seeing a psychiatrist, and the only thing she alleged against Tom was he was always drinking and drunk most of the time. There were zero allegations of physical or sexual abuse by Tom towards any of our teens, including her. Arina told investigators during that investigation that I was the one physically abusing her, not Tom. At the time of those interviews, she felt she was in a completely safe environment, was not going to be forced to come back in our home, and she would have spoken openly and truthfully had anything else been happening, or if such a story would have been to her advantage. Since then she had not been in our home AT ALL. Not for one minute. She had not seen Tom since she left for work that day back in early July. And knowing her, if there really was abuse, she would have told CPS, the police, and the couple she was with at that time. She hadn't alleged any such thing.

BUT, CPS still had to follow protocol. REALLY? Who wrote their ridiculous protocol? Why didn't anyone exhibit a little common sense?

Both Tom and Garrett moved out.

I drove with Rebecca to pick Arina up from the facility. We arrived at the facility and waited in the lobby for them to bring her to us. A woman from CPS was there as well as a police officer and someone from the facility. The woman from CPS asked in a snotty voice, "Has your husband left the home?"

I replied, "Yes. I reported to J. from Oakland County CPS earlier this afternoon that he was gone."

She said, "Well, I had to ask." I glanced at Rebecca and tried to hold it together.

They brought Arina to us. The CPS woman started to speak but I interrupted her and said, "Let me just go over the ground rules here. These are directly from the judge in Oakland County who oversaw her conviction of domestic violence against me in July, as well as the mediator judge from Children's Village when she was picked up from the suspected trafficker earlier in the spring. There will be zero computer or internet time. There will be no phones. If she is caught with a phone she will be turned over to the police. She will get up at 6 a.m. when the rest of the family gets up. Since she refuses to go to school, she will either do chores or find a job. She is not allowed to be in our home alone with me per the judge's orders and for my safety. When my other teens leave for school she will either leave for a job or go to the library. She cannot come into our home unless there is at least one other person there to protect me. Is that understood?"

CPS: "Um, I'm not sure about these rules."

Me: "Then you need to take it up with both judges. This girl physically assaulted me in a public place. She was convicted, as an adult, of domestic violence. She is a convicted felon. I'm afraid of her and what she will do to me if we are alone with no one to protect me. She has told me she wants me dead. She broke my leg and severely bruised my arms and head. It's why she made these false claims against my husband, who she hasn't even seen since the beginning of July. She turned the heat on us, instead of where it belongs, on her. In fact, since the last CPS investigation, where she alleged my husband was drunk all the time and she never said a word about being sexually abused by him, she has not been in our home or seen my husband. She is a liar. Like I said, if you have a problem with these rules, call the judge."

CPS: "Well, I guess. Okay."

I couldn't really enforce these rules because I was responsible for her and I couldn't force her to leave the home. But I said my piece in front of witnesses before walking out the door with Arina and Rebecca. I was, once again, in a no-win situation.

Rebecca sat in the back seat with Arina because I was afraid she would do something to me while I was driving. Rebecca attempted to talk to her and asked Arina why she accused Tom when she knew it wasn't true. Arina admitted someone in the shelter had told her it was a way to help her not be forced to go home and maybe be put with another family, so she lied.

No matter. The ball was rolling and Tom could not return home until the investigation was complete. We were told by CPS we should count ourselves lucky they didn't put Tom in jail during the investigation because that was the normal process. COUNT MYSELF LUCKY?? Seriously???? Where do they get the crazy idea we should feel lucky in all of this?

Tom stayed with one of our older sons. The other four teens were in school during the day and Arina refused to leave the house. So, there I was. Alone. With her. Afraid.

Garrett and Katherine were destroyed. Katherine burst into tears when I told her we had to let Arina come back home and Tom had to move out. Garrett was in shock. Our family was decimated by this one girl who held all of the power. They felt completely helpless. We all did. Garrett went to stay with his best friend.

CPS once again went to the high school to interview the four teens. Before Garrett and Katherine left for school they informed me they were going to refuse to talk to the CPS officer. They couldn't tolerate the thought of bad things being said about us. Sasha listened to them and nodded his head in agreement. He was going to refuse, too. They all walked out the door together.

Then minutes later Arina walked into the kitchen where I was cleaning up.

Arina: "I hungry. You make me breakfast."

Me: "Did you start cleaning your room?" I had told her the mess she left months ago needed to be cleaned today.

Arina: (laughing) "No. I no clean. I hungry. You make me breakfast. Then I go library."

Me: "Remember the judge said no internet."

Arina: "I do what I want. Give me food."

Me: "I made everyone oatmeal and toast this morning. There is some left for you on the stove."

Arina: "No! I no eat oatmeal. You make me eggs. Now."

Me: "If you refuse to eat what I make for everyone, then you can make your own breakfast."

I walked out of the kitchen, into my office and closed and locked the door. I decided I would stay in my office behind a locked door until she left. I heard her bedroom door slam, then open again, then slam again. Then the front door opened and slammed. She walked by the window to my office, turned to me, screamed something in Russian and gave me her fist before walking down the driveway and towards the library. I walked over and locked the front door and started crying. CPS was coming to see me after they finished at the school. I didn't know what to expect if Garrett, Katherine and Sasha stood up to him. My home seemed weird. Like it wasn't my home anymore. I wasn't safe in my own home.

October 27, 2015. Tom and Garrett were gone from our home for a full week. Accusations Arina made were hard to forget. And we were on guard. Constantly. The amount of time I was alone with her was small and during those times I stayed locked in my office. I could hear her ransacking the house, looking for anything she could find of value. I didn't care anymore. I just wanted to stay safe. She knew it, too. She knew I wasn't going to confront her with no one else at home. Things were being stolen right under my nose and I did not care. I stayed locked in my office. I left her food on the counter. She got what everyone else ate. I refused to make her anything special. I didn't engage with her at all. I never spoke to her. She only wanted ammunition to use against me. She tried to goad me by telling me what she was going to do to us. I wouldn't look at her or respond in any way.

I drove her to the CPS headquarters in our county for her deposition with a Russian translator. I was not allowed to be present during the interview, so I was on pins and needles. Even though she had told us she had lied, no one knew what she would say in the actual interview. I sat at a table in a huge room, by myself. Waiting. Praying. CPS guy came in after the interview and told me Arina had recanted her accusation and told the interviewer, through translation, she had lied so she would be given to a new family or if she had to go back to us, so she wouldn't be punished. He asked her what kind of punishment. She said she would be grounded from going to the library and getting on the internet. YUP. We are such bad people enforcing the rules of the judge. I asked, "Is there anything that can be done to her?" He replied, "No, that is not our responsibility." I looked at him and said, "You know she will just keep doing this stuff to us, right?" "Yes, I know, but there is nothing we can do."

The following was an email Tom sent to his men's Bible study group while he was forced to be out of our home due to Arina's false accusations. A group he had been a part of for more than 15 years:

Dear friends,

This is from the article by that pastor that Ralph shared with the group:

Happiness begins with choosing to accept life, yourself, others, and the world for what they are. It's a choice God has left to you.

Perhaps the pastor who wrote this could tell me how to find happiness in my current situation. I have been sent away from my own home and staying with my son Joe because Arina accused me of sexually abusing her, even though she wasn't even in our home during the time period she stated it happened. Seems CPS still had to do an investigation even though everyone knows she is lying. The CPS worker tried to trap Kathe in a lie. He didn't realize **my wife never lies**.

CPS workers have told us to our faces they are just doing their jobs, or they don't want to lose their job, or this is just the way it's done. I don't care about your job, Mr. CPS. I want to be home with my family and have this nightmare over with.

Mr. Pastor who wrote the article, Yes, I am still joyful and in a good mood, even though I have to eat this sh*t sandwich.

Tom came home but lived in our bedroom. He moved his computer there and he ate, slept and worked there. He only came out when Arina wasn't home. We now had cameras everywhere so there was always a record. The cameras protected us from Arina and Dima's lies. Tom was never home alone with either of them, even with the cameras. **Ever.** I was never home alone with either of them. **Ever.**

I found her a job working for a house cleaning company. She worked there for two weeks when I got a call saying they didn't think they were going to keep her. She couldn't (wouldn't) even clean a bathroom well and her attitude was defiant. Great! What the heck did this girl think? I know, I know. She wanted some guy who would take care of her and she wouldn't have to do anything. She could play on the internet all day and just be catered to. I was hopeful she would keep the job for at least a little while because she had over $1,000 in court costs to pay.

Her new goal was to pay off her court costs then, when she turned 18 the next July, move to Chicago with friends. First it was Ukraine, then she wanted to move to Syria with her "new" boyfriend, then Germany, now Chicago. The plan of the week. She said she would do better cleaning toilets because she wanted the money to move, so I hoped. She had another phone. She told me Dima had given it to her before he left. (I haven't told you that gem yet. He had three in his bag as he walked out the door. Stolen most likely. He had no money. He would earn, then spend.) What did it say that I didn't care anymore that she had a phone? I knew when she was on the phone at least she wouldn't hurt me or my family? I was beyond caring. I lived in a home which was a jail for all of us except the one who should be in jail.

Domestic Abuse

Let me lay out this scenario for you. A wife goes to the police because she has been battered. She has a broken leg and bruising over her body. They arrest the guy. They file charges. He goes to court. Then he goes to jail, for at least 90 days. There is a no contact order or PPO and he is not allowed near her. He finds a new place to live. That's what normally happens.

What if it really went like this? He went to court, and got time served of five days because the jail was full. He is let out. The police call the woman and tell her she must allow her husband to move back into the home or she will be arrested for keeping him out of his home and they will remove her children and put them in foster care.

If you anything like me you are screaming, "NO WAY!" No way should any woman have to be anywhere near a man who physically abused her.

Yet adoptive parents are told that very thing *all the time*. And the person who was the victim is now being threatened by the system and told she is going to lose custody of her bio children if she doesn't. **This is senseless injustice.** To add insult to injury the abused woman is not only forced to have the abuser back in the home with her, she has to cook and take care of her abuser. **SICK!**

CHAPTER 26

Back in Ukraine!

And now Dima! He was back in Ukraine. Yup! Hallelujah! Praise Yahweh! On October 24th he flew back to his country. One week before flying to Ukraine he told us he wanted to take a vacation to see his friends and family there. He had enough in savings for a one-way ticket plus $350 spending cash. At the time it was about 23 Ukrainian Grivna to the dollar and that was quite a lot of money for him in Ukraine. He kept most of it in his bank account and took his debit card, so it would stay safe. Or so we thought, anyway. When he informed us of his plan, Tom and I looked at each other with raised brows. I asked who he would stay with and he replied, "My father."

We drove him to the airport and I went inside with him while Tom waited in the car. I turned after seeing him through security and felt a huge sense of relief sweep over me. One troublemaker gone far away! I couldn't see him ever coming back, at least into our home. He was 18, and as he continually told us, he was a man and could make his own decisions. Everyone told him the idea of going back to Ukraine was stupid, there was no work in Ukraine, and he didn't have enough money for a return ticket, but he went anyway. Even the Russian lady at our bank told him he was stupid, that we were good people, and he was throwing away a good job and a future.

I checked his bank account the next morning and he was down to $5. He had spent his entire savings in the Frankfurt airport on stupid stuff. I wondered aloud to Tom "How is he going to pay for transportation from the Kiev airport into Kiev and then how is he going to get to Zap?" We both shook our heads. We did our best to teach him.

Shoplifting as income.

The night before his flight left I got a call at around midnight from the police. They had Dima in lockup for shoplifting. (I wondered to myself when I would stop getting calls and visits from police in the middle of the night.) The night before he had been in Walmart shoplifting, but they didn't catch him at that time. Not until Friday morning when they saw him on recorded security tapes did they catch what he was doing. He was easy to pick out because he always wore an oversized jacket with big red patches printed with SECURITY. They watched for him to return, which he did the following night.

He asked us if he could ride his bike to Qdoba to meet up with Sasha who was working and ride home with him. Instead, he went back to Walmart to steal more things. He told me later, "I want stuff for Ukraine. I sell there and get money. It worth more there." That was his plan; shoplift to live the high life in Ukraine.

He had to pay $100 bond to get out of jail. If we hadn't wanted him on the plane later that day, I would have left him in lockup. Instead, I picked him up from the police department, paid the $100 bond out of his account, and drove him to Walmart to retrieve his bike. He never said thank you. Nothing. He was angry. He thought if he didn't get caught it was okay to steal. In the car, he ranted. No matter what I said, he didn't see a problem with what he did. That's when I asked him why he stole, and he replied, "I no have enough money and I want more money for Ukraine. I sell stuff there and make money."

He flew out on October 24th. He called me three days later to say he wanted to come back home. Wow! That didn't take long! I reminded him I had said I would not pay for him to come back home. I already paid a lot of money to bring him here the first time and I wouldn't do it again. If he wanted to come back he would have to find a job, save his money and do it on his own.

The next day I opened an email from the wife of the pastor in the town of Arina and Dima's orphanage.

Dear Kathe, Dima is in Zap. He just called me yesterday from the train and told me that this night he will be here. I meet him on the train station. He will go to his aunt today. He had a breakfast and now he is resting after a long trip. "A".

The next day I received a second email from her:

Kathe, I did not know anything. Why you no tell me Dima is coming? Why he come all this way alone? Connect with Dima straight away and speak to him. He told for everybody: my Mam will buy me a ticket and at the end of the week I will have money to back to the States. Sincerely, "A"

I wrote to her and said I would not send Dima any money for a plane ticket. He went to Ukraine against the advice of everyone and had caused many problems since we left the orphanage and he was not allowed in my home any longer. I also told her in the email that he had a warrant out for his arrest for stealing if he does come back.

She sent me another email a few days later:

Kathe, please help with Dima going back to America. He has no place to stay here and you are his mam. Please send him money. "A"

(I found it quite interesting this was the same woman from whom I had received emails about Arina prior to traveling to Ukraine to adopt. In those emails she had made no mention of Dima, and she offered high praise of Arina.)

I replied, "Please understand I will not send any money for Dima. I wish we had not adopted him. He told us he never really wanted to be adopted. He just wanted to stay out of the Ukrainian army. He lied to us. Arina told us she never wanted to be adopted. She told us she lied to us, too. Everyone lied to us and it has been terribly hard on our family. Dima is on his own now. That is what he wanted. He will have to figure things out for himself now."

I never heard back.

She wanted to know why I let him come all that way on his own. Maybe because he constantly said, "I'm a man and I can do what I want." He was 18,

I couldn't stop him from buying a plane ticket and doing whatever he wanted. Maybe because I was sick of having a liar, a thief and a pervert who constantly tried to molest my daughter in my home, and I looked at this as a way out of hell. Maybe I was just done after 16 months of having these two, who, while we were in Ukraine, you told me were angels, rip my family to shreds. I didn't actually say any of this, you know. Just thought it. I was still too kind to say it, even in an email. But maybe they'll read our story and then they will know that I know how everyone there deceived us.

The next day my phone rang. It was Dima, again, asking for money. Nope. My Ukrainian facilitator messaged me saying Dima asked him for help at the embassy and he told him he couldn't help. Dima would need money for the embassy anyway. I said, "That's fine. I'm not going to help him either."

Then I got a call from a woman at the U.S. embassy in Kiev. She told me Dima wanted to come home. I said, "That's nice, but I will not help him." I think she was taken aback. I spent 10 minutes explaining the past 16 months to her and telling her several times we will not, under any circumstances, take him back in our home. I would not help him financially get back to America or send him any money. She told me he had a few other people on his list to call. I told her about the bench warrant. She had nothing to say about that. We hung up.

Dima persistently called me. Daily. Begging for the money to come home. Begging for another chance. I finally got him to admit to some of the things he had done. I was pretty sure he only answered truthfully because he thought I might send him the money to get back to America.

Me: "If you want me to even think about helping you I need you to be honest with me about everything."

Dima: "I will."

Me: "How much money did you steal from me and the rest of the family? Just you. Not anyone else."

Dima: "About $500."

Me: "And what about the others?"

Dima: "We all talk about it every day. Up in Viktor's room. We got about $500 each."

Me: "Where did you get all of the phones?"

Dima: "Some we stole. All of us steal. Not Sasha. Some we buy from money we stole from you and dad."

Me: "What else did you do that was wrong?"

Dima: "I want to be sexual with Katherine many times, but I no do it."

Me: "Why not?"

Dima: "She strong and other people come. I try when you sleep, but her door lock and knife didn't work like other door." I was furious at that moment and it was a good thing Dima was in Ukraine and not in front of me.

Me: "What else did you do?"

Dima: "We steal from stores every day. It fun to steal and have new things. I was mad get caught at Walmart. They are stupid."

Me: "Who did that – steal every day?"

Dima: "Me, Arina, sometimes Viktor. Me and Arina every day."

Me: "I have to hang up now."

Dima: "Now you send money go back America?"

Me: "No. Why would I help you come back to America just to do all these bad things again and especially after what you did to Katherine? That was very wrong."

Dima: "Bleep, bleep, bleep." I can't make myself write out profanity. I've been called worse names. I hung up. I thought, "No way am I helping you come back here! You confessed to all of that! You confessed trying to rape Katherine! There is NO WAY I'm helping you come back to my beloved America. To my family. Not a chance guy. Not a chance." He made me sick. I was devastated to hear him confirm what he did to Katherine.

Someone asked me how many children I had, and I stumbled over the answer. If you counted the four from Ukraine, there were ten. But some of them never wanted me as a parent and after having them in our home, I don't want them as my children. On paper, I have ten. In my heart, even that I don't really know. You're probably really judging me right now and guess what? I don't care. I've heard it all before. How can you say that? Would you say that if they were biological? Nothing in this world of adoption is that cut and dried. Feelings get all messed up and love is both an emotion and an action.

We took the action. They did not.

We worked at having loving feelings. They did not.

We treated them like our children. They treated us like caretakers in a boarding house.

We gave them a home, food, clothing, nice things, fun times and a family. They gave us lies, deceit, theft, and physical, emotional and sexual abuse.

To answer the question, what if they were biological? I don't know. Really. If my biological children were this way toward me I'm not sure I would feel any different.

You can't want something for someone more than they want it for themselves. And honestly, we were not even on the same planet for what we wanted vs. what they wanted. We wanted a family. Where we loved and supported each other. With love, respect, kindness and joy. They wanted freedom from all responsibility and unlimited money to buy anything they wanted. To be accountable to no one. Those two philosophies aren't congruent. And for the past 16 months we'd been forcing the issue to our detriment. There was not enough love on the planet for these two philosophies to mesh.

Anyone who is still considering adoption be forewarned that I'm no longer the person to ask for support. I'm convinced beyond a shadow of a doubt that helping them where they are is better for them, and for your family.

CHAPTER 27

Gone Again, and Again, and Again...

November 5, 2015. I had an almost 15-year old daughter, good student, top varsity runner in both cross country and track, who was literally falling apart in front of my eyes. She was constantly on edge waiting for the next problem to surface that would wreak havoc in her world. Her world was no longer the safe, stable, loving place it used to be. Happiness was fleeting and fragile. She lived in a dark basement behind a dead-bolt locked door for safety, instead of her sunny bedroom, which had been turned into a shambles. Her dad and mom had been accused of atrocious things and she had lost total control over her world, which broke apart even further in October when her funny, loving dad was forced to move out and Arina moved back in. Wham, wham. Her grades plummeted. She didn't care anymore. We found out that she had contemplated suicide. What had I done to my family? Her bright future was slipping away. She was slipping away.

Viktor left here in September and we learned he was in Detroit somewhere. Angry as the day we brought him home. Sasha told us Viktor had called him several times, asking for money. Since Viktor moved, we found out he had stolen so much more money from us than we ever knew, and it was confirmed by the call from Dima. Viktor spent it on clothes, cigarettes and liquor. Those times we thought he was making progress was a lie. What a waste.

Oh those sweet, needy, adorable orphans in Ukraine, and other countries, even here in our own America, who turn vindictive and criminal once they are with your family.

November 15, 2015. Arina had lost her job. Shocking. (Not.) She went back to being ugly with us. Not only couldn't she clean a toilet after being shown several times, she made no effort to learn English so it was almost impossible for her employers to converse with her. She sat in her room doing who knows what or would go to the library for internet access. (I had changed our access code so she couldn't get on the internet at home, but somehow she always had it figured out within 10 minutes.) She'd be up every night, all night long, making noises downstairs so I started sleeping on the couch as a deterrent to her doing any major damage. She sat at the kitchen table and talked loudly on Skype® to several male friends all at once, all night long. She was loud – on purpose. I'd ask her to be quiet as people were trying to sleep and she just laughed at me.

"Make me," she'd say.

She knew I had no power.

Then she would go to bed at 6:00 a.m. when I got up to start my day, and sleep until about 2:00 p.m. before leaving for the library. I was getting no sleep.

The daily calls from Dima stopped after our last conversation when I blocked his number.

I didn't know if he was dead or alive or with family or friends, or on the street. I thought I should feel something about this. But I didn't, except relief that he wasn't here, and he was too far away to cause any more trouble for us. Then I'd feel guilty. Then I'd work to overcome the guilt. It was a terrible cycle. I hated him for what he did to my baby. I'd never hated anyone in my life. Every day I gave my thoughts about Dima to Yahweh. I wondered if I could forgive someone, yet still hate them. In the Bible, Yahweh talks about hating Edom. If He could hate someone, maybe I could, too.

Arina started her cycle of running away again. I drove across town at 2:30 a.m. to pick her up from yet another police department. She had been with "Tattoo Man" again, then left him again, or he kicked her out. He would take her back, then one of them got sick of the other, so he would drop her off someplace far away from his house. Then I would get a call from the police to pick her up. He had given her another new cell phone with a plan. What was wrong with this guy? The police picked her up loitering at the local Walmart.

She was snotty to them, rolling her eyes and shrugging her shoulders every time they asked her a question. Sasha rode with me to pick her up. When I met with them to pick her up one of them said to me, "She's a piece of work. Trouble. If she ever shows up in our jurisdiction again we're taking her to lockup. It looks like you have your hands full with her." We spent ten minutes talking while she sat in the back of their patrol car waiting. I explained a little of what we had dealt with while they both stood there shaking their heads. "Unbelievable." They both said. "Let us know if there is anything we can do if she comes this way again." Then they gave me their cards. She started screaming in Russian and kicking at the inside of the car door. I told them, "Let me get her home. Thank you." They forcibly took her from their car and put her into mine and told her, "If you do *anything* to this woman we will find you and put you in jail. Do you understand?" "Yes." She said nastily. Then she folded her arms and sat back in the seat and said nothing the 40-minute drive home.

She was home two days and gone again. Somehow, she ended up with "Tattoo Man" again. Once again it was a few days, then he dropped her off at a mall. Mall cops called the police, who contacted us once they got our info out of her. It took several hours for her to give up the information so once again, I drove in the middle of the night to pick her up, this time with Katherine riding along. And, as usual, she was spewing hatred at both me and the police officers. I had a similar conversation with these two offices as I'd had with the others two days before. Home again for a day and she stormed out, screaming hateful words at me through my closed office door. Around 4:00 p.m. I started getting texts from her. I assumed she was at the library and was getting ready to run again. She couldn't just close a door. She had to slam it shut.

"I hate you."

"Really? Why this time?"

"You are bad mother. I hate you."

I said nothing.

"I am boss of house now. I do what I want. You no stop me. I call CPS if you try stop me."

I said nothing.

"Are you there?"

I said nothing.

"I hate you. F you. F you family."

I said nothing.

"F you. I never see you again. You not my mother."

Tom walked in the door.

Me: "I don't think she is coming home tonight?"

Tom: "What happened this time?"

Me: "I don't know. She just slammed the door and left. I think she is at the library. She is sending me nasty messages; burning bridges. I think she has a way out."

Tom: "Guess that means another long night."

Me: "Yup. The amount of venom coming from her means she has a backup plan."

It was far easier for her to be verbally abusive in texts because she translated them first. Some words got messed up, but I got the message, loud and clear.

I was right. That night about 11:30 I got another text. "F you, I hate you and I never see you again." So, I filed another report. I'd lost count how many I'd filed.

CHAPTER 28

Gone for Good!

Time did not fly by very fast in our home. Arina had come and gone several times over a few weeks stretch and we had just learned she was living with a 57-year-old man on the east side of Detroit. Lots of pictures were showing up on social media of her trying on clothes in dressing rooms and eating dinner out. She was smiling – a lot. Her relationship status was "married".

Arina's court day came and Tom and I left for the courthouse. We wondered if she would show. We waited a half hour past her court time. No Arina so we left. A half hour later our detective called to ask if we'd seen her. We updated him. He called the courthouse and they planned to issue a bench warrant for her arrest. While we were talking, his other line rang. It was the court. She was there. She showed up with "Tattoo Man". What? What happened to 57-year-old guy? The detective came back on the line to say they had sent a car to pick her up. That meant she would be back with us again. I told him I wouldn't be home again until after five. I asked him to call and let me know what I needed to do.

He called around 4:00 to update me.

Officer: "Mrs. Ray, I just spoke with the man who is with your daughter and told him that he had no reason to be with a 17-year-old girl. I told him he was looking for trouble and he needed to get into his car and leave the area immediately. I also told him he should not contact her again. Now I want you to know that I can't really enforce any of that, but the man did leave."

Me: "Ok, thank you. Now what?"

Officer: "The court has put her on a payment plan for the money she owes. We are taking her to the police station and will hold her there until you can get there to pick her up."

Me: "Okay. I will be there about 5:00."

There was pure hatred on her face when she saw me walk into the station. I don't know if through words I can tell you how painful it is to see that look on someone who you've done so much and gone through so much for? It crushes your heart. What a waste.

Officer: "She is a piece of work."

Me: "I know. I hate that I have to take her back home again."

Officer: "I wish there was more we could do. She is belligerent and this guy she was with was really bad."

Me: "I know. We know your hands are tied and so are ours."

I felt completely defeated as I walked out to the car with her.

Arina yelled at me: "You hate me. You no love me."

I said nothing. Really? Hate her? No. Love her? At that point it was true I didn't love her. Not a bit. My love was gone. Through her actions though, not mine. I said nothing in the car. She yelled F this and F that all the way home. "I hate you. I hate you family. You family not my family." Thankfully the police station was just a couple of minutes from home. She continued yelling as she ran into the house and up the stairs. Katherine was there just inside the foyer when I walked in. I was sad she heard the stuff coming from Arina, but at the same time relieved I was not alone with her. Arina started throwing things in her room. I heard breaking upstairs. I went up and told Arina through the door, "If I hear you throw one more thing or break anything I am calling the police officer we just met, and he will come and arrest you and put you back in jail." The noise stopped. Katherine was stuck to me like glue. Arina opened her door, ran downstairs carrying a bag, and then ran out the front door. A new record. Less than 3 minutes. I waited 10 minutes, then filed another report.

I slept off and on that night and woke up to a Facebook message from 57-year-old guy.

Arina is living with "Tattoo Man", a freak with tattoos all over his face. His phone number is 222-222-2222. Hers is 222-222-2223. Do not tell them where you got this information or he will kill me. Tell them metro PCS gave it to you.

How much more bizarre was this going to get? I now had two creepy guys telling on each other to me about her. I didn't respond to him.

I was living in crazy land.

I called the police to tell them about the message. I could hear an officer in the background asking if it was about Arina. Yup, she had successfully built herself a stellar reputation with our police department. They sent an officer from the local department to "Tattoo Man's" home where Arina stood on the front porch and refused to leave. She was 17 and they couldn't force her. I was okay with that. The last time, it took me five days of her not being there for the stress to subside somewhat and to quit being so jumpy. Now the drama was on full force again and I was just as happy she was off the street and the police knew her whereabouts. We were off the hook for at least a few days – hopefully.

I started out this adoption journey as a strong woman, or so I thought. I sometimes wondered how others who might not be so strong handled the trauma. I feel so damaged now. Hopefully not beyond repair. I'm certainly far different from what I was. My children are different. My marriage is different. None for the better. At least not yet.

Living with fear, regret, and overwhelming guilt.

Family X. Imagine yourself sitting at your kitchen table, head bent over reading an article in a magazine. The house is strangely quiet, but you are taking these moments to catch up, to breathe, and to relax a bit before the chaos starts again. The next moment you are screaming in pain, so much pain that you don't know how you aren't dead. You stand up and turn around and there is your adopted son, 9, holding a paring knife that he has just shoved into your upper back and pulled out again. He is laughing. I'm going to kill you he says. And you know he means it. You run out the sliding door, screaming for the neighbor to call the police. You have blood dripping down your back and the pain is so bad you can hardly think. You're afraid to look behind you because you know he can run faster than you can. Your neighbor hears your screams and opens the door to you. You run past him and yell, "lock the door, lock the door." He does. You yell to call the police. Then he sees the blood and grabs a towel. What happened? Call the police. He does and hands you the phone. You tell the police that your 9-year-old son just stabbed you in the upper back and you are bleeding. That you are at the neighbors and you think your son is still in your home with the knife, but you aren't sure. You can't see him from the window.

The police arrive. An ambulance. The police go to your house looking for your son. They find him quietly playing in his room on the floor with Lego's. As if nothing happened. There is no knife visible. They ask him what happened. He said he was just been playing Lego's while his mom was reading in the kitchen. As if nothing happened. During the investigation you are asked if you hurt yourself and are trying to blame it on your son.

WHAT?? The paramedic tells the police there is no way you did it and that the wound was done in a way it had to be by someone else, the police ask you what you did to cause it.

REALLY?? Maybe look in the file you have on this boy at your station. How many times have the police been called out to our home? The police search and find the knife wrapped in a blood-spattered shirt in the boys hamper. The boy is taken to the hospital for psych evaluation. He stays two days and you pick him up and bring him back home because there is nothing they can do. That's all. Until the next time. All you wanted was to make a difference in the life of a child. You live in hell. You wonder if you will one day be the subject of a news story. Dead woman found murdered by her son. What went wrong everyone will ask? Why didn't someone do something before it got to this point? Why didn't anyone say anything? What no one will know is that more times than I can count I've tried to get him help. Unsuccessfully. I know it will take my death for anything to change. I'm resigned to that.

Stories pop up in the news from time to time of children or teens killing their parents, or someone else. I now check to see if they were adopted. Many times they were. In the comments of the stories people will ask why no one said anything. We adoptive parents want to scream at how many times we've reached out about these behaviors and been told we are either crazy or we are causing it, or we have to wait until they really do something in order for authorities to act. A news story popped up about a school shooting in Florida. Yup. Adopted.

January 2016. "Tattoo Man" called. Why he thought he could talk to me like an old friend was beyond me. I thought, "I'm not your friend! You're a pervert! With a love/hate relationship going on with a RAD 17-year-old."

TM: "She is out of control."

Me: "Oh?"

TM: "All she does is sit on her phone looking at porn and if I ask her to do anything she just screams in Russian at me. She screams at me to get her food and if I don't get it for her right away, she screams more."

Me: "I warned you."

I hung up. Not my problem.

An hour later I got a call from our local police. She had been dropped off by "Tattoo Man" who then drove away. I had to go pick her up. Last time she was home a whole three minutes. I wondered how long she would be home this time. Katherine insisted on going to the station with me. Arina was silent on the ride home. I pulled into the driveway and Arina opened the door before I completely stopped and ran into the house. She was upstairs by the time Katherine and I got into the house. We heard her throwing things. Why was it that she was constantly in destroy mode? That girl could turn a perfectly good room into a disaster in mere seconds. She ran to her room and ran right back out again and then out the front door. One minute. A new record!!

"Tattoo man" called an hour later.

TM: "She is sitting on my front porch demanding to be let inside."

Wow! He lived 45 minutes from us. I wondered how she got to his house and so fast. (I found out later she had called Viktor, who had somehow gotten a license and a car, and he had driven her) Great! Now we had one messed up teen enabling another.

Me: "There is nothing I can do." I hung up. When would this guy understand that I was not going to help him? Even if I had driven out there I couldn't force her into the car and it would have been a wasted trip. I did, however, file another obligatory police report.

A few days later the police called to tell me she was now with some other guy. We called him "Auto Parts Guy". The police told me "Tattoo Man's" local police department had been called when "Tattoo Man" and Arina got into a domestic disturbance. "Tattoo Man" kicked Arina out and then he actually moved across town. You might think I'm heartless when I tell you I got a pretty good belly laugh out of that one. How many times had I wished we could move away from all this mess!!

Arina met up with this "Auto Parts Guy" who, according to the police, was immediately in love with her and wanted to marry her. OH! So, this is the third guy in just a few months she is going to marry because they fell deeply in love in what – two days???

I opened a peculiar message. A friend of mine was friends with a woman in Florida who had hosted Dima and Arina many years before when they were first in the orphanage. Arina had reached out to her the day before and asked for help. She asked if this woman would pay Arina's way to Florida. And asked if she could stay with the woman until she could get on her feet.

My friend was in the loop on what we were going through with Arina and told her friend, who backed out of the arrangements she had been making with Arina. Smart lady. Whoever she was.

The police called me and told me "Auto Parts Guy" had called them to complain about "Tattoo Man". I told the police I did not want updates on her, if possible. I told them Arina had made her choices and she refused to listen to me and it just made it harder to be constantly called with updates. They agreed with me and were fine with not calling me with the drama she was involved in.

That was a huge blessing for us. Not only our local police department, but all the other departments we worked with on a local, state and even federal level were so kind to us. There were so many stories of parents being put through the grinder by the authorities and that hadn't happened to us. (Apart from CPS) Law enforcement had been caring and understanding and seemed to know exactly who these teens were right from the beginning.

This cycle continued for the first six months of 2016. During this time we heard absolutely nothing from Viktor. I'd gotten a few messages via social media from Dima asking for money and each time when I'd say "No" he would spew profanity at me, calling me a bitch or other endearment. I blocked him. A few weeks later he would open a new account and stalk me again. Arina had not been in our home since the last time she stormed out to run to "Tattoo Man's" place.

I was in the basement, which had been the dumping ground for stuff the past few months. I was working to reclaim it bit by bit. On this occasion I was downstairs looking for any of Arina's stuff to give to her once she turned 18 on July 7th. I didn't want her possessions in my home anymore. I opened a black garbage bag and inside were several sets of Dima's clothes and shoes all covered in human feces. Gross. I don't know how I didn't puke. I thought I was done with his nastiness, but he left us a nauseating parting gift. He would do passive aggressive stuff like that. Gross bodily stuff. I'm sure when he did it he was excited thinking about us finding it one day.

He messaged me once again. "Please help me come back to America. I'm sorry for lying and stealing and breaking things around the house. I will work hard to pay you back for the window I broke and the door and for my plane ticket if you help me. Just one more time. Please." He never mentioned being sorry for what he did to Katherine.

I responded, "No, I will not help you." and he started cursing at me again. Of course. He was lying once again. He was not remorseful. He only said what he thought he had to in order to get me to help him. That train has left the station, buddy. I might have fallen prey to your schemes once, but never again. Never again.

Family X. If only we had known ... Poop!

- I didn't know that I would find a group online and realize that all the poop issues we've dealt with over the years would give me a sense of community.
- I never thought our home would look like this. He took scissors and knives to the furniture, the cabinets, and the curtains. Everything is ruined. He peed on the carpet so many times we had to rip it out and now just have some rugs down. One couch we had to get rid of

because he smeared his feces all over it because he was mad at me for not giving him candy 30 minutes before dinner. He is 13 and I can't leave him alone for even one minute. I'm in jail. A putrid, horrible jail. In my own home.

- I didn't know that hours long manic fits, wiping poop on everything, and self-mutilation would be part of our adoption story.
- I never knew that there was a human being on the planet who would regularly eat their own feces.
- I never thought I would find rows of human poop on my porch roof because RAD adopted daughter refused to do it in the bathroom and instead climbed out her window and used the roof.
- That someone would be motivated to touch feces in any way other than accidental. Every day.
- When we adopted I never imagined I would clean feces off of random surfaces nearly every day. So much for being a neat freak.

July 6, 2016. The day before Arina turned 18. We were calling July 7th FREEDOM DAY in our home. We had a big party planned with friends to celebrate her not being able to set foot in our home ever again. I would not have to accept phone calls at 3:00 a.m. I would not have to drive across town and be forced to bring her back home. I would not have to listen to her screaming at me at the top of her lungs about how she hated me and how I ruined her life. Freedom. Such a liberating word.

I got a message from her. She now had a different last name. Another man. Demanding. "I want my stuff. I want my papers." She had no idea how happy I was this day had come. A day I had dreamed of for months. I already had her things and her papers in a box ready for her. I told her, "Tomorrow the box will be on the driveway at 4:00 P.M. I've gone through the house and have put all of your things in the box."

I'd purged everything. It was all sitting in the foyer in a container. I wanted nothing of hers left behind.

A large victory came at midnight. At that moment, the balance of power shifted from her to us. She no longer had dominance over us. No more police, no more CPS, no more middle-of-the-night calls. I could leave my phone off and not worry about someone banging on my door at 3:00 a.m. I could sleep in pajamas again. I could sleep for more than an hour or two again!

FREEDOM! THIS. IS. AWESOME!

Ah! July 7, 2016. Our Freedom Day! With just a small hitch, she came and went. Tom and I sat on the porch. Her new boyfriend peeled off with her in his muscle car and she was hateful as usual. She dumped out the big container with all her stuff, pulled out her official papers and left everything else behind. She took nothing, not even her mementos from Ukraine. (I will never understand this behavior. I do know unless she decides to get help she will never get better. That makes me sad. But I also know that I couldn't help her. I was still the enemy.) For the last time, we cleaned up her mess and dropped the leftovers into the dumpster.

Chapter 29

Surprise! You Don't Instantly Feel Great Again!

I know that much of what Arina and the rest of the Ukrainians did stemmed from deep trauma. I know in her case she has RAD which requires RAD trained professional help to even begin to live a normal life. Viktor and Dima also suffer from RAD. The biggest problem with these children/teens is unless they agree they need help and choose to go through the healing process you cannot make them. They are stuck. I have friends who have adopted as young as birth whose children have RAD. Even through years of therapy there are still enormous issues. It makes me sick. On so many levels. And helpless.

July 7th we had our Freedom Party! Many of our friends came over to celebrate with us. We had a huge cake and bar-b-que. The sense of relief was and is still enormous. I knew then that no matter what happened with Arina, I would never again be forced to allow her back into our home. I can, and will, say no. The countdown clock Tom had on his phone for over 16 months clicked to zero! That was a huge milestone for him. She no longer had any power over him or his home.

It was a great day. Sort of.

Garrett and Katherine were quiet, and I felt very sad. Somehow, I thought we would all feel better instantly. That didn't happen. In fact, it's now February

2018 and we are still recovering. Bit by bit things come bursting out, then that piece gets healed. It's been 18 months since Arina's 18th birthday and I still beat myself up because the heaviness still has such a hold on me. I feel like I should have been able to shake it off and get back to the business of life. Why is the weight still so heavy? I still cry – a lot. It's hard to get motivated over any of the things that had, before adoption, gotten me excited. I get angry quickly. Katherine does, too. I walk around with a smile on my face, crying inside. And then I get mad at myself for feeling so sad all the time. I am doubly angry because I really thought that on July 7th everything would be just fine again. It wasn't. And I don't know when it will be. Maybe I'm scared it never will be.

I want my family back – NOW! I want my daughter and son to laugh and smile again – NOW! I want my funny husband back – NOW! When that didn't happen instantly my sadness reached a whole new level. More regret. More guilt. Letdown.

And it's taken a huge toll on my business. It's impossible to put a good face on things when your family is so broken. I feel like I'm in a vortex spinning down and down and down. I just want to hide out from the world. I don't know how to make myself feel different – feel better.

CHAPTER 30

Hollywood Lies about Adoption

Hollywood. Several T.V. shows and movies have come to my attention that concern adoption in one aspect or another. I made myself sit down and watch them all to gain some perspective on what viewers are shown about adoption.

Hollywood's portrayal of adoption is much skewed and contributes, I believe, to the overall reasons why many are led to adopt. This idea of "saving" a child and doing what "God led us to do". None of these adoption stories are even close to real life. Except for the mom in the last scenario who is treated like a criminal. That is more real than any of us would want to think.

So much of adoption is based on emotion, which I have already addressed should NEVER be a part of the decision. These three glorifying adoption scenarios completely play down all negatives, if there are any to begin with, and show these adopted children/teens to be well worth the time and money spent. They show zero negative impact upon the adoptive family or bio children.

First scenario. A movie where a loving, godly couple with a younger teen son adopts a teenager who is troubled and older than their bio son. The bio son is against the adoption and the couple overrides his feelings with "we are being led by God to do this and we will do it and you have nothing to say in the matter". **BLECH!** I'll bet you're going to care when your bio son becomes suicidal because of abuse by the adopted son or when he completely turns your home upside down and you don't even know who you are anymore. Oh wait! This is a Hollywood movie. Not real life.

Before long they bring this teen home and trouble immediately starts, but it's nowhere near the magnitude of the troubles I talk about in this book. In fact, had our adoptions been like this Hollywood version this book would not have been written at all. We would all be living happily ever after with no PTSD, no trauma, no picking up the pieces of our lives that are in shambles.

In this story, after being brought into the home the boy was slightly argumentative. He went into his room and slammed the door. Wow! That's rough. No screaming profanities, pure rage or breaking furniture and dishes or anything else in his sight. I rolled my eyes at the T.V. screen. Where is the "I hate you and you're not my mom" or "you're a bitch and I'm calling the police on you and reporting you for abuse for telling me to do the dishes?" I said to myself.

Later the boy climbed out of his bedroom window because he is angry. He vandalized some property. He apologized, and the owner forgave him if he promised to clean up the mess. He apologized profusely and did all the clean up without ANY complaining. Not only that, he did such a professional job he was offered several jobs by community business owners. He worked later than asked and did more than the job required. The adults talked to each other about how special this teen was. (If you're an adoptive parent you're probably ready to puke right about now.)

WHAT? You mean the parents didn't have to threaten the boy to get him to go do his community service? To remind him if he doesn't show up he will have to do jail time and the parents didn't get any bad mouthing in return? That the teen didn't complain the entire time, waste a lot of time and got barely anything done so the owner had to call the parents several times and eventually the parents had to drop everything to drive over and practically stand over him to get him to do the job? And then he complained the entire time the parents were there and told them this was all their fault anyway, so they should be the one doing the work. Of course, the parents forced the teen to run off, steal stuff from the store owner and then damage her property.

Later in the movie he was late to an appointment and they were all disappointed. They were so sure he had turned a corner. Soon they found out he was helping someone who was in trouble, so all was forgiven. REALLY? That is a troubled kid? Even the bio teen within a day or so of the adopted teen coming into their family was all lovey-dovey and how can I help you transition into our family and I will have your back and not tell our parents you are doing something wrong and you are my brother and blah, blah, blah. By the end of the movie everyone was living happily ever after with the adopted teen fully integrated as a family member as if he was born there, and even had his own little thriving business, was an upstanding member of the local church and dating the pastor's daughter, who he just happened to help through a traumatic experience. SCREAM!!!!

I told Tom no wonder people go out and adopt. They want this fairy tale. And in fact, this is pretty much what we thought it was going to be like. We were wrong. Hollywood is WRONG!! THIS is **NOT** real-life adoption and if you believe it is like this and you adopt you're in for some BIG trouble.

Second scenario. Highly rated T.V. show. Famous actress travels to a third world country and adopts a little child. They are home and all of a sudden the biological father shows up and wants his son back. Seems the child was taken from the parents by an orphanage who told them they were going to give the child a free education. The orphanage then makes money by selling the child through adoption. The parents find out the child has been adopted and follows the child to America to get him back. The woman goes to court to keep "her" child. Everyone feels sorry for the woman. And I agree it wasn't her fault in the beginning. Her heart was in the right place. This is where reason should have taken place and not emotion. Before going to this country, she had zero intention of adopting. She hadn't researched it. She didn't even know the right questions to ask. She did no investigation on this child or even on adopting. Pure emotion.

However, once she found out the child had a set of parents, and siblings, back in their home country, she should have returned the child to where the child belonged. Period. This happens in real life, more than you think. Here is a CNN article with real life situations. This story has a somewhat happy ending though. Thank goodness for good people who do the right thing even when it is incredibly hard.

CNN: Kids for sale: My mom was tricked. In this true story, a 7-year-old little girl from Uganda is reunited with her birth family after her adopted family in Ohio learned the little girl was stolen from her family by the orphanage in order to make money by adopting her out.

(http://www.cnn.com/2017/10/12/health/uganda-adoptions-investigation-ac360/index.html)

Third scenario. This one made my blood boil. Police found some children who had been taken by traffickers. One boy about 9 years old was traced back to a couple who adopted him from Asia. Seemed the father traveled a lot on business, so mom was left with adopted son plus twin daughters who were little. Mom ended up re-homing without dad's knowledge when he was gone on another business trip. The plot unfolds with police learning the re-homing website was really a front for traffickers. Now in real life, re-homing does take place, and I'm sure there are some scary organizations (because there are a whole lot of bad people who want to make money off children) but there are also many who are working to do the right thing. There are home studies, attorneys, and the whole gamut of adoption requirements that take place and the show took great liberty here showing a worst-case scenario to show this wife to be a nut case. Quite unfair and that's only the beginning. Where do they get this stuff?

When the police show up at the home the father is incensed at the wife. How could you? He is my son. He is such a good boy! The wife, of course, saw the real child. She looks like one of us; drawn, exhausted, not really alive anymore. She tells police that the child was constantly lying, stealing, abusive, and that she was afraid for her daughters. Boy did that hit home. The police and her husband treat her like a criminal. No way is that sweet boy like you say. (Triangulation and manipulation at its finest). They don't believe a word she says. In fact, all the times she told her husband prior to this he blew her off. **HUSBANDS believe your wives!!** I wanted to slap this man!

The program goes on to show how loving the boy is to everyone he meets and the mom, who has borne the brunt of his brutality is now under a cloud of suspicion.

In a real life scenario, she will get divorced and lose custody of her daughters, who now live with her ex-husband and the boy who is now physically and sexually abusing her girls and there is nothing she can do about it because she is not even allowed visitation. THAT is real world. Where is Hollywood on that one?

Stupid! Stupid! Stupid! After those three shows I realized if Hollywood is this messed up it is no wonder many of us have a skewed perspective on adoption! We are set up for failure from the beginning. We expect the fairy tale and we end up kissing toads.

Seriously this is like watching Cinderella® and after she got married not only is her new husband not Prince Charming at home, but he is a drunk and a verbally and physically abusive man. To everyone outside the marriage he is still Prince Charming. Once in the home with Cinderella® he is a monster. She tells a few of her friends and someone at her church. They tell her one or more of the following:

I can't believe that, he is such a nice prince.

He just needs more love.

What are you doing to him to cause this behavior?

Just give it more time.

He had a bad childhood. Just love him through it.

You should get some counseling to be a better wife for him.

Are you sure? He seems amazing to me. I would love someone like him.

NO! They don't say things like this if you have an abusive spouse. Or at least I hope they don't. If they do, you need better friends and a new church. People don't say these things if you have an abusive spouse. They tell you to get the heck out of there – FAST. And they are there to help you move. BUT people have no problem saying it to you about your adopted child/teen.

Back to Hollywood. Hollywood has it WRONG when it comes to adoption. Totally wrong. It's a fairy tale no different from anything else they put out. It has zero basis in truth.

Once more I will offer the disclaimer that yes, there are some good adoptions. If you have one of those or you know someone who does, good for you. I'm over the moon happy for you and your family. In the lottery of adoption, you won big. But there are far more losers than winners in the lottery and in the adoption world. I would like to see some reality from Hollywood so more families at least know the truth of what they just might be getting into instead of believing the fairy tale which could potentially destroy their family.

Family X. Boy X – six years old - is home today and kicked me, HARD. He threw his breakfast at me, then fell to the floor screaming that he hates school, and everyone hates him. He refused to do any homework last night and just sat there breaking pencils. Yesterday he told his teacher that he was "done with her" and told her to F off. I'm just not sure what else to do, or how much longer we can control him. He's getting so big, too big for me to handle, too big for his teachers to handle. And honestly, he is starting to scare me.

He is still urinating everywhere. On my walls, beds, furniture, everywhere. We finally just took all his bedroom furniture to the dump because it was so ruined with pee and smelled horrible. His psychiatrist has tried so many meds. None of them are working and some make it even worse. I can't get him into the car by myself when he has a melt-down. Everyone else is at work. I'm so tired I just want to give up. Why didn't we dissolve this adoption? I feel like a total failure. I wanted to help him, change him, and give him a shot at a future.

His psychiatrist told us to get a thick but small mattress to put in the hall next to the bathroom door. We did and are taking turns sleeping on the couch to keep an eye on him. We are all so exhausted. I want to just put him on a plane back to Ukraine with a note and just go ahead and be THAT CRAZY WOMAN! I truly think it would be well worth the humiliation. Do you think my report to the Ukrainian consulate this year will matter?

Annual Reports

When you adopt a child/teen from Ukraine you are required to file annual reports with the consulate. I'm sure other countries have something similar. They ask you questions like date of last medical exam, height, weight, information on child's personality and physical development, new accomplishments, daily routine, diet, eating habits, sleeping patterns, likes & dislikes, adjustment to new family, interaction with family, acceptance by extended family and additional comments. And they want 8 – 10 recent photos, along with copies of any recent medical, therapist and/or psychological reports.

(It would have been completely amazing if only the Ukrainian government had given us a portion of the stuff they wanted from us in these reports prior to us adopting. Had we gotten truthful information like they wanted from us there would have been no adoptions by us or by a lot of other people. We didn't even get school or medical histories for our four even though we requested them. For Viktor we received one tiny notebook, written in Russian, with some medical history.)

Let me just say right here **THEY DO NOT WANT THE TRUTH!** They want a fairy tale. The first year I did my best to tell a positive story about Viktor. Hopeful. Then, after the second adoption went all to hell, I finally told the truth. NOTHING. Not one response. The next year rolled around and they harassed me for the report. Since I could barely hold my head above water, I wasn't up to spending days writing out four individual reports just so they could file their papers and check their little boxes. I wrote this instead:

To whom it may concern:

I have been so busy managing trauma issues in my family and dealing with the police after adopting these four teenagers from Ukraine that honestly, I don't have the time nor the inclination to fill out your reports. We were told so many lies by those in Ukraine about these four teenagers. The last several years with them in our home has absolutely devastated our family. My biological children have had great harm done to them and we barely manage to get through each day. I believe adoptions from Ukraine (and other countries) should be stopped until the process is more protective of the adoptive families. I have had the local police, county police, state police, FBI and Homeland Security in my home many times because of the teenagers we adopted from your country. Maybe it's time for Ukraine to take some responsibility for the destruction American families are experiencing because of adoption from your country. For your information here is the only update I will give on them:

Viktor. We bailed him out of jail and are paying court fees to three different courts - over $5,000. He lies continually and has stolen thousands of dollars from us. He thinks nothing of lying to get what he wants. He drinks and smokes cigarettes continually. He is an alcoholic. He should never have been adopted as he has biological family in Ukraine who he could have gone to once out of the orphanage. He causes continual problems. He is very, very angry all of the time. He is aggressive. He never really wanted to be adopted, he just wanted out of the orphanage. I'm sure Ukraine was happy to get rid of him.

Dima. After he turned 18, we put him on a plane back to Ukraine, so he is your problem once again. I'm sure you will find him about where he was when we adopted him. The night before he left he was arrested, once again for stealing from Walmart. All he did while here was lie and steal from us. He ran away countless times with the police bringing him back. He was indecent on several occasions to my 14-year-old daughter and myself. He tried to rape and molest her several times – she was 15 years old. While in Ukraine we were told by officials that he was such a good boy. He told us once here those people lied about him to get rid of him over there. He never really wanted to be adopted, he just wanted out of the orphanage and to stay out of the Ukrainian military. He should never have been adopted since he has biological family near the orphanage and could have gone there once aged out.

Arina. I could write a book. OH wait! I am writing a book. People need to know how adoptions like ours are ruining good families. She is a LIAR. She lied to be adopted so her brother would be adopted so he wouldn't have to go into the Ukrainian military. ONE WEEK after coming here she told us she hated us, and that she and Dima had lied to us, that everyone in Ukraine lied to us, and she started running away. She lied to everyone about us. She ran away with men over and over again. She prostituted herself – the very thing we tried to avoid by adopting her. She broke my leg while in a grocery store. She went to jail. She stole money and other things from us. She threatened to harm us to get her way. She falsely accused both my husband and myself of abuse when she was the one abusing us. She did it to get what she wanted from us. We were literally held hostage in our home for two years. When she turned 18 she ran off with another guy. We have not heard from her since. She never wanted to be adopted. She lied. Everyone in Ukraine lied to us about these teenagers. She has been gone since July a year ago and we are still trying to heal. She almost destroyed our family. She should never have been adopted as she has biological family near the orphanage and could have gone there once aged out.

Sasha. He is the only one doing OK. Not great, but OK. He is still in school. He lies, all the time, as if it's no big deal. It's as if they were taught to lie and steal and they think nothing of it. We were told many, many lies about him in Ukraine. To make him seem better. Perhaps he would be doing better, but for the other three. He should never have been adopted. He has biological family where he could have gone once out of the orphanage.

I understand there are hundreds of cases just like ours where Ukrainian government employees (orphanage workers and social workers) lied to prospective adoptive parents from America and those families are living with the same things we did. I will be writing about many of those stories in my book.

It's not right that these children were taken from their country, language and way of life. Wrong for them and wrong for all the families over here now dealing with them and their mental and emotional problems.

I won't be doing any reports. I'm sure that violates some agreement, but you are welcome to take them all back. Just let me know when you want to pick them up. I'll have them ready for you. Dima is already there.

Sincerely, Kathe Ray

HA! Wouldn't you know but I never heard from them again. I wish everyone who has had a bad adoption would write a letter like this. Maybe something would be done about it.

It reminds me of a line from a movie. *"You can't handle the truth!"*

CHAPTER 31

Viktor Reappeared

August 2016. Viktor was getting deeper into trouble all the time. He had never changed his address, so all his mail continued to come to us. Demand letters from the bank where he owed over $700. Several different courts had warrants for his arrest for one thing or another. I kept writing on them "return to sender/addressee no longer lives here" but they kept coming. I counted what I thought he owed and it came to well over $5,000. I felt bad we brought him here to be a drain on our country.

Sasha bought himself a moped.

Tom: "If you're going to get a moped it is up to you to know all of the rules and get it licensed properly. Understand?"

Sasha: "Yes, I will."

Tom: "A moped is not a car. You cannot ride it in the middle of the road. The top speed is 30 miles per hour. You must ride alongside the road. Do you understand?"

Sasha: "Yes."

Well, of course he got the moped and drove it like a car.

Tom: "Sasha, it is only 50cc and the top speed is 30 MPH. We already told you that. You must drive alongside the road, not on the road. You can't impede traffic. Do you know what that means?"

Sasha: "Yes. I will."

One day while driving, Tom just happened to be following Sasha who was riding in the middle of the road like he was driving a car. Sasha blew through a stop sign as if it didn't exist. Then when they both were home Tom told him, "Sasha, if I catch you riding in the road again you are grounded from riding your moped for one month. It is dangerous to ride in the road and if a police officer sees you doing it, you will get a ticket."

Of course, there was the attitude. "It's my moped and you can't tell me what to do. I bought it with my own money."

Right. The next day he was riding it to his summer school class and got into an accident. I was driving home from taking Katherine to cross country practice and got a call from the police asking if I could get there right away. Sasha had been riding in traffic, in the road, and the car in front of him stopped. He didn't. There was no damage to the car, but his moped was beat up and Sasha complained that his knee hurt where he bumped it against the moped. He got a ticket for impeding traffic and driving without a license. He had never gotten proper licensing, even though he told us he had. Now there was a misdemeanor traffic charge he would have to pay. It ended up costing him $600 and 2 points on his license. He kept telling us, "This is stupid. The sun was in my eyes and I couldn't see, and I shouldn't be in trouble for that."

NO ACCOUNTABILITY – EVER! He was angry at everyone but himself. We made him sell the moped so he could use the money to pay his fines. Later that week he asked me, "Can I take drivers training and drive your car?" HA! "You can take drivers training, but you will have to buy your own car and insurance." No way was he going to drive my car with that entitlement attitude!

October 2016. We found out through Sasha that Arina was pregnant. I don't even know what to write about that. A selfish girl with RAD taking care of a baby. A recipe for disaster. Soon after we learned that news, she was in the hospital with a "miscarriage". Honestly, I was relieved. She was not capable of taking care of a baby. What a nightmare.

We heard Dima was working in Ukraine loading steel trucks for $6 *a day*. Wow! And he was upset because the restaurant where he was working here only paid him $9 *an hour*. For washing dishes. Inside. Out of the bad weather. He had it so rough here in America.

We heard from Sasha that Viktor was in jail, then he got out and started back working in the same restaurant as Sasha. At least for one week. Then he got fired for being lazy and stubborn. He didn't believe the rules applied to him. Then he got picked up by the police for sleeping in his car in the parking lot of the elementary school up the street from us. The high school called us that he was there to try and enroll again. They told him they were sorry, but he was now too old, and they sent him to community education.

January 2017. News was quiet about Arina. News was quiet about Dima. We were muddling through the days trying to figure out where to go now in our family. Everything felt fragmented. We were all in our own little worlds with walls up. Not much connection between us. Days passed.

A call from Viktor. He was in jail and asked if we would bail him out. Tom drove to the jail to find out what was going on. Viktor was picked up for driving on a suspended license and had a bench warrant from two other courts for the same thing. Tom brought him home.

He walked in the door, walked up to me and said, "I'm sorry mom. I did a lot of bad things to you. I'm sorry."

I was wary. I didn't believe he was sincere. I was sure this was only because he had nowhere else to turn. He had no job, no place to live and his car had been impounded so no place for him to sleep. He was in debt up to his eyeballs and three different courts had citations and warrants out for him. What a mess.

Tom and I talked. We agreed to do what we could to help him get back on his feet one last time.

I know, I know. I'm shaking my head at myself as I write this. Another mistake by us. We should never have believed him!!!

I helped him get two jobs and I, once again, took control of his finances. I attended court hearing after court hearing with him and helped him whittle down what he owed. He also owed over $1,000 to the IRS because he worked all of 2016 on a 1099 and paid no taxes. He was clueless. And he still owed the bank over $700 for being overdrawn, plus fees. He told us that once he had everything paid off he was moving to Siberia. Okay then. We were hoping he would be done with his debts by June and able to move out on his own again. It actually would take us all the way to November 1st for that to happen. In the meantime, just his presence in our home was a gigantic setback to our family healing.

October 2017 - *Funny story – not!* I came home from a cross country meet to an empty house – miracle. On the kitchen counter was an envelope with $700 cash and a $250 paycheck for Viktor from his job. He was saving money to move out and get his own apartment. I put the envelope into safe keeping, waiting for him to say something about it. Nothing on Saturday. Nothing on Sunday. (Now this is a boy for the last five years has lied to us on a regular basis and had admitted to stealing hundreds of dollars from us on a regular basis. He is a pathological liar and thief. He frequently loses things. Seriously, he had to replace his driver's license four times because he kept losing it.)

I decided I wouldn't say anything about finding the money. I wanted to know how long it would take for him to miss it. I'd told him I would put his savings into safekeeping for him, so he wouldn't have to carry it around with him. Nope. He didn't trust me. He'd told me to my face that he didn't trust me, even after all I had done to help him get out of trouble, even after helping him resolve his court issues. That hurt like a knife in my heart. I asked myself what was the point of all of this? I still don't have an answer. It made me angry, and sad.

Finally, on Monday morning he burst into my prayer room in the basement – without knocking – shouting, "There is an emergency!"

Me: "What is wrong?"

Viktor: "There is an emergency!"

Me: "You said that, what is the emergency?"

Viktor: "Someone steal my money!"

Me: "Where did you have it?"

Viktor: "I don't know, someone steal it."

Me: "I have it, Viktor. I got home from Katherine's meet and the envelope was on the counter. I put it in a safe place. Why did it take you so long to know it was missing?"

Seemed he had a deal with Sasha, the 18-year-old senior, to keep his money safe for him. They were going back and forth about the envelope and both left the house without putting the money away. Real safe. Ugh. Two totally irresponsible teenagers trusting each other. Sometimes you just must laugh. (To myself, by the way, not out loud.)

I was baffled. I asked, "Viktor, why would you have someone that is not good with money, who has been caught stealing and who lies all of the time, hold on to your money?"

He replied, "I trust Sasha. He my brother."

"Have I ever lied to you?"

"No."

"Have I ever stolen money from you?"

"No."

"Have I ever done anything to hurt you?"

"No."

Mind boggled. Seriously. And that's after I'd had his money for three days and not one penny was missing. And he had lived with us for almost five years and I'd bailed him out of so many jams I've forgotten many of them. I just helped him pay off $5,000 in debt to three different courts.

At the end of the conversation I asked him, "How did it feel to think someone stole your money?"

"Bad."

"How do you think I felt when you stole money from me?"

"I guess you felt bad."

No remorse, no "I'm sorry" or "Thank you for holding onto my money for me." He just shrugged shoulders, pocketed his money and walked away.

November 2017. Just shy of three weeks after he moved, we received a notice in the mail that Viktor owed $350 for a traffic violation. The actual violation was $18 for parking in front of a fire hydrant. Because he did not pay the fine he had a court date which he didn't attend so costs got added on. I was furious. All we did the past 10 months and now this!! We should have told him way back in January 2017 to figure it out for himself. The aggravation it caused for our family and the setback to our healing was just not worth it if he was just going to get himself into another bad place. On the day he moved, Tom and I sat him down and told him that we had helped him all we could and if he got into more trouble we would not help him again. We were worn out from trying to help this person who refused to learn from his mistakes. All we had done was enable further bad behavior.

CHAPTER 32

Working to Recover

January 2018. It's the beginning of a new year. Where is my family now? Still working to recover. Working to overcome the trauma. Working to figure out how to overcome the ramifications of things that happened to our bio teens, so they can move forward into their futures. Decisions were made to do things during that time they now regret and that are having an impact on what they want to do for their futures. That is hard. I'm not one to place blame or justify. At the same time, the things that happened to them during this time was not their doing. And they were holding on the best they could during a time when many adults would have made bad choices.

One of the hardest things I'm finding right now is filling out college applications for Katherine. Some of the worst trauma to her happened during her freshman and sophomore years and her grades suffered. She wants to go to a D1 university to run with a top notch cross country and track team. Those average grades just don't cut it. Now that three of the adoptees are gone and she is a junior, she is getting back on track. We just don't know if it's going to be enough, or in time. Garrett has been set back, almost a year, from what he wanted to do. It's so hard to watch my teens suffer for something we allowed to happen in their lives. Another round of guilt ensues.

On the positive side, I am choosing to believe they will be better people for enduring what they did in the long term. They are learning to be overcomers. They are learning to talk things through instead of keeping their feelings inside. We have all learned it isn't circumstances that define us, but how we handle those circumstances. We talk constantly about not giving someone else power over us. I ask the question almost every day to one of them, "Are you giving them (or that) power over you right now?" Especially someone who isn't even in your life anymore. I ask myself that same question. We are learning that someone or something else can only control us when we allow them or it to do that. We are hoping these lessons serve them well in their futures. And we are here to help them navigate the healing and teach them these tools which they will need to rely on in the future should there be bumps in their roads, which inevitably there will be. They are definitely much more mature than the average teen.

We are feeling lighter and more joyous, on most days. Laughter comes more easily. There is more family time and less time spent alone in bedrooms. Bringing our puppy Reagan home a year ago has helped. He inspires laughter and all he cares about is loving on us, which all of us need desperately – unconditional love. We are back to having family time on Sunday, like we did pre-adoption. We are slowly finding our groove again as a family, although we are taking far longer than I imagined we would.

There are still signs of trauma. I still jump unconsciously when someone pounds too hard on the door. Katherine gets highly emotional way too fast and allows others to pull her into their drama. Garrett requires constant reminders to open up. Tom is focused on work and robotics. He is stoic and keeps his feelings inside. Sasha is happy and on track to graduate in June, then has plans to go into the Air Force along with Garrett. Some days are harder than others. We take them as they come.

I get up each morning at 5:00 to have quiet time to read, study my Bible, pray and think. Most times these days I'm thinking about what to write to you. Especially this part. Where are we now and some words of wisdom should you find yourself in trouble, adoption or just life trouble. The words of wisdom must come from Him, not me. He is the author of wisdom and no real wisdom is found without Him. I ask Him to speak through me, to you. The words you need to hear.

Here are some of the things I've learned and decisions I've made to do things differently in the future because of everything we've gone through.

I stop and think – long and hard – before allowing anyone to have an impact on me or my family. I stop and ask Yahweh what He wants. Then I listen. I am Gideon with his fleece asking for a sign. (Judges 6:36-40) I am very protective of me, my time, and of my family.

I have learned that seeking first His Kingdom is not just a saying. It's the only truth that matters in my life. When I put Him first I will have all that I need. I have changed. Now I make Him and spending time with Him a priority – every day, all day.

I have learned to better prioritize my days. Yahweh, Tom, taking care of me, my children, my work. If it doesn't fall into one of those categories there is a high probability I'm saying no.

I no longer care what others think of me. Their opinions of me are none of my business! I live for the One and I know what He thinks of me. That's all that matters. There is only one Judge I care one whit about anymore. Judgmental people have zero power over me anymore!

I will never again let emotion dictate my decisions. Decisions must be based on facts known and I will always get Yahweh's input.

Proverbs 3:5-6: Trust in Yahweh with all your heart and lean not on your own understanding; in all your ways submit to Him, and He will make your paths straight.

Not taking care of myself is not an option anymore. It's difficult enough going through this life without being sick, tired or hurt. It has become one of my new priorities. Getting to the gym, eating right, getting enough sleep and saying "no" to a lot of things where I used to say "yes".

And I have learned to obey Him no matter what. If He tells me to do something, and I'm certain it has come from Him, I no longer question it; no longer procrastinate. I jump in. 100%. No more being a Jonah.

Family X. A woman reached out to me. She was in Asia and had picked up her six-year-old adopted son from the orphanage and was waiting in country for the paperwork to be finished. She was six months pregnant and alone, her husband stayed in America to take care of the rest of their family. The two of them were in their hotel room when the child raged at her and kicked her, hard, in the belly. She messaged me and asked what I thought she should do. I said, "Immediately call your facilitator. Tell him you need to disrupt the adoption and take the child back to the orphanage. Do not let him try to convince you otherwise." She replied, "That is what my husband told me to do." She left the country without the child.

I was so relieved. One tragedy avoided.

CHAPTER 33

Some Final Thoughts

Family X. We had absolutely no idea when we entered into our double adoption about RAD. We went through extensive training by our adoption agency, but we weren't told RAD was a possibility. We weren't told what signs to watch for. We weren't encouraged to put the boys, ages 11 and 12 at the time of the adoption, into counseling immediately. They exhibited most of the symptoms of RAD and they were persistent, pervasive, destructive and chaotic. The younger one was a pathological liar and, after I grounded him for a month for refusing to tell the truth, he ran away for six days and convinced local law enforcement I'd abused him. His older brother backed up his story. It was found out later they had been planning this for quite some time and were just waiting for the right time to act.

During the time the boy was missing local law enforcement was convinced I had actually murdered him because they claimed I was the last person to see him, which was not the truth as there was a confirmed sighting of him in our town the morning he ran away. They even dragged our pond, sprayed down our kitchen for blood and required an officer to keep watch over me even when dressing in my own bedroom. The boys were found a few days later, laughing because they caused us so much trouble. They were sent to a residential treatment facility until they were 18. We don't know where they are now.

Two and a half years later, after spending $150,000, our names were cleared of any wrongdoing, the charges were dismissed and expunged. Our reputations have been damaged beyond belief and we are always fearful of the boys coming back to harm us. If it weren't for the grace of God and a wonderful family, we would have been broken apart. These RAD symptoms are real. They cause real damage. Good people trying to do the right thing for others are destroyed. Law enforcement, teachers, child "protective" services, all need more and better information on what RAD looks like and how it destroys.

Empathy

I want to make this crystal clear. I completely understand that our teens, and the other children/teens stories in this book, have had terrible trauma in their lives. The one person who was supposed to love and nurture them, their biological mother, was absent, either physically or emotionally. It is not their fault they have attachment and other issues. I feel terrible for them. I can pretty much guarantee all parents caught in this nightmare feel the same as I do. We wish, more than anyone can imagine, these children/teens had never experienced any of what they have, and they were living happy and healthy lives with their biological families. Adoption does not happen unless there is a negative reason for it. There is no such thing as a positive reason. Someone gave up, or had taken away, their baby, or child, or teenager. That is not normal. A baby/child/teen who was meant to be with their mother is not. Period. There are going to be problems. Some are minor. Many are not. It is not, I repeat, it is not the fault of the adoptee.

BUT it is not the fault of the adoptive parents either. This is something which needs to come out into the open with adoptions so:

(1) Potential adoptive parents are fully aware what attachment disorders are and they can make an informed decision to move forward on the adoption, or not,

(2) There is transparency from adoption agencies, orphanages, facilitators and the like about behavior and emotional issues,

(3) There is ongoing support for the entire adoptive family with the ability to disrupt if necessary without further financial and emotional burden on the family, and

(4) There is money available for RTF's (Residential Treatment Facilities) so that short and long-term care for adoptee's who cannot stay in the family home does not put families at further risk financially.

A Changed Perspective

I remembered a story from back in 2010 about Torrey Hansen who sent her 7-year old adopted son back to Russia.

(http://abcnews.go.com/WN/anger-mom-adopted-boy-back-russia/story?id=10331728)

At the time I had zero experience with adoption and was horrified by her actions. Oh boy, has my tune changed. I can 100% understand how she got to this point. I've done what she did with the only difference being our adopted son was 18 so we were in the clear. I personally know several adoptive parents who have returned children to their home countries being unable to handle the enormous trauma the child/teen brought to their family. Many will say "oh! But he was only 7". Yeah. I have a friend who has a 7-year-old with RAD who beats her up daily. They have no respite. No one believes them because he is only 7 and cute as cute can be. He is a master manipulator. She spends a good part of her day protecting her little's from this boy and takes the brunt of the abuse herself because of it. The "he is only 7" doesn't matter when you are talking RAD and trauma.

The story really hit home when Torrey said, "He drew a picture of our house burning down and he'll tell anybody that he's going to burn our house down with us in it," Hansen said. "It got to be where you feared for your safety. It was terrible."

I can relate to this and so can many of my adoptive parent friends. One friend of mine is paying $10,000 a month to have her 7-year-old in a therapeutic group home because she couldn't take the risk of the child burning down the house with the rest of the family inside. More financial burden, but there are no other choices. So, Torrey, I get it. And so do hundreds of other families. I can't tell you how many times I thought of you and wanted to do what you did. I just couldn't figure out how to bundle up a teenager who was bigger than me and put them on a plane.

Humiliation because of fundraising

This was very hard for us and for many others. For months and even years in some cases we begged money to help us fund our adoptions. I hate asking people for anything, and here we were asking for money! We adoptive parents hold yard sales, bake sales, puzzle fundraisers and envelope fundraisers. We constantly beg our friends, family and strangers to help us rescue these orphans. People gave of their hard-earned money to help us. Some even did fundraisers themselves to support us.

I have a friend in another state whose entire Bible study group of women, who I do not even know, raised funds for us. We had teenagers of friends do fundraising for us. A group of children cleaned out their piggy banks. One woman I know, who barely makes ends meet, gave us more than she should have. Now I trust Yahweh He is going to bless all of them for helping. At the same time, it is part of what holds some people back from being truthful about how their adoption is really going.

It's difficult to face people who have helped you to rescue a child. It seems easier somehow to just put a happy face on it. And at this point I would tell them they did a good thing and Yahweh always makes things right. What they did, they did from their heart and that will be counted as good by Him. I'm sure of it.

Satan

I want to talk a bit about this evil being and the part he is playing in all of this adoption chaos. The number one target of his are families. Break down families. Destroy them. And if he can take out the mom, then he has pretty much won the fight.

If ever there comes a time when the women of the world come together purely and simply for the benefit of mankind, it will be a force such as the world has never known. Matthew Arnold, 19th Century Poet and Philosopher.

I read that in a book the other day. It hit me then. If the enemy can take away the witness from women (moms), take away their physical and emotional health, their strength, and their joy, then he has gone a long way to destroying the family. The number of women who have asked, "Where is God in all of this?" breaks my heart. Women are falling away from Him through post-adoption trauma.

When the enemy causes triangulation through manipulation he makes craters in family relationships. Who then is at the heart of the deceptions of adoption? Who wins in this battle of the heavenlies? He loves to cause problems in families. And I believe that through the adoption industry he has found a perfect way.

All in the Name of Yahweh.

Adoptive parents stand strong in Yahweh, no matter what. Gird yourselves with the Armor of Yahweh.

> *The Whole Armor of God - Ephesians 6:10-20. Finally, be strong in Yahweh and in the strength of his might.*
>
> *Put on the whole armor of Yahweh that you may be able to stand against the schemes of the devil.*
>
> *For we do not wrestle against flesh and blood, but against the rulers, against the authorities, against the cosmic powers over this present darkness, against the spiritual forces of evil in the heavenly places.*
>
> *Therefore take up the whole armor of Yahweh that you may be able to withstand in the evil day, and having done all, to stand firm.*
>
> *Stand therefore, having fastened on the belt of truth, and having put on the breastplate of righteousness and as shoes for your feet, having put on the readiness given by the gospel of peace.*
>
> *In all circumstances take up the shield of faith, with which you can extinguish all the flaming darts of the evil one; and take the*

helmet of salvation, and the sword of the Spirit, which is the word of Yahweh, praying at all times in the Spirit, with all prayer and supplication.

To that end, keep alert with all perseverance, making supplication for all the saints, and also for me, that words may be given to me in opening my mouth boldly to proclaim the mystery of the gospel, for which I am an ambassador in chains, that I may declare it boldly, as I ought to speak.

I'm all alone

This is something I've heard way too often when talking with an adoptive parent, mostly moms. I've lost my family. I've lost all my friends. My church turned away from me. My husband left me. I've been abandoned by everyone I care about. No one believes me. I'm incredibly sad all the time because I have no one who understands what I am going through. No one cares about me anymore.

Complete isolation. Another tool of the enemy. If he can get us alone, he's got us. We humans are not meant to do life alone, especially during difficult times. We need our tribe. I can't tell you how many times someone in surprise has reached out to me after a blog posting, realizing what she is experiencing is not uncommon. That others are dealing with it, too. It makes me so sad to think of how many are out there even now who think they are the only ones to whom this is happening.

In some cases, it even becomes "I'm afraid to say anything". They feel humiliated they've "let" this happen, or they've been pressured by the abusive teen that no one will believe her, and most times they don't. Or they've attempted to tell someone, and that person has shut them down, belittled them, told them it can't be that bad, told them if God wanted them to adopt then He will get them through it, or the like. The number of people who have told us that all the problems were caused by something we were or were not doing is ridiculous. It's hard enough to go through adoption trauma without having to do it all on your own and being told it is all your fault.

The Church

I want to know where the Church is in all of this. The ones who have spearheaded this entire adoption business. They promote adoption. They talk about helping the widows and orphans. They have "Orphan Sunday" and "Orphan Weekend" and "National Orphan Month". They invite hosting and adoption organizations in to speak during church services. Then, willing families step up and commit and when it all goes horribly wrong, the church moves onto a different mission field, conveniently forgetting they ever talked about adoption. They have no resources to help the family or families. In fact, in many cases families have been asked to leave the church because the children/teens have been too disruptive. OH MY WORD!!! Are you kidding me, you ask? NOPE!

The Church now has a responsibility to share this information and refuse, at this point, to allow one more loving, godly, and unsuspecting family walk into disaster without knowing ALL the facts. Spread this information like you spread the word about adopting. Help your families who are living in hell. Quit judging them. Love on them. Support them.

Family X. If only we had known...The Church

- I didn't know adoption meant alienation by family and friends. What hurt the worst were the looks on faces at our church. They would ask us how things were, but they didn't really want to know the truth. They wanted the fairy tale. After we opened up and told a few people what was really going on we were completely ostracized. We were given a myriad of recommendations such as: just love them more, maybe you're being too harsh with them, would you give up on them if they were biological, and God told you to do this, so you really need to think about how you're handling yourselves. Suffice to say we don't attend church anymore. We've experienced more judgement in the last few months than we have in our entire lifetimes.
- We have no friends left and plan to move as he goes to placement. Our older children will stay in their schools, but our other child in

elementary school will be in a different school. We have no idea if we will be able to stay at our church or not. We've been abandoned.

- That the people who were our biggest supporters through adoption are now judging us the harshest for how we are trying to parent. They are elders of our church and I really thought they had our back. We've left church for good after all of this.
- I never realized we would be asked to leave the church we adopted through because they believed the lies about us abusing our adopted children. Even after the truth came out they were "uncomfortable" with us being a part of their church. I hate church.
- We never thought that the church that we both grew up in would someday ask us to leave because our adopted teens were causing problems. We adopted them after hearing a host organization speak one Sunday. We were encouraged by the pastor and several members of the church to adopt. Once the trouble started those people were nowhere to be found. Until the day we got the call that perhaps we should look for a new church. A call! After 40 plus years! We are done with church!

Our government

Where are they in all of this? USCIS – United States Citizenship and Immigration Services. The U.S. State Department. The embassies that are run by the State Department in these other countries. They are right there front and center to collect all the "necessary" (exorbitant) fees from the adoptive parents going through adoption, but where are they once things go south? Nowhere to be found. One employee of USCIS, who asked not to be named, told me they are well aware of adoption fraud in international adoptions and how many families are in trouble with the children/teens they have adopted, but it's not worth losing his paycheck to actually talk about it openly.

Adoption fees paid for international adoptions to these government agencies is more than $2000 per child/teen. (Rates may have changed since our adoptions, so it may be more/less.) All this for some paperwork. This is a huge money maker for our government and yet when an American citizen needs help to disrupt or even find resources, the bureaucracy is insane. There is NO help! Or it takes years and years, so by the time something is actually done, it becomes a moot point.

Family X...

- When I adopted I didn't know it was possible to hate a child. And what that does to you to feel that way.
- I didn't know adoptions didn't work out. I never heard of the negative side of adoption that would destroy our family.
- I never realized how much destruction guilt could have over a person. I feel so damn guilty about everything I've done that's wrecked damage on my family by bringing one little person into it to help them have a better life.
- When I adopted, I never dreamed that I would watch as our adopted son was arrested in our family room by three police officers.
- I didn't know I would live everyday walking on egg shells, not knowing when, <u>not if</u>, my child would rage. I didn't know loving was so tough.
- I never liked horror movies. Now I live in one every day. How did this happen?
- I didn't know that one day I would lock myself in my bathroom to call 911 because my 9-year-old son was trying break down the door to try and kill me.

CHAPTER 34

The Last, Last Word!

Before I give *my* last word I'm going to share some last words from my family; Sasha, Tom, Katherine and Garrett. I asked them to write out some of their thoughts now that the post-adoption battles have subsided. It's not pretty and honestly, it was like a punch in my gut to read the stories from Garrett and Katherine. I share them with you just in case what I've written has still left you with any doubts the current adoption process must be changed. These words tore my heart to pieces. This should never have happened to my children. We've got to stop it from happening to any more families.

Thoughts from Sasha – January 2018

Before I was adopted I thought a lot about being on the streets or what else I would do after I finished with school. I wouldn't have opportunities like here. Probably, I would have gone to college and lived in the dorms. After that, I don't know.

I did some mistakes when I came home to America with my family. When Viktor, Arina and Dima were here I was following their direction most days. Maybe I wasn't used to it here. I wasn't used to having a family. The other adopted kids were Ukrainian like me and spoke Russian, so it was easier to follow them. I felt bad that all that stuff was happening to my family with the three of them making so much trouble, running away and talking to the police.

Now they are gone, it feels calmer here. No police at the door. I have improved my English more. I will graduate from high school in June, then I am maybe going in the Air Force. I am happy about my future.

(I had been contemplating how to help orphans while still in their own country. While driving Sasha to school one day I asked him what he thought about an idea I had. "If dad and I had known about you and instead of adopting you, we helped you get into college or a good trade school in Ukraine, with an apartment, so you could later get a good job to support yourself, what do you think about that? He responded with an excited, "Yes, that would have been great!") Hmmm…

Thoughts from Tom – January 2018

Kathe wrote of much of the story, including my discussion with CPS when I was falsely accused of sexually abusing Arina at a time when she wasn't even in our home. It was a very challenging time for me. As the dad of the house, I had no actual control over anything that was happening. And I couldn't protect my family from any of it. My biggest burden was what happened to us financially.

We had our share of ups and downs prior to the adoptions but saw Yahweh's hand in our lives and it was good. Then one day in the summer of 2012, the SOS message comes before me regarding Viktor. Things were not going well for the family who was hosting Viktor in Minnesota and he needed three weeks to be with another family before he returned home to Ukraine. It was summer. Kathe was a stay home Arbonne mom making a portion of our income. She assured me that she could keep an eye on Viktor and make sure our two bio children would be ok. I agreed to him being hosted for the next three weeks. To me, it was no big deal. I had no idea what went on in Minnesota but didn't care; what is the worst that could happen in Michigan? I could have said "No" but I said, "Yes". This was the first of my decisions that changed the life of countless, including my own family.

During the three weeks stay, Viktor acted like a recluse unless we really encouraged him and this should have been our first clue. We had a swimming pool and he didn't want to swim. We would finally get him in the pool, then he'd have a great time. He didn't want to do family things, but again, once firmly encouraged he would go along with it. He definitely did not want to do any family chore stuff like set the table, do dishes, clean the floor, vacuum. He mostly wanted to stay in his room and be on his phone to watch Russian YouTube or VK. We surmised he must just be traumatized by the Minneapolis to Michigan ordeal and given time, it would work its way out. We were sucked in to all the same lies that floated out there regarding adoptees from Ukraine. The lies like, at 16 years old, they are shown the door and they are out on the streets fending for themselves. Or, they have no family. Or, the girls will end up in prostitution. Or, the boys end up in prostitution or organized crime. It is all B.S. Maybe a small percentage is true.

All we were told was doom and gloom for him. All the lies told us were that if he went back to Ukraine un-adopted, there was a high percentage chance that he would be dead within one year. Untrue, untrue, untrue. With this erroneous belief, I made the ultimate decision that we would adopt Viktor, and that is where this whole mess started. ***All because I said yes to him being adopted.***

In life, you have things that you need, things that you want and things that you just must do. You need to take the trash out. You don't have to, and you may not want to, but you need to do it. Unless you want trash piled up high in your house. You want butter on your toast. You don't need butter on your toast and you don't have to have butter on your toast. Adoption is a different category. It doesn't fall into a need, want or must. You're led to believe adopting is something you're inspired to do because it is the right thing to do. There is only one problem with it. Yahweh said to help the widows and the orphans, He never said to bring them into your home. Yahweh also never said to borrow money to do His work. If it is meant to be, He will see fit it will happen and that includes financial. We didn't have the money to adopt. The urgency is presented, the aging out at 16 and if you don't help, it will be too late, that it's a matter of life or death. How can you put a price on life? Again, B.S., B.S., B.S.

We went into debt rather quickly thinking it would all work out. Yes, we did get some private donations, but it didn't compare to the huge amount of funds needed to adopt four Ukrainian teenagers. It is like getting involved in a bad relationship, going into debt to cover all the bad debts of the other person and then that person walks out of your life and you are left with the debt. It is a hard pill to swallow. Here we are now, straddled with credit card debt and an adoption loan for a multiple adoption that brought hell into our home.

At my age (almost 60), I should not have to think about how much things cost all the time. This financial burden, because of this decision, will take years just to get back to a zero point. Decisions about money today which should go to benefit my biological children and grandchildren, can't be made. We go on family vacations and yet have no money other than for basic lodging and travel. There is no additional money to cover anything fun. From pictures, I notice Kathe and I are wearing the same clothes we've been wearing for many years. There is no buying new clothing or anything else for us. But, we are surviving the ordeal. Arina did not win when she accused me of sexually abusing her or when she repeatedly reported us to authorities for some made up offense. Dima got his just rewards when he went back to Ukraine to visit with no plan on how to get back to America. Viktor finally moved out at the end of October 2017 with zero "thanks Dad for getting me out of jail and for bailing my butt out of the trouble I got myself into" or for showing him how to make a living and to live on his own debt-free or "thanks, I appreciate everything you have done for me." And he doesn't even visit us now. A simple thank you would have been nice.

The debt looming over our heads is tough, but it doesn't compare with the thought that if I just would have said no to adopting them, they would not have existed in our lives and we wouldn't be living with this financial burden, or the trauma my family is working to overcome. Other families we influenced would not have adopted and would not be living in hell. Adoption is a ticking time bomb. I hope our story makes a difference.

Thoughts from Katherine – January 2018

Before we adopted my life was normal. I was home schooled by my parents. Life was normal. It was good. I didn't really have any problems. Life was actually pretty boring.

After we adopted, I was surprised. I expected them to be nice people. I was looking forward to it. Excited. Before long I regretted we adopted them. They lied, they stole, and they physically, emotionally and sexually hurt me. I was terrified they were in my house. I had to move into the basement to try and stay safe from them. Arina took over my room and I can't go into that room anymore. She ruined that room for me. I hate Ukrainian colors and I hate minions. They bring back horrible memories. I never understood why Viktor got his own room and why I had to share a room with Arina. He started the whole mess and he caused so much trouble and he got a room to himself. I was anxious and depressed and hated life. I didn't know how to fix my life. One night I was so upset with how everything was in our house that I climbed out the upstairs window and sat on the roof. I wondered what would happen if I jumped off the roof. Would I die? Would that make things better? What if I just got hurt and couldn't run anymore? I don't remember how long I sat up there. I remember wishing I could make it all go away. Make all of them go away. I hurt so bad inside.

Now they are gone. I am learning to enjoy life again. Running is better. For a while I didn't like running and it's my favorite thing in the world to do. It's like getting into a car accident and not being able to walk. Then you go to physical therapy to learn to walk again. It takes a long time. That's how my brain is. I'm learning, slowly, to love life again. I am retraining my brain. It's hard to trust people. It's hard to meet new people. I am more introverted than before. I used to love making new friends. My parents used to say I would walk into a room and in five minutes I would have a bunch of new friends. I'm not like that anymore. I didn't deserve to be kicked out of my own room by her and be treated like crap whenever my parents weren't around by the people we tried to help. I didn't deserve to be abused. It makes me angry and I would give anything to see them one last time and kick the crap out of them. I know I could do major damage. I know I'll never get that chance. They did all that stuff to me and I couldn't do anything to stop it or do anything back to them. I struggle with forgiving them. I want the feeling of not feeling terrified every time Arina makes a fake social media account and tries to follow me. I want to stop feeling like crying just getting a friend request from her. I wish she would just leave me alone and never try to contact me ever again. I want to forget it all happened. I wish we never adopted.

Thoughts from Garrett – January 2018

Mom, I cannot even fathom where to begin writing this. The raw and broken emotions buried deep within threaten to break free from their chains that bind them with every word I write. I want to keep it all buried. To split up my life into eras of the period when "they" were here is almost impossible. The days, weeks, months and years are a blur. I cannot remember dates, I cannot remember when it began, how old I was during events, and what I was doing. I used to think it was my crummy memory, now I realize it is the culprit of something far worse.

It is a defense mechanism to prevent my fragmented mind and hollow heart from descending further deeper into the darkness that they brought to our family. I faintly remember a life before the darkness. A life of happiness, free of the pain. Sure, it had its times of struggle, but it was nothing like the nightmares to come. My worries consisted of beating a video game or getting over some social anxiety to make friends. Grades and homework were my problems. Life was simple, and I can truly say it was a happier time.

But, they came. They came under the promise of us doing the right thing. I went along with it, for I really had no say in the matter. I did not realize the horrors that they would bring at first. First, it seemed like rebellious behavior, and my parents seemed to be in denial. I started trying to stay as far away from home as possible, because it became less and less of a home. They were demons. They were vile demons that corrupted everything they touched. They stole, they lied, and they cheated. They did what it took to gratify their perverted, selfish desires. I had never truly felt pain until they came. I started thinking of myself as "cold, hollow and broken" to shut out their darkness. I never talked to my parents about what I was feeling. They were completely overwhelmed.

"The brightest light will always cast the greatest shadow." I had once thought to myself, "So why bother being a light at all?"

I realized the way to keep their darkness out was to create my own. I was never rebellious, I merely corrupted myself in secret, drowning the pain out in my activities. I started doing things I shouldn't just to escape the pain of my home life. Yet the pain was still there. The pain persisted through any masks I put up. I hid my suffering from my family and friends.

I stopped caring about me or anything else. I kept "them" out of my life at the cost of me. How could they try to corrupt me if I already corrupted myself? Viktor tried to assert his dominance over me like he did the others, but I would not let him. How could I? He was nothing to me. I had given him the privilege of being my brother, my equal, yet he tried to subjugate me like I'm worthless? No. He deserved everything that came to him, as did the rest of them. We tried to give them a great life. The life I had before they came into our home and they ruined it. Not only for themselves, but for us as well. They didn't deserve what they were given.

Even when they left I kept the mask of hatred up. It was bound to me and I was bound to it. This persisted for months after. It is still lingering. So much hatred and suffering sealed within. I saw some of it come out, once with my online friends, another time with real life friends. No matter how much I try to lie to myself of how I'm "getting better" I have to accept this pain will remain for as long as I am still alive.

Broken Darkness by Garrett Ray

I am the broken one

Born into solitude

One with darkness

All alone in my suffering

Afraid of the next day

When will the light come

Why can't I feel the warmth anymore

I miss it

The feeling of joy

I miss the feeling of being painless

Unmarked, unhurt

Away from the inner terror

I don't want to be afraid

I don't want to be hurt

I am tired...

I have no conclusion. I have no conclusion because there is no conclusion. I feel as if I was born into this pain and that it will always be there to poison me. Every day is a new one and I'm tired of fighting an enemy that no longer exists. I'm sorry Mom.

Thoughts from me – January 2018

Just like my introduction in the beginning, talking about myself is difficult. Mostly because I haven't figured out yet who I am after all of this. Some days the tears are ready to spill out. Some days I have to force myself to take a shower. Other days I feel like my old self again. I catch a glimpse of who I used to be, then the rug is pulled from my feet and I want to curl up and hide again. Watching Garrett and Katherine struggle is absolutely the most difficult thing I've ever had to witness. It tears my heart up. I trust Yahweh that He can turn all things to good. I trust Him that He will make good for my teens. It's a rough road I'm traveling right now.

Little things get to me more than big ones. A random picture on social media from that time hurts my heart. Talking to Garrett about something we did as a family before they came into our lives makes it hard for me to breathe. Looking around my home seeing things they destroyed, and we can't afford to replace make me want to curl up and hide. I live in a home filled with trauma memories. I wish we were in a different house. I'm afraid I will open the door one day and one of them will be standing on the front porch. I want to go someplace they can never find me. I wrestle with regret, and guilt and see-saw between those emotions and forgiveness and trusting Yahweh. I want to be healed. To put it all behind me. Move on. Be positive. That's been the mode of operation my entire life. This hasn't been so simple. And I can't figure out why. Why can't I just block it out and move on like I have done so many times? Maybe because everywhere I look I see them; I see the spot she screamed at me, the broken window or door, or the bedroom door I walk by every day which remains closed because it's where she was. I can't get away from the trauma. There are days I hate my home.

I start thinking like that, then stop myself and look at one of the yellow sticky notes on my desk.

Isaiah 40:31: Those who trust in Yahweh will renew their strength; they will soar on wings like eagles; they will run and not grow weary; they will walk and not faint.

I feel hopeful, and I smile. I trust Yahweh, so I choose to trust Him that everything will turn out exactly as He planned. I will be healed and so will my family. For His glory! It's a minute-by-minute thing some days.

I struggle most with the fact there are some good adoptions. Our Sasha is one of them. We had some difficult times with him, but today he is a loved member of our family and we can't imagine our family without him. We are proud of how he has turned things around, how hard he has worked, how well he has integrated into our family, and we are excited for his future plans. I wish I could say to STOP all adoptions and go to battle to make that happen. But what about the other "Sasha's" out there? Don't they deserve a chance at a future? But how do you know who is a "Sasha" and who is a "Dima or Arina"? Is there a way to know? To ensure your family will adopt a "good one"?

AND what if when we had learned about Sasha, instead of adopting him, we spent our time and money to support him in Ukraine? Maybe helped him get into a good college and get an apartment so he could get a good education. Or helped him find a good job and learn how to do life on his own. For the amount of money we spent (and still have to pay back) we could have helped Sasha and several more orphans get a good start to a life in Ukraine. And it certainly would have been a more positive experience for our family. And for him, as well.

A friend adopted a teen girl from the same orphanage as Sasha. Once in the U.S. she became much like our Arina. She practically destroyed her family. I asked Sasha what this girl was like while in the orphanage as he had grown up with her and lived with her for many years. He told me she was a very good girl and one of his best friends; like a sister. He can't comprehend her behavior now. It's as if she is a different girl than the one he knew at the orphanage. I wonder had the money been spent to help her there, would her future be brighter than it is now. It makes me incredibly sad to think what we have done to these children/teens by bringing them here instead of helping them there. All with good intentions, certainly, but the fact remains we have done them no good service.

I have had hundreds of conversations with other adoptive parents trying to figure out the secret formula to a "good adoption" vs. what we and others in this book experienced. Does it matter if they have biological family? Does it matter what age they went into the orphanage? Does is matter if they have biological siblings? Does it matter if their biological parents were alcoholics? Does it matter if they were from a "good" or "not so good" orphanage? Does it matter if they were hosted? Does it matter if they were hosted more than once, or for how long? Does it matter how long they were in the orphanage? Does it matter how much freedom they had in their orphanage? Does it matter if it was a city or farm-country orphanage? Does it matter what country they are from: Ukraine, Bulgaria, Latvia, Uganda, Russia, Columbia, Guatemala, Haiti or another country? Does it matter if it's a Hague or non-Hague country?

In my opinion – **NO!** None of that matters. There are children/teens from each of the above who adjust with few problems and there are children/teens from each who will make their adoptive family's lives a living hell.

There is no definitive answer I can give to you. There is no magic formula. It's like playing a game of Russian roulette. In our case we had a gun with room for four bullets in the chamber. Our chamber held three bullets with only one empty slot. Had we known what we know today, we would have left the gun on the table and walked away as fast as we could. The odds were against us.

If after this you are still convinced adoption is good and you are going for it, at the very least, you have learned what's possible and you can be prepared for the worst. Build around you a network prepared to support you no matter what happens. If that storm never happens, great! Thank you for your sacrifice.

Let your faith be bigger than your fear and fuel up with Yahweh!

Before I end this saga, I want to talk to all of you who are in the trenches, or maybe you are just someone going through a difficult time in your life. I have no idea where you stand with Yahweh. I've talked about Him throughout this book and you may, or may not, have a relationship with Him and if you do only you know how strong that relationship is.

> *Abraham Lincoln wrote, "I have been driven many times to my knees by the overwhelming conviction that I had nowhere else to go. My own wisdom and that of all about me seemed insufficient for the day."*

I know how he felt and I think you do, too.

On more days than I could count the only One who got me through was Him. I have no other explanation as to how I'm standing here today.

> *Psalm 91:14-15: Because he loves me, says Yahweh, I will rescue him; I will protect him, for he acknowledges my name. He will call upon me, and I will answer him; I will be with him in trouble, I will deliver him and honor him.*

As I was reading through my Bible during the hardest of times a message really spoke to me that Yahweh does not save us from bad experiences, but He is there with us to help us through them. In so many instances in that amazing book, from David, Daniel and Jeremiah all the way to our Savior Yahshua, Yahweh was right there to help them through it. Like Shadrach, Meshach and Abednego in the fire He didn't keep them from the fire but went into the fire with them. He didn't keep Daniel from the lion's den, He kept him safe from the lions.

The enemy of this world wants you to give up and as Job's wife said to him, "curse Yahweh and die". That's his goal. And especially for us women – can you imagine his glee if he can get you to turn away from God? If he can do that the whole family comes apart at the seams. He is using adoption to kill families.

Jeremiah reminds us in Lamentations.

Lamentations 3:19-26: I remember my affliction and my wandering, the bitterness and the gall. I well remember them, and my soul is downcast within me. Yet this I call to mind and therefore I have hope: Because of Yahweh's great love we are not consumed, for His compassions never fail. They are new every morning; great is your faithfulness. I say to myself, "Yahweh is my portion; therefore I will wait for Him." Yahweh is good to those whose hope is in Him, to the one who seeks him; it is good to wait quietly for the salvation of Yahweh.

Yahweh does have plan and purpose for you. You may be right in the middle of the burning hot fire right now as you read this book. Know this. He is right there with you if you want Him to be. Ask and you shall receive. Ask Him to be with you every minute. Ask Him to guide you in your decisions. Ask Him to protect you from the evil intent of the enemy. He is waiting for you to call on Him. Call on Him from your knees, in the shower, driving in your car, loading the dishwasher. Cry out to Him. And then trust Him. Trust no matter what you see with your eyes and no matter what you hear with your ears. He knows the end from the beginning and He will right all wrongs. We don't know how, and we don't know when. But He will. Trust me on that. I've seen it with my own eyes.

Talk to Him. Cry out to Him. You can tell Him the deepest secrets of your heart. He will listen without judgement. He will have your back when no one else does. He already loves you more than anyone else ever has or will. Do you really accept the message that Yahweh is head over heels in love with you?

Jeremiah 29:11-13. "For I know the plans I have for you," declares Yahweh, "plans to prosper you and not to harm you, plans to give you hope and a future. Then you will call on me and come and pray to me, and I will listen to you. You will seek me and find me when you seek me with all your heart.

Believe Him! Trust Him! Obey Him!

Finding purpose through the pain!

Rise up! Rise up! Rise up all of you battered mothers and fathers and sons and daughters. Stand strong with Yahweh by your side! Rise up and let us take back our families! Rise up and let us make a difference! Rise up knowing you are not alone in this battle. I honestly believe the battle is already won. We just have to walk it out! Rise up and be brave! Be brave knowing that the One has your back! The God that resides in us is so much stronger than the enemy who is in this world! Put on your armor and stand strong against the enemy and his forces which are trying to decimate our families.

2 Chronicles 32:7-8: Be strong and courageous. Do not be afraid or dismayed before the king of Syria and all the horde that is with him, for there are more with us than with him. With him is an arm of flesh, but with us is Yahweh our God, to help us and to fight our battles.

If you can do what you did to adopt, then you can do this! I believe in you! I believe in Him!

Isaiah 40:31: Those who trust in Yahweh will renew their strength; they will soar on wings like eagles; they will run and not grow weary; they will walk and not faint.

If you don't currently have a relationship with Yahweh, then I humbly suggest that you search Him out and make a decision to follow Him. It's the best decision I've ever made in my life and it made all the difference in this horror show we lived through. Please feel free to contact me if you want to talk about Him and giving your life over to Him.

Some of my favorite "go-to" Bible verses that help me through challenges in life

Honestly, some days all I could do was lock myself in my bathroom and cry and pray through the Psalms with David. Or Ephesians. Or go into the lion's den with Daniel. I held on to Yahweh's promises. I lived through their trials and tribulations. Daniel is just one of my heroes. I thought that if they could do it, so could I. I received hope to make it through the next few minutes of my day. So many nights instead of sleep I just prayed through Scripture. If you could see my house you would see yellow sticky notes everywhere. Big ones, little ones. His words stuck everywhere so no matter what I was dealing with HIS words were close by. I can't tell you how many times that by glancing at a sticky note it stopped me from completely breaking down. Or losing it completely. I'm praying these Scriptures will help you do the same. Sometimes I did break down. And cried out to Him for help. He will be our strength through our weakness.

> *Awake, and rise to my defense! Contend for me, my God and Lord. Vindicate me in your righteousness, Yahweh my God; do not let them gloat over me. Psalm 35:23-24*

> *May He give you what your heart desires and fulfill your whole purpose. Psalm 20:4*

> *Whatever you do, work heartily, as for Yahweh and not for men knowing that from Yahweh you will receive the inheritance as your reward. Colossians 3:23-24*

> *And He spoke a parable to them, that they should always pray and not lose heart. Luke 18:1*

> *Your strength will come from settling down in complete dependence on me. Isaiah 30:15*

> *In all things Yahweh works for the good of those who love Him, who have been called according to His purpose. Romans 8:28*

A woman who fears Yahweh is to be praised; give her the fruit of her hands, and let her works praise her in the gates. Proverbs 31:30-31

The earnest prayer of a righteous man accomplishes much. James 5:16

Draw near to Yahweh and He will draw near to you. James 4:8

Because you have made Yahweh, who is my refuge, even the Most High, your dwelling place, no evil shall befall you, nor shall any plague come near your dwelling. Psalm 91:9-10

But the Fruit of the Holy Spirit is love, joy, peace, patience, kindness, goodness, faithfulness, gentleness and self-control. Galatians 5:22-23

Strengthening the souls of the believers and encouraging them to continue in the faith and that through many pressures and trials we enter into the reign of Yahweh. Acts 14:22

As for me, I trust in You, O Yahweh; I say You are my God. My times are in Your hand. Psalm 31:14

I say to you, all things for which you pray and ask, believe that you have received them, and they will be granted to you. Mark 11:24

Because such is the desire of Yahweh, that by doing good you should put to silence the ignorance of foolish men. I Peter 2:15

Trust in Yahweh with all your heart, and lean not on your own understanding; in all your ways acknowledge Him, and He shall direct your paths. Proverbs 3:5-6

And the peace of Yahweh, which surpasses all understanding, will guard your hearts and minds in Yahshua your Messiah. Philippians 4:7

Let all bitterness and wrath and anger and clamor and slander be put away from you, along with all malice. Be kind to one another, tender-hearted, forgiving each other, just as Yahweh in Yahshua has forgiven you. Ephesians 4:31-32

Make me to know Your ways, O Yahweh; teach me Your paths. Lead me in Your truth and teach me, for You are the God of my salvation; for You I wait all the day long. Psalm 25:4-5

O Yahweh, open my eyes that I may see. 2 Kings 6:17

Satan has demanded permission to sift you like wheat; but I have prayed for you, that your faith may not fail. Luke 22:31-32

Be anxious for nothing, but in everything by prayer and petition, with thanksgiving, present your requests to Yahweh. Philippians 4:6

You have said, "Seek My face." My heart says to you, "Your face, Yahweh, do I seek." Psalm 27:8

For I have walked in my integrity and I have trusted in Yahweh without wavering. Psalm 26:1

Have I not commanded you? Be strong and courageous. Do not be afraid; do not be discouraged, for Yahweh your God will be with you wherever you go. Joshua 1:9 (Joshua 1:1-9 is an amazing promise!)

And lastly, my mantra is this, which I have on sticky notes all over my house.

More of you! Less of me.

I repeat the phrase over and over and over…

And just in case you have a few moments to read an actual book...

I built my armor by reading my Bible. In addition to that amazing book here are a few other books I rely upon for support and inspiration.
- Fervent by Priscilla Shirer
- The Power of a Praying Woman, The Power of a Praying Wife, and The Power of a Praying Husband by Stormie Omartian
- The Resolution for Women by Priscilla Shirer (There is a Resolution for Men by the Kendrick brothers)
- Sun Stand Still by Steven Furtick
- Greater by Steven Furtick
- Choosing Forgiveness by Nancy Leigh DeMoss
- The Circle Maker by Mark Batterson
- The 4:8 Principle by Tommy Newberry
- The Battle Plan for Prayer by the Kendrick brothers

You'll notice that none of them are about adoption, parenting, trauma, etc. I found that by grounding myself in Him I could handle all the rest. Not that those other books aren't good, but I didn't find my way through this hell by reading those kinds of books. I read many of them, but they weren't nearly as helpful as being immersed in Him. That's my story anyway. Seek first His Kingdom! It was the only thing that got me through the war.

Family X. It truly is hard to find joy when you feel like you could throw up, are shaking like you're cold but it is really anxiety, my body reacting to stress creating adrenaline and causing me to shiver. I find no peace or joy in that. You can't explain this pain to someone who hasn't adopted one of these children. You just can't. I've tried, and it only makes things worse – on me. It helps me to know there are others that live like I do. I'm thankful for other adoption parents who reach out.

Reading my Bible this morning made me more anxious. I am a wreck beyond wreckage and trapped in my home that is normally joyful, peaceful and happy, but the past years have put us someplace completely different. And

YES, I realize and understand these kids are damaged. I get that and know that but living with it is beyond difficult, it's frightening. And the constant chatter that goes around and around in circles that YOU CAN'T MAKE THEM STOP because they WON'T!!! It practically drives a person insane listening to it.

As of now, I no longer feel I was called. My heart hurts, it's heavy and it's broken and it's empty! The constant lies, the attacks, the projection, the manipulation, the RELENTLESS agonizing chatter. I am damned if I do and damned if I don't. I don't know how much longer I can handle this. It's not giving up. It's getting out of something so horrible that most people can't even comprehend it. It's taking back our home if that's even possible now. It's bringing peace back into our hearts and home.

Imagine living with people who constantly twist everything that we advise or give them. They just told us that "we don't believe in your God" and as hard as we have tried to show God in our home, not by pressure or force but by love and actions, they take it and throw it back at us. Everything we've done for them was because we thought God wanted us to do it. Without God in our lives we wouldn't have them here now.

I am weary, and I am exhausted and I want to live in peace and love without the added STRESSFUL chaos that is present. Life IS hard, LIFE is stressful, but this is beyond! People will say that God takes us to hard places to refine and I believe that. I really do. Right now, I'm at a loss and I just want out. Now!

So, to all of the hurting moms out there (and dads, too) I want to just hug all of you. I wish I could wave a magic wand and make it all right again. I wish so much joy for all of you who've put your whole lives on the line for a child or teen who is now making your life so horrific. I know it feels like your future is broken. And that hope is far, far away. I read a quote the other day.

> *"Where there is ruin, there is hope for a treasure. Rumi."*

I pray a treasure from Yahweh over you and your families for the sacrifices you have made. Please follow my blog and feel free to reach out to me. **(www.simplymyopinionbykathe.com)**

Tell Your Heart to Beat Again by Danny Gokey©

You're shattered, like you've never been before
The life you knew, in a thousand pieces on the floor
And words fall short in times like these,
When this world drives you to your knees
You think you're never gonna get back
To the you that used to be, tell your heart to beat again
Close your eyes and breathe it in, Let the shadows fall away
Step into the light of grace, Yesterday's a closing door
You don't live there anymore,
Say goodbye to where you've been
And tell your heart to beat again
Beginning, just let that word wash over you
It's alright now, Love's healing hands have pulled you through
So get back up, take step one, Leave the darkness, feel the sun
Cause your story's far from over, and your journey's just begun
Tell your heart to beat again, Close your eyes and breathe it in
Let the shadows fall away, Step into the light of grace
Yesterday's a closing door, you don't live there anymore
Say goodbye to where you've been,
And tell your heart to beat again
Let every heartbreak, and every scar
Be a picture that reminds you, who has carried you this far
'Cause love sees farther than you ever could
In this moment heaven's working, everything for your good
Tell your heart to beat again, Close your eyes and breathe it in
Let the shadows fall away, Step into the light of grace
Yesterday's a closing door, you don't live there anymore
Say goodbye to where you've been,
And tell your heart to beat again
Your heart to beat again, Beat again
Oh, so tell your heart to beat again.

Resources

Following are some resources that I've found for different issues concerning orphans including orphan care in country, dissolution of adoption, attorneys who specialize in dissolution, help with CPS issues, etc. These are current as of the time of publishing and is not a comprehensive list but meant to help get someone started.

I highly recommend that rather than adopting spend your resources helping them where they are instead. Your resources will go much further, you will be following the directive of helping the orphan, and you will protect your family in the process. And the orphan is much better served keeping them in their familiar culture, language and social arena.

I have no personal knowledge of these resources but gleaned them from people in groups to which I belong. Please do your own due diligence as I can take no responsibility for them. Things change rapidly in the adoption/orphan world, especially in other countries.

In Country Sponsorship Opportunities

Orphan Sponsorship International - http://www.orphansponsorship.org/
Antares Foundation - http://www.antaresfoundationinc.com/
Romanian Orphan Ministries -
https://www.facebook.com/romanianorphanministries/
Kings & Queens International - https://www.kingsandqueensint.org/
Agape Ukraine - http://www.agapefororphans.org/
Open Arms Ukraine - http://openarmsukraine.org/
Life2Orphans – Sponsorship program (not the adoption program)
http://www.life2orphans.org/cms/sponsorshipprogram
Youth With A Mission - http://www.ywamvinnitsa.com/

There are other programs out there to help orphans in other countries. Again, do your due diligence to find out if your money will actually be used to help an orphan either while in the orphanage or to transition into real life.

Attorneys who specialize in adoption related matters.

Again please do your due diligence. Ask for recommendations. I cannot personally recommend any of them due to the fact that we did not use them.
American Academy of Adoption Lawyers (Dissolution of adoption)
http://www.adoptionattorneys.org/aaaa/home
Arizona – Brent Ellsworth (Mesa) 480-654-3668; brent.ellsworth@asbar.org
Arkansas – Sherry Balmaz (central)
Colorado – Virginia Frank; Grob & Eirich LLC
Florida – Paul Consbruck (Sarasota); Mark G Capron (Lakeland); Molly Gutcher (Tampa)
Georgia – A. Keith Logue 770-321-5750 (Paulding County)
Illinois – Sheila Maloney; Charles Alexander 815-226-7700 (Winnebago County)
Indiana - Allison Breeden in Evansville and Mark Phillips in Boonville
Kansas – Tish Morrical
Kentucky – Carol Arnette (Louisville)
Maryland – Peter Wiernicki
Michigan – Rick Persinger (Grand Rapids); Evelyn K Calogero (Olivet)
Minnesota – David Gapen; Jessica Maher
Missouri – Jim Waits
New York – Elizabeth K. Joggerst (Binghamton)
North Carolina – David Thurman (http://www.twbglaw.com/); Brinton Wright
Ohio – Mike Vorhees (Cincinatti); Lisa Thompson (Columbus)
Oklahoma – Virginia Frank; Davis Cole (Tulsa)
Pennsylvania – Joseph Francis (http://www.sasllp.com/)
South Carolina – http://www.adoptionlawsc.com/ and http://dovelawgroup.com/

Texas – Luis Corona (Corpus Christie); Sumpter and Gonzalez
Utah – Sophia Moore (Salt Lake City); Hillary Pavia (Draper). http://www.tyshlaw.com/)
Virginia - Jessica Foster in Manassas, Virginia. Foster &McCollam
Washington – Craig Smith (Spokane); Tierra Busby
Wisconsin – Joe Pozorski Jr. (Manitowoc); http://www.ghnlawyers.com

Respite and (RAD) Residential Treatment Options; Dissolution agencies; Information on RAD; Information for Trauma from a parent's perspective and from a child's perspective and more.

Most of these facilities have specific placement criteria. Some are any age, some have age or gender requirements. Some have certain medical or behavior requirements. Some take with sexual aggressive behaviors, some do not. Some are free while others may have a cost (low or high). Some are only good if you live in that particular state. Some are short term, some long term. Internet search is your friend. Research these facilities and look for reviews from other parents who have used them.

Some of these links are simply great places to go for more information. They are here as your starting point.

There are also links here to help you find the information you need to help dealing with your child/teen with RAD, FASD, trauma, etc.

www.radadvocates.org
https://sites.google.com/view/radvocates/home?authuser=0
www.themotherranch.com
http://www.jobcorps.gov/home.aspx
http://parentingallies.com/respite-care-for-adopted-children-part-2-finding-respite-care/
http://www.attachmenttraumanetwork.com/index.html
http://christhaven.publishpath.com/
http://archrespite.org/
http://ranchforkids.org/
http://www.evergreenpsychotherapycenter.com/
http://instituteforattachment.org/ - excellent resource

http://caloteens.com/
http://www.abcofohio.net/
http://www.chaddock.org/
http://www.intermountain.org/
http://www.villasantamaria.org/
http://www.mercyministries.org/
http://www.jaspermountain.org/
http://www.attachmentnewengland.com/website/index.html
http://www.acadiahealthcare.com/locations/resource-treatment-center
http://www.youthvillage.org
http://www.helpinghandhome.org/residentialtreatment.html(Located in Austin, TX)
http://www.heartlightministries.org/
http://www.trtc.net/
http://www.youthvillage.org
http://www.attachment.org/therapists/find-a-therapist-in-your-area/
http://site.iwebcenters.com/louiscompanypublishing/Attachment2016.pdf
http://www.nhfaik.org/
https://www.nightlight.org/renewed
http://ranchforkids.org/
http://www.wiaa.org/secondchance.ht
http://loveandhopeadoptions.org/blo
http://www.specialangelsadoption.org/
http://www.chask.org/adoption/waiti
http://ahome2come2.com
http://www.intermountainresidential.org/
http://www.come-over.to/FAS/RADparentsPSTD.htm Family Trauma issues
https://www.youtube.com/watch?v=byQBP7fq5vQ Child Trauma issues
https://www.pinterest.com/pin/214484000978247319/
http://healthland.time.com/2013/04/30/abused-children-may-get-different-form-of-ptsd/
https://www.youtube.com/watch?v=5ypmGTGGN7A RAD
http://johnmsimmons.com/rad-stealing-reactive-attachment-disorder/

http://www.nacac.org/adoptionsubsidy/factsheets/childsupportenforcement.html

Twenty RAD symptoms by Todd Friel

(My comments as a RAD parent in parentheses)
1. Superficially charming. (Never real. Fake. Good enough to fool people who don't know them well. Used extensively for manipulation purposes. Example: I love you mommy, all super sweet, after being abusive for days because they realized they want something that only you can give to them.)
2. Lack of eye contact on parents' terms. (Will not engage with a parent unless they want something. They will only have direct eye contact when they want something from you. If you attempt a conversation with them they will look everywhere except at you.)
3. Indiscriminately affectionate with strangers. (Ours point blank told us that they trusted the stranger they met just that afternoon more than they trusted us, their parents. Hugging and snuggling with complete strangers within moments of meeting them. Stroking other people including their hair and rubbing their backs. They have ZERO natural boundaries.)
4. Not affectionate on parents' terms. (Only when the RAD wants something will they say I'm sorry, I love you or show any signs of affection. Sometimes this means you give in on something simply to see a glimpse of the child/teen you thought they were even knowing once they get what they want they will go back to the same ways.)
5. Destructive to self, others and material things. (Talked about in this book.)
6. Cruelty to animals. (They love to torment those who are weaker than they are to show their superiority, and even more so if this animal is one that you, their enemy, shows any affection.)

7. Lying about the obvious. (Example: see RAD take money from the counter. I say put the money back it isn't yours. I didn't take any money. It's in your hand. No, it's not. I can see it right there in your hand. No, you can't. This will go on forever unless you threaten to take something from them. No amount of reasoning will do anything except cause you frustration.)
8. Stealing. (Constant.)
9. No impulse controls. (What they want, they take. What they want to do, they do. They care nothing about consequences and in fact will be surprised if caught and then mad that they got caught for something they don't think is a big deal. It is narcissism gone wild. They can only think about themselves and what they want. You cannot reason with this mentality.)
10. Lack of conscience. (See above with no impulse controls.)
11. Abnormal eating patterns. (They do whatever they can to disrupt family meals. They can eat enormous amounts of food or no food at all for days. They will eat strange combinations like an entire container of sour cream with a cup of sugar on top. They will ask for a certain food and once you make it refuse to eat it and tell you it looks like garbage. Stealing food and then letting it go to waste. Spitting on food that you just made so no one can eat it. And on and on and on.)
12. Poor peer relationships. (Making friends is literally impossible. It goes back to it's all about them. No one, even another small child that starts out as their friend, will put up with that behavior for long. They will keep up the relationship as long as there is something in it for them. After that they will walk away without a second thought.)
13. Preoccupation with fire. (Talk about burning the house down, burning the car, burning everything meaningful to the family and even burning the family. Playing with matches and lighters. Drawing vivid pictures of building burning. Lighting trash cans on fire to watch them burn. Burning down a neighbor's barn.)

14. Preoccupation with blood and gore. (If not watching porn on their phones they will migrate to the most violent shows possible. They spend hours watching the news and the worse it is the more they are enthralled with it. A fellow adoptive mom said that her daughter would only watch the beginning of a particular show because she liked watching the murder happen. The mom said she liked watching the criminals get caught and brought to justice. That RAD said, "That's boring.")
15. Preoccupation with bodily functions. (Painting with feces is common. Urinating on things of importance, into heat vents and urinating to ruin furniture and paint on walls. However, this bodily function focus does not mean they have good hygiene, in fact in most cases they have terrible hygiene.)
16. Persistent nonsense questions and chatter. (Non-stop questions about mindless things. "Why" questions constantly. And if it's not questions it is either meaningless chatter or noise. Imagine someone who will not get more than 2 feet from you who constantly clicks their tongue over and over for five or six hours just because they know it is making you crazy. And if you ask them to stop, they just do it louder because they know they are achieving their goal.)
17. Non-stop demanding of attention. (They must be the center of attention. If someone or something else has your attention they will force themselves between in any way they can. One dad told this story. He was playing cards with another child at the kitchen table. RAD attempted to sit on dad's lap – this is a 16-year-old male – and when that didn't work he pulled up a chair to touch dad's chair and leaned heavily against dad, talking and disrupting through the entire game and even put his feet up on the table and asked dad to rub his feet. AND this was *after* dad asked RAD to play the game with him and RAD retorted with a profanity that he hates playing games and stomped off to his room. It was only after dad started playing with the other child that RAD was interested.)

18. Triangulation of adults. (Most times this is pitting dad against mom. There is an entire section on this.)
19. False allegations of abuse. (This is more common than any sane person would think, and I've written much about it. This is the number one go-to for RAD children/teens to get back at the people who are not giving them what they want or to try and get what they want.)
20. Creating chaos. (They are experts at creating commotion so they can be the center of attention and/or cause your attention to be elsewhere so they can get away with a planned activity such as causing a fire in your kitchen, so they can go through your purse to steal money and credit cards. Or doing whatever they can to disrupt a family dinner or outing.)

The following video is a must watch for anyone who is a friend or family member of someone who has adopted. Please watch and then ask them how you can support them. Todd Friel on RAD
(https://www.youtube.com/watch?v=5ypmGTGGN7A&feature=youtu.be)
Excellent Resource for RAD families: http://instituteforattachment.org/
See more about the Pirtle family here:
https://pirtles.blogspot.com/2015/12/please-dont-correct-me-correcting-my.html
TedX San Antonio – Alicia Arenas – Recognizing Glass Children:
https://www.youtube.com/watch?v=MSwqo-g2Tbk

What to do if CPS (Child Protective Services, aka Child Welfare, The State) shows up at your door

http://journeyboost.com/2015/05/21/what-to-do-if-cps-shows-up-at-your-door/

http://seasconsulting.org/ Help with navigating CPS, residential treatment, State services for your child, and educational services. Run by Toni Hoy, author of "Second Time Foster Child". Toni was forced to relinquish her parental rights to the state of IL, for her adopted son to get the mental health help that he needed. She then fought the state to get her parental rights back and she won. She now helps families navigate "the system".

There are more organizations out there than I can possibly list here but this will get you started. There are also groups on social media with parents who are going through, or have been through, the same things you are going through now. Search them out as there is a wealth of information there. And no judgement on how you are handling things as a parent of your trauma teens/children.

The Four Stages of Cultural Adjustment

This was shared with us by our Novi High School ESL teacher, who by the way, is simply the most amazing and wonderful woman on the face of this planet. Shannon Hadley loves, loves, loves on these teens from so many different countries who are working to fit into American life. Love you lady!! She has been a **huge** blessing to our family. Most of the teens she works with moved to America with their families. They live in "normal" families and don't have the diagnosis' that many adopted children/teens have. These following four stages will be greatly exaggerated by adoptees.

She made a point that this is quite eye opening for **anyone** who moves from one country to another. For adopted children/teens it is **exponentially harder**. THIS is one reason I would love to see more done "in country" for these children/teens rather than adopt them into another country and culture. The money spent on adoption could go a long, long way to making a difference for them right in their own country. I have given some resources on how you can help orphans in their own country.

The most common problems include: information overload, language barrier, generation gap, technology gap, skill interdependence, formulation dependency, homesickness (cultural), infinite regress (homesickness), boredom (job dependency), response ability (cultural skill set). There is no true way to entirely prevent culture shock, as individuals in any society are personally affected by cultural contrasts differently.

Though each person is different and will have a unique experience settling in to their new home, many people will go through four common stages of adapting to life in a new culture, often referred to as "culture shock."

Honeymoon phase - During this period, the differences between the old and new culture are seen in a romantic light. For example, in moving to a new country, an individual might love the new food, the pace of life, and the locals' habits. During the first few weeks, most people are fascinated by the new culture. They associate with nationals who speak their language, and who are polite to the foreigners. Like most honeymoon periods, this stage eventually ends.

Frustration Phase - (For teen adoptees this becomes the stage where you wish you had never adopted them in the first place. Your home becomes chaos. Some adoptees never move out of this phase.)

After some time (usually around two to three months, depending on the individual), differences between the old and new culture become apparent and may create anxiety. Excitement may eventually give way to unpleasant feelings of frustration and anger as one continues to experience unfavorable events that may be perceived as strange and offensive to one's cultural attitude. Language barriers, stark differences in public hygiene, traffic safety, food accessibility and quality may heighten the sense of disconnection from the surroundings.

While being transferred into a different environment puts special pressure on communication skills, there are practical difficulties to overcome, such as circadian rhythm disruption that often leads to insomnia and daylight drowsiness; adaptation of gut flora to different bacteria levels and concentrations in food and water; difficulty in seeking treatment for illness, as medicines may have different names from the native countries and the same active ingredients might be hard to recognize.

Still, the most important change in the period is communication: People adjusting to a new culture often feel lonely and homesick because they are not yet used to the new environment and meet people with whom they are not familiar every day. The language barrier may become a major obstacle in creating new relationships: special attention must be paid to ones and others' culture-specific body language signs, linguistic faux pas, conversation tone, linguistic nuances and customs, and false friends.

Most develop additional symptoms of loneliness that ultimately affect their lifestyles as a whole. Due to the strain of living in a different country people often feel anxious and feel more pressure while adjusting to new cultures—even more so when the cultural distances are wide, as patterns of logic and speech are different and a special emphasis is put on rhetoric.

Adjustment Phase - Again, after some time (usually 6 to 12 months), one grows accustomed to the new culture and develops routines. One knows what to expect in most situations and the host country no longer feels all that new. One becomes concerned with basic living again, and things become more "normal". One starts to develop problem-solving skills for dealing with the culture and begins to accept the culture's ways with a positive attitude. The culture begins to make sense, and negative reactions and responses to the culture are reduced. This seems to parallel learning the new language.

Mastery phase - In the mastery stage individuals are able to participate fully and comfortably in the host culture. Mastery does not mean total conversion; people often keep many traits from their earlier culture, such as accents and languages. It is often referred to as the bi-cultural stage. There is going to be much less inner and outer conflict in this stage and the person has integrated fully into the new culture.

Kathe's Note: Teen orphans can also regress and go back and forth several times from stage three back to stage two. Running into a roadblock or memory jog can take them right back to stage two. This is common. Many adoptive teens, especially those with FASD, RAD or other emotional and attachment issues never move out of stage two.

I Am Grateful

See that no one repays anyone evil for evil,
but always seek to do good to one another and to everyone.
Rejoice always, pray without ceasing,
and give thanks in all circumstances;
for this is the will of Yahweh in Messiah Yahshua for you.
I Thessalonians 5:15-18

I am grateful for the following incredible people
who made this book possible.

First, my King and Messiah, Yahshua; and my Father in Heaven, Yahweh. To You belongs all the glory. Without You there is nothing. You are my world. I could not have written this book without You. I could write here all the Psalms giving you praise and it wouldn't be enough to tell you how much I love You and am indebted to You. My life belongs to You! I pray that my life gives You the glory You so richly deserve!

My husband Tom. My love. I can't imagine having gone through this adoption experience, or the experience writing this book, without you by my side. Thank you for talking things through with me, and for being steady and sure, no matter what. I can always count on you. You are a priceless gem of a man for me and for our family. You are the best husband a woman could ever hope for. Thank you for being an amazing father to our children. Thank you for being my best friend. Thank you for hanging in there through the rough patches. Thank you for "No Matter What."

Garrett & Katherine. Thank you for reading parts of the book and giving me your input. I know it was exceedingly hard. Thank you for opening things you had deeply hidden. I pray blessings over your lives for sacrificing so much, so young. I pray Yahweh fills your lives with incredible blessings. Thank you for being my children. I love you more than you'll ever know. Thank you for giving of yourselves in hard ways. I pray for complete healing for you both and that your lives are filled with Yahweh's abundance. I pray you live for Him all your days.

Yuri. Thank you for being one of the good ones. I'm grateful you are a part of our family and I pray blessings over your future. I'm grateful you got through the hard parts with us. And I'm so grateful that you chose wisely in the end. I know you are going to do great things in your life and I'm happy to be your mom.

Rebecca Bailey. Friend, confidant, protector, and author in your own right. Not only were you there with me through some of the darkest times with support and love, you gave many hours of your time to edit this book, a bigger project than I ever imagined going into it. You protected me when otherwise I would have had to be alone in potentially dangerous situations. When I called, you said, "No problem, I'll be there." You always make me laugh. Thank you for all your hard work to make this book a reality and for your constant encouragement. Encouragement that it needed to be done and most importantly, you believed I could do it. Thank you for your feedback. I see red pen markings in my sleep now. I love you and will keep you in Arbonne Blackberry Fizz Sticks as long as I am able. I pray huge blessings from Yahweh over your life.

Kristen Stewart. Author and new friend. Joy filled woman. Thank you for all the input given to get this book published and out there in the world. I am so grateful for you and grateful you were put in my path at exactly the right moment. He knew.

Becca Hill. Friend and fellow adoptive mama. Early on you sent me a letter with a pendant. On it was written the famous quote. "For such a time as this." You will never know how many times I looked it and you gave me the strength to keep on writing through the rough patches. Thank you for your prayers. Thank you for always being there with the right words to keep me going. Thank you for believing in me. I pray many blessings over you and your family. Thank you for your sacrifice through adoption.

Miss Shannon Hadley. ESL teacher extraordinaire. Thank you for the uncountable hours you gave to these teens, and all the other teens under your care. Thank you for mentoring Yuri and giving him encouragement. Thank you for being my eyes and ears at school and for the many emails keeping me informed. I appreciate all you've done more than you'll ever know. You were truly a gift to all of us. I pray many blessings over your future.

My Arbonne family and especially my team. Honestly, I don't know how I would have gotten through those adoption years without you. Each time I was around you, I felt uplifted and knew that I could get through one more day. I've never been around such a group as you. Positive, encouraging and so others-focused. There were so many times, through the worst of it, when I went to a meeting I didn't want to attend, only to come home refreshed just by being around all of you. My team, I thank you from the bottom of my heart. Your efforts gave us a continual paycheck despite me barely being able to breathe on most days. I ask Yahweh's blessings on all of you for all you did for us. I love you all so much! You are amazing!

Jeanine Cushion, the most amazing cosmetologist, who always makes me look better in the hair and makeup department. You know how to take this "low, low maintenance" girl and turn her into someone glamorous. I appreciate you!

Donna at Beaux Arts Design. New friend and amazing graphic artist. Thank you for designing an amazing cover for the book and all the do-overs!

The officers and detectives at the Novi Police department. Thank you once again for all you did for my family through these trials.

To the many, many adoptive moms and dads who wrote to me with your adoption stories. Your voices will now be heard. I am so grateful you dug deep and shared for this book. I know how grueling every single day is in your lives, and how hard it was for you to relive your stories by writing them. I appreciate you and I pray for you all to come through these trials better than ever. Let this book be *"our voice crying out in the wilderness"* and let it make a difference!

ABOUT THE AUTHOR

Kathe Ray is a daughter of Yahweh and serves Him first above all things. She is a speaker and an executive regional vice president, independent consultant, with Arbonne International. She has studied health and wellness, culinary arts and nutrition for more than 20 years. Her hobbies include reading, writing, cooking, hiking and traveling. She has a blended family of ten, four of whom were adopted as teenagers from Ukraine, and she is a grandmother of seven.

To book a speaking engagement please contact Kathe
www.adoptioncombatzone.com
248-704-6677
Follow Kathe on her blog: www.simplymyopinionbykathe.com